The Daily Life of the Greek Gods

Mestizo Spaces

Espaces Métissés

V. Y. Mudimbe
EDITOR

Bogumil Jewsiewicki
ASSOCIATE EDITOR

The Daily Life
of the Greek Gods

Giulia Sissa and Marcel Detienne

Translated by Janet Lloyd

Stanford University Press
Stanford, California 2000

Stanford University Press
Stanford, California

© 2000 by the Board of Trustees of the Leland
Stanford Junior University

The Daily Life of the Greek Gods was originally
published in 1989 as *La Vie quotidienne des dieux
grecs*, © 1989 Hachette.

Printed in the United States of America
CIP data appear at the end of the book

For Maurice

Contents

The Greek Aegean world

Sky—Earth

Ocean—Tethys   Coios—Phoibe   Hyperion—Theia   Japet—Clymene   Rhea—Cronos

Oceanids   Asteria   Leto—Zeus   Eos   Helios   Selene   Atlas   Prometheus—Celaino   Epimetheus—Pandora   Hestia   Demeter   Zeus   Hera   Poseidon—Amphitrite

Artemis   Apollo   Deucalion   Lycos   Chimairea   Pyrrha   Persephone   Athena   Ares   Hebe   Ilithyia   Hephaestus

The table shows the main lines of descent from Sky and Earth. Note that Hephaestus and Athena are each born from a single parent.

Chaos

Erebus   Night

Aether   Day

The genealogy of Day, a power who is descended not from Sky and Earth, but from the Abyss through Night.

The Daily Life of the Greek Gods

Introduction

"Life must be changed": only yesterday that was a slogan scrawled on our walls. Today, it is a commonplace in our exhibitionist society. As the experts constantly tell us, every evening, from screens both large and small, the "quality of life" has become everybody's concern. As early as the time of Fourier and of Etienne Cabet's *Voyage to Icaria* (1840), daily life was already a favorite topic. Philosophers who studied Marx and Engels continued to elaborate a critique of daily life, until, as May 1968 approached, others interjected new violence into their attack on the industrial age, capitalism, the hellish world of the underprivileged, and the exploitation of demeaned workers who slaved in chains twenty-four hours a day. Daily life meant alienation; its end would bring the end of all that, Revolution, a repudiation of the existing division of labor, and an end to humankind's alienation.

In a book written in 1968, entitled *Everyday Life in the Modern World*, Henri Lefebvre disparaged the idea of daily life "a la Hachette"–that is, daily life everywhere, among the Incas, the Etruscans, the Romans, and even the Greeks, as well as the daily life of Billancourt, that at the steelworks of Lorraine, and even that of the Hotel Matignon.[1] Hachette, he thought, had got it wrong, had evidently failed to see that daily life was synonymous with alienation, that it had only made its appearance after the generalization of the market and monetary economy, and that it had nothing in common with the kind of material life and culture studied by Fernand Braudel. The Greeks, Romans, and Etruscans had strayed by mischance into the Hachette series, or rather had been wrongly annexed, misdirected, pushed off course. For, clearly, the Greeks, Romans, and Etruscans belonged to a time that predated that kind of daily life, "when the world's prose was inseparable from its poetry." The Etruscans, Romans, and Greeks had been blessed with a *style* that marked every last detail of their civilization.[2]

However theoretically pertinent the parting of the ways represented by alienation may be, in truth, reflection upon daily life and the category of "everydayness," the kind of life subjected to a daily program, had anticipated this type of denunciation of the modern capitalist economy. When Joyce decided to recount the daily life of the world of 1905, encapsulated within a single, long drawn-out day in the lives of Bloom and Molly, lasting from 9 A.M. to 3 A.M., he may secretly have been inspired to do so by the revolutionary failure of the Paris Commune or possibly some other, less-well-known revolt. But when he wrote *Ulysses*, Joyce was also, or perhaps even more, writing in the Western literary tradition initiated by Homer's *Odyssey* and *Iliad*. It was a tradition that had never desisted from exploring "everyday" values and comparing different ways of living reflected in the mirror of a single day. Jean-Jacques Rousseau, Pierre de Ronsard, François Rabelais, Seneca, and the disciples of Pythagoras had all done exactly that. In his brilliant study, "The Order of the Day," Jean Starobinski picked out a number of major figures associated with that tradition: Ronsard, with his "plural days," amid the euphoria of humanism, with its thousand ways of living multiple lives; Rabelais, with Gargantua's day, from three o'clock in the morning until nightfall, with its care for the body, its physical exercises that were inseparable from the intellectual activities of an encyclopedic education; the daily habits promulgated by Protestantism, in which an individual had to be "a person unified by his/her responsibility before God"; and the Christians' injunctions to prepare for the coming of the eternal day by dividing up every day according to the monasterial discipline instituted by the great religious orders from Cassian down to Saint Benoît.[3]

Earlier, working back through time, there had been Seneca, with his Roman Stoicism, his inventory of the events of the day, recording in writing all its happenings and all its doings, and engaging in an examination of his conscience, to the end of mastering forgotten time so as to construct an identity for himself by remembering all the thoughts and actions of the dying day.[4] Under the sign of Pythagoras, the Greeks discovered the spiritual virtues of daily life, of "everydayness," with the effort of "remembrance," or memory, which made it possible to work back up the chain of successive incarnations and to choose a new kind of life, a kind of life that altogether transformed being.[5] Each day: because, as Seneca points out, each day encapsulates the entire life of an individual.[6]

Ever since the earliest times, in particular since Homer's epic in the eighth century B.C., the human race has been marked, even stigmatized, by the notion of a *day*, a brief span of time, a passing moment. For example, the word *chronos*, which was to develop into the god Time, or the Father of the Days, in the *Iliad*, has the meaning of "an instant, one particular, fleeting moment."[7] Beneath the walls of Troy, human existence is colored by the "day-to-day," by the "day when" something or other happened, or by whatever each morning brings, be it good or bad.[8] As Homer has Odysseus, the hero of the *Odyssey*, remark, "The view we mortals take of this earthly life depends on what Zeus, the Father of gods and men, sends us day by day."[9]

The "day-to-day," the vital force of what is short-term, is thus the lot of mortal men, "always" being reserved for the gods, who enjoy a vital power that lasts,[10] which assuredly implies a kind of life very different from the "day-to-day," the *ephemeral* that pervades the *Odyssey* from beginning to end.[11] The notion of a day implies a notion of a particular kind of life, for those two terms are linked in the idea that so strongly shapes the Greek concept of time, namely the idea of *life*. *Aiōn*, the term Greek doctors used to designate "life," meant the spinal cord, the substance of the vital energy that abandoned a man on the day of his death, but it was also the energy that gave existence its duration, its extent, its more or less long, more or less short, form.[12] It was vital energy, that is to say, *life*, that differentiated humans from the gods. For there was, after all, a difference in vitality between them, even when the Immortals and mortals all ate at the same table, seated alongside one another. Although humans and gods seemed to live according to a regime of parity, in truth they were not equal in "vitality," in *aiōn*, as Hesiod puts it when describing the Golden Age, that is to say, the time before the Prometheus episode, before the theft of fire and the scandal over the shares of the fraudulently presented sacrifice.[13]

In the *Theogony*, Hesiod sets out the dominant version of the origin of humans and the gods: they were all born from the same mother, Earth or Gaia. The Greek gods, like the human race, are part of this whole world. They are not transcendent powers, creator-gods who are masters of the physical universe and can deal in sovereign fashion with the creatures of the sky, earth, and sea. To be sure, each of the two races accomplishes its own destiny. And it is true that some of the Olympians heap scorn upon the mortals "who are like leaves–for a time they flourish in a blaze of glory and feed on the yield of the earth; and then again they fade lifeless."[14] There is a difference of power, of *dunamis*, between them, as Pindar says when recalling the original shared parentage of the gods and the mortals: the bronze sky, where the gods dwell, is unshakable, whereas man is nothing, less than a leaf fallen from a tree.[15] Compared to the great Immortals, the human race seems to have lost its way, for it presents the spectacle of a congenital inability ever to find a remedy for aging and death.[16]

Nevertheless, because of their common origin, comparisons are constantly drawn between the lives of humans and the lives of the gods. Throughout the tradition, ever since Homer and Hesiod, life as it is lived by mortals is referred back to the life of the gods, the gods who are so close, so similar that they are imagined as anthropomorphic (*anthrōpophuees*).[17]

In Greece the gods were born on earth.[18] Anyone approaching pagan theology, whether to study it closely or not, has at the back of his or her mind the memory of Apollo and Artemis, born in Delos; Hermes, born in a cave; Aphrodite, emerging from the Aegean Sea. Greek theological thought was well named by the Greeks. They called it *anthrōpologein*: "a knowledge of gods who are represented as men."

The gods lived on Olympus, high up in the sky. It was a space where the seasons did not come and go, where time never changed. But a mountaintop, however lofty, is still attached to the earth.

Even up there, where the gods lived, it was still the earth. The gods never died, they were *athanatoi*, immortal, *aeigennētai*, born for always. But that did not prevent Ares from coming close to death, and we even know of a tomb of Zeus. Their bodies were vulnerable; they suffered from wounds. Fed as they were upon ambrosia, nectar, and smoke, they had no blood, but beneath the surface of their fine skin their flesh was prey to other humors.

The Immortals were *akēdees*, free from cares. Life slipped by easily (*rhea*) for them. Yet, despite this typically divine carefreeness that the poets constantly ascribed to them, they worried (*kēdesthai*) about all kinds of things, forever involved in the current age, alongside men. They were blessed in happiness (*makares*), yet were subject to anger and pity, fear and desire, affected by everything distressful and upsetting.

It was often said that, face-to-face, they were terrible to behold. Nevertheless, they were always appearing to human eyes, sometimes in disguise, but sometimes openly, and those who saw them were not overwhelmed.

To judge from the Homeric poems—our foremost source—the representation of the gods is thus ambiguous. On the one hand, we are told they are radically different: they have their own time, their own space, non-human bodies, and they are serene and terrible to behold. On the other hand, the hectic story in which they play their part, move about, live their lives, masks their otherness, almost negates it, by placing them in a setting remarkably like that of humankind. One typical feature of this ambiguity is their language. Homer attributes to them their own way of using it; yet in Homeric poetry the mouths of the Olympians speak the Greek of mortals, just as if it were their mother tongue. All that remains irreducible to the identity of human beings is their immortality, their changeless age, together with a collection of extraordinary *powers*: swiftness, strength, invisibility, the ability to fly.

Among themselves, the Olympians constitute a society. They are linked by kinship, allied by endogamous marriages, and they form a closed group composed of three generations in which each individual remains forever in the same age-group. Apollo is the *kouros*, the beardless youth; Zeus is bearded, an adult. Plenty of children are engendered outside this group by one Olympian or another seducing a mortal woman; but rarely are these semi-divine bastards recognized as gods in their own right. Heracles, the son of Zeus and Alcmene, is an exception, admitted to Olympus after performing a daunting set of exploits. Dionysus, the son of Zeus and Semele, a princess of Thebes, protests against that general rule. Denied recognition by his own family, Dionysus plots his pitiless revenge: he afflicts his mother's sister, his Aunt Agave, with madness and makes her kill her own son, tearing him limb from limb like a wild animal. Generally though, the offspring of gods or goddesses do not inherit the status of their immortal parent. They remain heroes, beings who are remarkable by virtue of their courage, beings privileged by the divine favor that attends them throughout their lives. But those lives are destined one day to come to an end.

The family—hence, hierarchical—structure of the society of the Olympians engenders power relations. The supremacy of Zeus, as represented by the epic tradition, has an entire history behind it. Zeus seized power, revolting against his father, Cronos, who, earlier, had dispossessed his own father, Sky (Ouranos). In a dynasty of Immortals, the transmission of power is always violent. But Zeus is not an only son; he has brothers and sisters. He enters into sexual relationships with his sisters, marrying one (Hera) and fathering the child (Persephone) of another (Demeter). He draws lots with his brothers in order to divide the world in an egalitarian (and classically fraternal) fashion. Hades receives the world of the dead, Poseidon the world of the seas, Zeus himself the world of the sky. As for the earth and Olympus, they both remain common to all three, and undivided. However, that triple division is only equal in appearance. From high in the sky, Zeus dominates. As the *father* of gods and humans, he imposes his authority upon all his siblings because he is the strongest, the only one who can outweigh the rest altogether. That he can do so, physically, is clear from the remarkable challenge that he issues to the other gods: If a rope be stretched between the heavens and the earth and all the other gods pull on one end, at the bottom, he alone will pull on the other end, at the top. And it will be seen that all the other Olympians put together cannot match the power of Zeus on his own. His brothers are seriously affected, for despite their claims to be his equals, they are sharply called upon to bow to the order of precedence. Poseidon, for example, wants to in-

tervene in the Trojan War, despite Zeus having forbidden this. He
tries to do so, with Hera acting as his accomplice, distracting the attention of her husband. But as soon as Zeus awakens from the
amorous slumber that has closed his eyes, the audacious Poseidon
is forced to give way and bow to a will that brooks no disobedience.
Zeus is the father of gods and humans–before whom the other
gods and humans sometimes seem to feel a very similar inferiority–
and he does not consider himself bound by democratic laws. It is he
who makes the laws. Athena warns of this: he is to be feared, for he
chastises the innocent and the guilty alike. The exercise of power
certainly involves considerable brutality: rages, threats to strike
other gods down and hurl them from the summit of Olympus, for
them to be shattered on the ground. In highly colorful fashion, the
language of the gods conveys the potential for conflict within this
group bound together under a despotic authority. It also manifests
the extraordinary versatility of these beings, said to be *makares*,
happy, yet infinitely sensitive to the smallest offense, to any slight
made to their honor. Zeus tramples upon the "legal" demands of his
brother; yet he responds to Thetis when she begs him to avenge the
dishonor of her son. In a matter of *timē*, of honor, the father of gods
and humans immediately feels involved.

It was not long before these gods who interfered so much in the
affairs of humans would attract all sorts of criticism. The philosophers claimed that their forms were merely shadows cast by those
who invented them (Xenophanes), or that their manners and their
proclivities were unworthy of the perfection that is inseparable from
the notion of divinity (Plato), or that their lives, wracked by passions
and cares, were not compatible with humankind's natural belief in
their absolute happiness (Epicurus). Nor was it long before they
were reduced to mere allegories of natural phenomena. The thought
of the Greeks thus prepared the way for the polemics of the Church
Fathers.

But what would become of the Olympians, the great gods known
to us from mythology, once they were plunged into human time?
Would they be as pervasive in daily life once the Greeks were organized into cities? For the world of Homer and of the epic was con-
temporaneous with the appearance of the first Greek cities, the
most ancient communities of citizens. Would the gods keep on in-

terfering in the affairs of the new citizens? Would the inhabitants of the cities continue to feel dominated by the divine powers? The gods were certainly present in the city, to the extent that no political community could be founded or instituted without its gods. There was always the first altar to be built, the inaugural sacrifice to be offered up; every new city even planned for a special area to be reserved and devoted to the gods. Politics in Greece needed the divine powers. But at the same time, the stories tell us how, one fine day, the Olympians discovered the existence of the cities, cities entirely invented by these mortals who were "just like leaves." And the gods now jostled to obtain a place, the foremost place, of course, in these little societies that were so well planned that the sites for their temples had already been chosen by the architect-townplanner or the official city-founder. The gods were delighted with their new citizens' clothes, enchanted to become "city-gods."

In the cities springing up on every side, there was even special time set aside for the gods, for the affairs that concerned them: the festivals, the sacrifices, the time allowed for ceremonies, the ritual details, the organization of the calendar, the days particularly allotted to each one of them. The gods were not forgotten; their concerns always took precedence over those of humans. On that score, the citizens were unanimous. And they also agreed, indeed, took it for granted, that their own political assemblies should decide in sovereign fashion on all the gods' affairs. These were gods who were certainly extremely active, very much present in social life as a whole, in all men's relations with one another, in their behavior and their public and private attitudes. And they were gods who were several times a day involved, through prayers and through sacrifices, in the lives of the citizens, whether they were attending the assembly, preparing for war, or waiting for the fruits of the earth to ripen; they were gods who used their autonomous powers and gave advice through oracles, through special signs. But they were gods whom the city deliberately decided to keep an eye on, so that the citizens in general should never feel themselves to be under their thumb.

The city-gods are presented very differently from the busy, activist powers of Homer, who are prepared to submit to terrible torments imposed by one another in order to indulge an almost morbid need to involve themselves in the affairs of mortals. Nor are they the indifferent figures imagined by Epicurus, distant gods confined to their beatitude, in self-contemplation, in no way affected by the bustling life of public squares. The city-gods are powers who, by virtue of their specific modes of action, are involved in all the actions of those who set out to "lead a citizen's life."

To set on stage a number of these gods implicated in the world of men, we have given precedence to the feminine over the masculine and chosen to show how great powers such as Hera and Athena, the one in Argos, the other in Athens, wielded their sovereignty over the city territory, reigning over not only the activities of women as a whole but also the molding of future citizens. Then we turn to Dionysus and follow the evolution of one of the forms that he adopts, that of a phallus paraded in processions. Under the sign of this god, so attentive to all things feminine, we shall be able to explore the typically civic ways of thinking about the relations between natural fecundity and the sexuality of daily life.

I Homer as an Anthropologist

1 Literature? Or Anthropology?

The daily life of the gods. That is a delicate matter, for the anecdotal waits to trap us mortal readers, and futility threatens, along with the boredom that some people associate with the gods. But, at the same time, it is a fascinating subject. Given that these are gods, would it be a tasteless misconception of theology itself if, shamefacedly, we were to acknowledge our curiosity as to the lives of these figures? How did they live? How did they spend their time? What did they enjoy doing? If we are intrigued by reality, we should tell ourselves that that is no bad thing, that little nothings and factual details such as these always and everywhere constitute a challenge to both mythical and "logical" thought about the divine. How did the gods use their time? The very association of those three words–gods, use, time–indicates obstacles to be surmounted: how does one define a god, imagine his experience of time, explain how he relates to the world?

As we shall later see, faced with these problems, ancient philosophy plumped for the most fatally contradictory choices. Nor is that all: when, for Plato (in the fourth century B.C.) or for Cicero (in the second century A.D.), the debate on the nature of the gods takes the form of an explicit dialogue, it turns out that there is one basic reason why the controversy is rife with so many disagreements and refutations centered on the very idea of divinity. That reason is an obscure question that is the source of all the arguments: namely, do the gods take action or not? That is the question that divides the various schools of thought, for it presents two diametrically opposed options.

For Plato, and later for the Stoics, too, action in time and in the world–the then-current century–is not simply a possibility that is accidentally relevant to the identity of a deity. *Action* seems to constitute a presupposition for the very existence of the gods, for it is their raison d'être. So, to acknowledge that there are Immortals while denying that they are active is, tacitly, to deny their existence. In contrast, one recurrent critique of the religious tradition, the Epicurean version of which is the best known, rules out any hypothesis of gods leading a busy life so as to concentrate on the notion of the Blessed in full possession of their perfection.

Active or not active. Ever since the Greeks, the question of the existence of the gods, of a God, has been posed in those terms within a tradition, initially polytheist, then monotheist, that postulates the need to explain "being" as the ability to act. I act, therefore, I am: that could well be the motto of the gods fashioned by the theologians–pagan and Christian alike–which contrasts with the Epicurean gods, who, on the contrary, aspire to logical recognition by laying claim to a sovereign and essential idleness. To illustrate the pertinence of this debate and its permanence across the centuries, we need only recall Diderot and d'Alembert's *Encyclopedia*, whose definition for atheism, an attitude that is "not limited to disfiguring the idea of God, but . . . that destroys it completely," boils down to resuscitating the ever-looming fantasy of the pupils of Epicurus:

> Atheism is the opinion of those who deny the existence of a God who is the world's creator. . . . I have added the words *the world's creator* because, in order not to be an atheist, it is not enough simply to use the word *God* in one's system. The Epicureans spoke of the gods, and recognized a large number of them; yet in truth they were atheists because they attributed to those gods no role in the origin and preservation of the world, but relegated them to a soft life of leisure and indolence.

If Greek culture had taken the Epicurean path, if the gods of Olympus had been as Olympian as the Immortals of Daoism, or if they had been like the gods in Confucius's Heaven, which, as the Je-

suits were to discover in the seventeenth century, did not even
speak, then, to be sure, a *Daily Life of the Greek Gods* would have
been unthinkable. But the Olympian gods woke up each morning
when Dawn brought them, as well as us, the orange-tinged light of
the new day. And each day, motivated by love, fury, or passion, they
got up, propelled outdoors by some plan, intention, or desire, entering into the sublunary world that they shared with us, a world
where they thought they were born to be forever, and where they
burned with a desire to live. Once upon a time, there was Homer's
Greece.

Far, far away from the disillusioned discussions and parodies of
later years, rhythmic hexameters, trustingly and without irony, recalled the acts and days, the *lives* of the ancient gods. In the cities of
classical Greece, where the *Iliad* and the *Odyssey* were sung every
year in the presence of all and sundry, those who listened were
vouchsafed a glimpse of that life.[1] A large expanse of time, inhabited
and fashioned by the gods, was revealed to humans through literary
images, through stories.

The World of the *Iliad*

As sunny days and dark nights follow one upon another, a series of
remarkable and sudden events takes place against a background of
sure, continuous temporality composed of habits and full of trifling
details. As the narrative sweeps along, in the foreground there is a
clash of incidents and setbacks in a war which, all of a sudden,
turned epic and febrile when the anger of one hero exploded over a
point of honor. The battlefield is situated in the land of men, on the
banks of the Scamander, but the gods are deeply involved: they direct the war, keep it going, are obsessed by it. They make decisions
and take up arms. The Trojan War is theirs. Who is it that wrests the
armies out of their torpor, out of an immobile tension and empty
waiting in which whole years have slipped by in vain? Who decides
the strategy of those memorable days of sallies, ambushes, assaults,
and duels? Who? The father of the gods and humans. It is Zeus who
shatters the monotony of the siege when he responds to the complaints of a goddess wounded by the dishonoring of her son. It is
Zeus who decides when to order the resolution and end of the conflict. He sends a message to the sovereign of the people of Argos, a

misleading dream that triggers the formidable confrontation that ends with the capture of the town. And the dream, although it deceives Agamemnon as to his immediate chances of success, does not conceal the *divine* nature of its source. The figure who speaks to the sleeping king through the countenance of Nestor, his venerable counselor, actually mentions the assembly of the Olympians: "The immortals who live on Olympos are no longer divided in purpose—Hera's entreaties have turned them all, and sorrows are in store for the Trojans."[2] It was a disagreement between gods that had been paralyzing all activity. It is at a sign from a god that the inertia is eventually broken.

For the poet of the *Iliad*, the dynamics of the Trojan War and the hectic story of its battles lie in the hands of the Olympians. The quarrel between Achilles and his king simply provides Homer with an opportunity, a primordial chance. The opening words of the poem are: "Sing, goddess, of the anger of Achilles, son of Peleus." But the instigator and extremely active motivater of this disagreement between a hero, the son of a goddess, and a sovereign of mortal descent, is a god. It is true that the poet asks the goddess to have the story begin with the time "of the first quarrel which divided Atreus's son, the lord of men, and godlike Achilles."[3] But behind that beginning lurks another. Upstream from the altercation that sets a king and his best paladin against one other, another crucial, divine, cause can be glimpsed. The poet asks, "Which *of the gods* was it who set these two to their fighting?"[4] And now Apollo appears upon the scene as a protagonist. It is the son of Zeus and Leto who is at the origin of the dispute, he who, having seen one of his priests slighted by the king of the Achaeans, strode down "from the peaks of Olympos with anger in his heart,"[5] seeking vengeance. Agamemnon had refused to restore to Chryses, the priest of Apollo, his daughter, a young woman whom Agamemnon had selected as part of his booty after the conquest of Chrysa. But the god reckoned that he himself had been insulted, through the person of his minister. The presumptuousness of the king upset and affronted him. His reaction was to burst into that dull stretch of time in which nothing had happened for so long. So it was Apollo who inaugurated the time of the active war of which the poet tells. As for the initial source of

Agamemnon's insult to the priest and his god, that seems to have been the king's own, all too human, arrogance. However, as we should never forget, the entire unfolding of the war is part of the designs of Zeus.

To intervene in the human world and position himself, like night, close to the Greek fleet, Apollo leaves his house, a well-built dwelling located in the mountain fiefdom of the Immortals, at the summit of Olympus, in the northwest of mainland Greece. Like all his peers when they decide to mingle with mortal men, the Apollo of the beginning of the *Iliad* has to make a journey, that is to say, he must pass rapidly between two separate spaces: from the place of his day-to-day existence to that of his present actions, which happens to be the Plain of Troy. Two spaces, each with its own time. The drama of chivalrous high deeds, which occupies the forefront of the stage, is set against a background of customs and habitual, repeated gestures. As has been noted above, it is a background we glimpse from time to time, through rapid indications slipped into the narrative in passing, in a pause, such as in the allusion to the great cloud that the Seasons push aside, using it as a door at the entrance of Olympus,[6] or as in a fleeting mention of table manners.[7] But such hints of the life of the gods that suggest a barely sketched-in landscape do, in fact, together compose a separate theater for the exploits of the gods, where their own divine lives take place, autonomously and in parallel with the world of humans. Long scenes–assemblies and conversations, banquets and altercations–take place there, in the palace of Zeus or on the peaks that surround it. There are journeys, meetings, quarrels. Here, in this elsewhere, is where the gods move and have their being, with one day following upon another in a rhythm exactly like the rhythm of days known by mortals. They are busy, take action, move about; but they also relax here: they know how to let time slip by idly, hour after hour. To Homer's readers, the totally separate and independent society of the Olympians seems very real. It is relatively animated, and what happens there is not invariably interwoven with what happens in the world of the human eaters of bread. It has undergone changes of power and experienced sedition. Its hierarchical and genealogical structure is constantly exposed to the risk of conflict. But it is a society that also possesses a profound stability, one that is based upon a system of customs and representations: the Olympians obey rules, observe customs, and have a very clear idea of their ethnic identity.

The society of the Immortals constitutes a veritable gift to history and ethnography. The great cultural divide that cuts the world of the *Iliad* in two is not the separation between the Greeks and the Trojans, for the resemblance between the men on the two opposed sides is almost total. All mortals, whatever their origin, be they Hellene or Asiatic, speak the same language, don the same, interchangeable, arms, eat the same food in the same fashion, and sacrifice to the same gods. Compared to them, taken as a whole, it is the Immortals who appear as a completely different nation. They have a language of their own, their own kind of food, and they use metals in their own idiosyncratic ways: bronze for houses, gold for crockery and furniture; and they themselves are filled with a vital substance that is not blood. Quite apart from their specifically divine characteristics and the countless powers that they manifest—moving from one spot to another with a speed that erases time, undergoing metamorphosis, making themselves invisible, bestowing power or removing it—the Olympians manifest a whole set of traits that are strictly cultural. They are not simply gods, supernatural beings distinguished by a virtual, unchanging omnipotence. They are the inhabitants of Olympus, eaters of ambrosia, specialists in Apollonian music.

History means a sequence of recounted events, a cultural depth, a whole collection of data about a particular system of life—and the *Iliad* shows us the Immortals in just such a double dimension. We have both an account and a description: the sample of days taken up by war is supposed to be representative of other possible days, either similar or passed in other ways, which, however, the Homeric text encourages us to guess at, for even as it carries us along with its hectic narrative of factual events, it offers us glimpses of the material life of the Olympians. If there is any point in writing a *Daily Life of the Greek Gods* today, it is thanks to Homer. Neither Hesiod's *Theogony* (written in the seventh century B.C.) nor the mythographical literature offers us such a precise picture of the existence of the gods in time. Day-to-day life—that compound of inventiveness and routine, of the automatic and the unexpected–cannot be reconstructed by accumulating exploits and biographies. In the *Iliad*, this double aspect of life is never forgotten: so, let us be guided by the Homeric narrative. For it would be a shame simply to wonder, "What do the gods do when they are not taking part in the Trojan War?," when we actually have the means to know all about those days, which are so full and so typical. Part I of this *Daily Life* will thus unfold within the chronological framework of the Trojan epic.

Detailed Time

If we really seek to discover what the Greeks called the *ephemeral*, that is to say, the day-to-day, we must seize upon the pertinence of all the rules and manners that could so easily pass unnoticed. "What do they eat? What do they drink? How do they dress? What are their houses like?"[8] If such questions sometimes seem incongruous where human beings are concerned, they may well seem positively risible in connection with the gods, this "leisured class" whose existence belongs in the dimension of exploits. And yet all those little nothings, all those tiny details are what create the powerful illusion of reality in the epic fiction, in its depiction of the gods even more than in its depiction of humans. Thanks to Homer, even among the gods, there is reality. And it is this reality, among other things, that distinguishes the epic form from mythography. A *muthos* recounted by Apollodorus, to whom a large collection of myths entitled the *Library* is attributed, is defined as an account purged of all non-factual dross. Any element whose function is not strictly necessary to the development of the plot will be left out. The compilers of myths aimed to be economical. Pindar, for his part, is more concerned to censure anything that might tarnish or diminish the image of the Olympians; so, in his work, too, there is no room for daily business, for what is ordinary, for the underside of the decor. As for Hesiod, he recounts, names, lists the doings of the gods, but he leaves days and daily life to the world of humankind.

Let us consider an example. A typical moment in the married life of Zeus and Hera is that of their quarrel over the birth of Heracles. One way of recounting the episode is the following: "When Hera-

cles was about to be born, Zeus declared among the gods that the
descendant of Perseus then about to be born would reign over Myce-
nae, and Hera, out of jealousy, persuaded the Ilithias to retard Alc-
mena's delivery, and contrived that Eurystheus, son of Sthenelus,
should be born a seven-month child." That is a fair presentation of
the chain of events, and nothing essential for an understanding of
the plot is left out; and that is how Apollodorus tells the story in the
Library.[9] But if you read the "same" story in the *Iliad*,[10] you find the
same meager narrative elements deployed to formidable effect.

What, in Apollodorus, is reduced to a succession of purely temporal actions, lacking any spatial context, in Homer's poem constitutes
a series of carefully constructed "acts," in the theatrical sense. The
first act is set on Mount Olympus, where, in the presence of all the
gods, Zeus boasts of the birth of a child destined for the most glorious position of power among the mortals. Then the scene changes.
Hera leaves the mountaintop and makes her way down to Argos to
organize her double trick. The third act is again set on Mount Olympus and presents the sovereign's imprecations against Ate, the
power who so blinded him as to make him forget to be cautious.
Zeus then seizes Ate and hurls her down to the world of humans.
Homer introduces *space*, the primordial condition for the day-to-
day. And he marks out that space with aesthetic and toponymic con-
notations that determine its quality. Olympus is steep, with a starry
sky; Argos is located in the land of the Achaeans. The epithets used
are not merely decorative; their primary purpose is to confer upon
things and people their distinguishing features. And Homer also introduces *time*: everything takes place within a single day. It is, indeed, this introduction of time that imparts such a sharp savor to
Hera's ruse, for she makes Zeus swear that the child of his blood,
born *this very day*, will be the one invested with great power.

From the point of view of the construction of the account, the difference is even more striking. In the *Iliad*, the narrative is constantly infiltrated by descriptions and interrupted by direct speech.
Even when he has to convey a very rapid sequence of events, the
poet persists in explaining, glossing, clarifying, and the effect of
this is to make his highly colored accounts a thousand times more
vibrant than the texts of the mythographers, who are so parsimonious with details. In a comparison, the latter emerge as monoto-

nous, just worthy to be classified and compared at an extremely general level, on which any hero could quickly become *the* hero performing *the* exploit, with the assistance of *the* god. With Homer, we are plunged into a wealth of detail and unique, particular situations: that specificity is conveyed by the details, both in the texture of the account and in the rich vocabulary. The poet *takes the time* to have the gods speak, to let them explain at length how and why they are going to take action in a particular way, to give them things to say, things that may indeed be redundant from the point of view of the plot, but that are precious because of all they tell us about the gods themselves.

The fact that they talk to one another transforms the "actors" who are silently present in the mythography into "subjects" whose actions are conditioned by experience, by memories of what has happened in the past, by life. The Zeus who, we are told by Apollodorus, announces the forthcoming birth of one of his children, and Homer's Zeus, who cannot wait to boast of it to the first comer, are as different from each other as an automaton is from a real person. For, in the first case, our sense of what is happening is conveyed by the "observer," who ascribes to his "actors" the minimum of necessary motivation, just what is sufficient to justify whatever they do: here, all Apollodorus mentions is Hera's jealousy. In the second case, dialogue introduces an entire gamut of subjective attitudes and feelings, seized upon as they affect the speaker. It is true that Zeus vents his ire upon Ate, the redoubtable sibling who so blinded him as to make him foolishly boastful, thereby damaging Heracles' chances. So in the poetic account, as in the mythographer's, there is an external force directing events. But in Homer's narrative this force is herself a character. She does, to be sure, have the power to affect the behavior of another character, but the latter can, in his turn, round on her and punish her. There is a cause behind the events, but here the causality takes a conflictual and dramatic form.

In contrast to the mythographers and their parsimonious narratives, which certainly do not favor procrastinations or digressions, poetic speech is powerful enough to depict a perfectly repetitive and static swath of time. Alongside the *lives* of the gods, and their tumultuous events that are briefly recounted, the *Iliad* sets the *life* of the gods, presented as an indefinite, virtually eternal continuation of a particular way of behaving, a particular state. In Hesiod's *Theogony*, the gods spend their time in two completely separate and independent fashions. In the background, their history and the vicissitudes of their genealogy are set out in linear time. Births, marriages, and conflicts follow one upon another in a narrative that never flags. That is their past. Next, they are imagined as at last leading a peaceful existence, in the predictable present of Zeus's reign. This is a time for enjoyment, a time for musical rejoicing: "Unwearying flows the sweet sound from their lips, and the house of their father Zeus, the loud-thunderer, is glad at the lily-like voice of the goddesses as it spreads abroad."[11] Their indefatigable voices raised in song and feasting constitute the very condition of the sweet life that is led on Mount Olympus. But, here, the music does not simply fill in the intervals that occur in an eventful and dramatic existence. For the gods presented by Hesiod, the time of their life of activity is past. "Unwearying," the voices recount their tales, carry afar, flow on and on.

Is there any such thing as a *daily* life in the *Theogony*? How do the gods spend their days, according to the author of the *Works and Days*, that astonishing manual for the life of humans? Ever since Zeus set his world in order, the gods have been happy on Mount Olympus. They listen to the eternally sweet (*glykera*) singing of the nine Muses. Theirs is a voice that reminds the gods, ad infinitum, of their own past exploits. The same song that from time to time diverts unhappy mortals soothes the heart of Zeus constantly. The same music that distracts mortals from their awareness of their sorrows also plunges the gods into a ceaseless contemplation of their own image, their own history. Delight in themselves, self-fulfillment, perfect satisfaction. What more could they desire; what could be better for these melody-loving gods?

The Muses, who are the daughters of Zeus and Mnemosyne (Memory), were born to perform a very particular and precious task: to blot out the memory of misfortunes, to offer respite from cares, to contrive to introduce pauses, periods of forgetful happiness in the laborious, wearisome, hard life that is the lot of mortals. They themselves *have no cares*, their hearts are entirely free from them (*akēdes*). Their sole interest is their singing. They are beneficent sirens, the bestowers of a revivifying oblivion, who quickly blot out the sorrows that beset the soul.[12] Whoever hears the voice flowing from the mouth of a poet beloved by the Muses ceases to remember his own troubles (*kēdea*). Listening to the exploits of heroes and dreaming about the gods in their Olympian dwellings, the listener is distracted from the difficulties of a life that will be cut off by death. Just for a fleeting while, the Muses, those carefree goddesses, assuage the cares of human beings, replacing the obsessive thought of death with the recollection of another life, the life of the gods and the heroes, the very life of which they sing to the gods themselves, to help them indulge in their own self-satisfaction.

Another prestigious thinker uses a different language to speak of this entirely reflexive enjoyment. For Aristotle, it is no longer a matter of Zeus listening over and over again to his own story and deriving delight from it. Rather, the principle that rules the world, a principle of movement, the supreme and supremely desirable good, is a pure intelligence perpetually occupied by the action of thinking. The aesthete is replaced by the intellectual: "His life is like the best which we temporarily enjoy."[13] This philosophic god, Thought, thinks; that is his life, his joy: "For the actuality of thought is life, and God is that actuality; and the essential actuality of God is life most good and eternal."[14] God is "a living being, eternal, most good"[15]; it is the continuous and eternal duration of his life of an intelligent subject that is itself God. And what is the object of this thought? Itself, thought. God thinks of himself thinking: that is the only thought worthy of him.[16]

The philosophical insistence on perfection engages an active god in vertiginous self-reflexivity. There is constraint, too, in the idea that to be a god is a pleasure, but a pleasure that cannot be caused by anyone else, anything else, for if it were, God *would depend*, would need someone/something else. God must be self-sufficient, while being the cause of desire in others. This is a far cry from Hesiod's Olympians with their vain, naive self-consciousness sustained by stories and flattery. Aristotle has no use for that kind of happiness: nectar and ambrosia, music and poetry. He mocks Hesiod's Olympians, cannot make out whether they cultivate their ambrosian diet out of taste and for pleasure, or whether it is a necessity for them.[17] Hesiod does, after all, mention gods punished by fasts, who become debilitated, extenuated.[18] The economy of divine desire is none too clear.

And yet, when you compare the philosopher to the poet, each with his determination to conceive of the gods as closed upon themselves, you realize the extent to which they both squeeze out the daily life of the Olympians, making it unthinkable. Time does not pass; it is frozen, locked in an eternal present. No day-to-day in the mythographers, too much of it in Hesiod. The mirage of the eternal today, the *sempiternum hodie* of Christian theology, is already detectable on the horizon.

The Structures and Invention of Everydayness

Until the advent of the novel, epic was the only genre that combined narrative and dialogue, and scholars have written at length about this, wasting their time reconstructing the mechanism of factual links, which can be quickly summed up as an alternation of narrative, itself rich in minute details, and the presentation of scenes consisting of moments in which nothing happens except an exchange of words in real time. Put another way, the epic is characterized by dispersion, dissipation, waste. If what is considered essential is the plot, Homer, it must be admitted, is full of "detail."

But detail is essential to everydayness. That has been demonstrated clearly enough by the historians of the *Annales* school, by anthropologists, and also, in their own ways, by the authors of other *Daily Lives* in the series for which the present work was originally written. But they were working in the context of the history of mankind and with the conviction that anything day-to-day belongs to the time of those destined eventually to die. "I believe that humanity is more than half-buried in the day-to-day," Fernand Braudel declared in 1977, while reminding his audience at Johns Hopkins University of his reasons for deciding to write "The Structures of Daily Life." Where it is a matter of the gods, do the details of daily life cease to be "banalities," do they cease to be that "generally ill-perceived mass of history lived in a mediocre fashion"?[19] One answer might be that in the gods' case it is not a matter of history, or even of mythology—since all that is necessary for the latter is a plot—but rather, it is a matter of literature. And detail is also an essential element for literature. Thus, the same Roland Barthes who in 1957 so caustically mocked the petits bourgeois who were curious about

the private lives of the stars[20] later confessed to his own longings as
a reader:

> Why do some people, including myself, enjoy in certain novels, bi-
> ographies, and historical works, the representation of the "daily life"
> of an epoch, of a character? Why this curiosity about petty details:
> schedules, habits, meals, lodging, clothing, etc.? Is it the hallucinat-
> ing relish "of reality" (the very materiality of "what once existed")?
> And is it not the fantasy itself which invokes the "detail," the tiny pri-
> vate scene, in which I can easily take my place?[21]

The day-to-day means detail, and detail is a fantasy, the kind of fantasy that makes me enjoy reading, so the day-to-day constitutes a
pleasure of the text. All the same, it was a somewhat shamefaced
Barthes who succumbed to that pleasure, embarrassed by his incli-
nation to garner in "the more tenuous" and "insignificant notations": "Are there, in short, 'minor hysterics' (these very readers)
who receive bliss from a singular theatre: not one of grandeur, but
one of mediocrity . . . ?"[22] And there you have it: no sooner is it regarded as fantasy and literature than the day-to-day once again becomes the time of mediocrity, of insignificance, of guilty voyeurism.
On this point, the man of letters and the historian are united, for
Braudel himself certainly preferred the day-to-day, the long-term,
in which things are slowest to change and ways of life are preserved.
He explored the day-to-day in order to draw attention to its importance. All the same, he did so still convinced that this was the domain of unconscious habits, of routine, of "history lived in a
mediocre fashion."[23] Insipidity, sadness, airlessness; some might
say: inauthenticity.

And yet, some authors declare that the day-to-day not only has
structures of its own, rules inherited and repeated, by which it is organized; it can, moreover, be inventive, it can improvise, create itself out of nothing. I am thinking of Michel de Certeau and his attempt to reveal the innovative, ingenious, heuristic dimension to
the kind of time that is the time of real life, in which individuals
make efforts, endeavor, try–to make things happen.[24] I am also
thinking of Paul Ricoeur and his way of thinking, which makes it
possible to rethink the day-to-day, seeing it as the time when a subjective experience of the long-term coincides with the world.[25]

A Scratch and a Glimpsed World

But, above all, I am thinking of Homer, and I would now like to offer an example of how his narrative intermingles the commonplace with what is exceptional, and of how it sets out the general rules that govern the social life of the gods even as one of their number flouts them.

One day, Aphrodite, maternally bent on protecting her son Aeneas, a mortal warrior, intervenes in the fighting. She protects her child with her arms, enfolding him in her fine gown. Goddess though she is, she looks vulnerable, and Diomedes, a particularly aggressive hero, seizes his chance, "discerning that she was a weakling goddess and not one of those that lord it in the battle of warriors—no Athena she, nor Enyo, sacker of cities." So Diomedes makes for the beautiful, vulnerable body of Aphrodite and wounds it, not without giving her a piece of his mind: What does she think she is doing in the midst of the carnage? Her place is elsewhere, among the weak women! From the graze above her wrist a humor escapes, the immortal blood that is produced in the gods' bodies by their particular diet. Feeling a sharp pain, Aphrodite has herself wafted back to Olympus, where her mother, Dione, consoles her, and her father, Zeus, also reminds her of her own proper vocation: "War's work, my child, is not your province. No, you busy yourself with marriage and the work of love."[26]

The episode shows clearly that the society of the Olympians is structured around strictly opposed powers, yet that it is possible for an individual to overstep his/her own particular powers, and that whoever so transgresses will be recalled to order and will pay dearly for forgetting his/her limitations. All this we learn from the very minor episode of the wounding of Aphrodite. This single, tiny happening opens the doors of Olympus for us, revealing the relations that exist between the gods and telling us of the vulnerability of their bodies and blood, and of their fears. It is also the pretext for a lamentation—to which we shall be returning later—on the divine condition. The scratch on Aphrodite's lovely skin reveals many aspects of the life of the gods. For one thing, on the basis of this extremely individual episode, and thanks to its being so full of detail, we can imagine others for ourselves. The story has the force of an example. It is an emblematic part of a larger, implicit, and imaginable whole. For another thing, the movement of the narrative follows the movement of the life of a society in which the customary constraints are, like anywhere else, strong but not insuperable, and in which the actions of individuals fall sometimes within the law, sometimes not, are sometimes predictable, sometimes unexpected.

In Homer, particularly in the *Iliad*, the life of the gods is revealed in all its depth through the mixture of events and routine by which it is characterized. So, let us be guided by Homer's narrative, pausing at points where, in the chain of recounted facts, windows open up on to the theater of, not mediocrity, but the *vita*, the existence of the gods. Umberto Eco would call this "Salgarism."[27] And that is exactly what our method will be. There is the narrative, a chain of events, carefully constructed, closely linked, and only occasionally, when it stumbles, do we get the chance to slip into the background against which it rests. But I would venture to claim the word *anthropology* to describe this process. For the "science of man" stole its name from the Greek term *anthrōpologein*, which meant precisely this: "the representation of the *gods* in the shape of man."[28] Homer is, quite literally, an *anthrōpologos* when he brings his Immortals to life. And we have but to read him to discover how much an anthropologist, in the modern sense of the term, can also learn to his/her advantage here.

2 The Gods: A Particular Nature, A Particular Society

When submitted to an ethnographic and comparative inquiry, the gods are discovered to possess a status which, compared to that of mortals, is both exceptional and heterogeneous. Their attributes give them a systematic superiority over humans; and they are also different from them in very specific ways. The gods are seen to be "other," both because they appear to be *greater*, *more* powerful, *more* knowledgeable than humans and also because, to regulate their existence, they choose ways of proceeding that are exclusive to themselves. "No man, not even the strongest, can resist the purpose of Zeus, since his power is far greater than ours."[1] Nor, one might add, could any mortal outrival Hermes, surpass Apollo, outstrip Hera . . . ad infinitum. Whatever their personal characteristics—and even if Zeus is, on his own, far stronger (*polupherteros*) than the rest of the Olympians[2]—all the Immortals, all the gods, as such, are a hundred times stronger (*polupherteroi*) than the boldest of the heroes.[3] Men know that, or painfully learn it, and the gods themselves never forget it, as they look down from on high upon the natural deficiencies of mortals. Age, death, and pains see to it that "there is nothing more miserable than man among all the creatures that breathe and move upon the earth,"[4] as Zeus remarks, regretting having entrusted his divine horses to a pathetic mortal. But the otherness of the gods does not reside solely in their strength. Their felicity, their condition of being immune to cares *(akēdees)*[5] sets them in radical opposition to poor mortals, who are destined to live in grief *(achnumenoi)*. Beatitude, like immortality, is a qualitative attribute.

However, by laying over much emphasis on their difficulties and the distance that separates them from men, an ethnologist of the Olympians lays himself open to remarkable embarrassment. That very remark made by Achilles, which seems to establish such a clear-cut separation between the miserable mortals and the carefree Immortals, represents no more than an entirely relative personal opinion. As we shall see, that absence of cares is inconsistent with the activities, commitments, and ceaseless preoccupations of the gods. Moreover, it is not only human beings who experience grief or even pain: gods such as Hephaestus and Thetis are known to describe themselves as literally *achnumenoi* (affected by pain).[6]

Immortal Blood in Context

We are also told that the gods have not blood but a different humor, *ikhōr*.[7] And that is on account of their diet, which excludes both cereals and wine.[8] When Aphrodite is wounded by the impetuous Diomedes, "immortal god's blood dripped from her ichor, which runs in the blessed gods' veins. They do not eat food, they do not drink gleaming wine, and so they are without blood *(anaimones)* and are called immortals."[9] So here is another mark of their otherness, and one that is all the more important because it is said to be a cultural practice, their diet, that determines this natural quality, this presence of *ikhōr*, instead of the blood that humans possess and that flows from them so copiously. To be a god is to belong to a society in which one eats—or rather does not eat—in a particular fashion, and so to possess a nature in conformity with accepted dietary rules. Although poles apart from man, a god, too, is what he eats. On the basis of this distinctive characteristic of the eaters of ambrosia, it is certainly tempting to infer a whole anatomo-physiology. For, if the text is as materialistic as this on this point (since they eat a particular substance, they must develop a particular metabolism), it would seem reasonable to expect a no less strict concept of the nature of the gods' bodies as a whole.

However, it must straightaway be admitted that, on the question of *haima* (blood), there is no coherence. Zeus himself, the lord of the gods, does not hesitate to speak of his blood, literally, of his *haima*, and in circumstances in which his proximity to the human race is particularly evident. It is when he is congratulating himself upon awaiting the birth of a child destined for glory, a child of his own blood, his *haima*, just as human children are descended from the blood of their forefathers: "Today Eileithyia, goddess of birth-pains, will reveal to the light a man who will be king over all those who live around him, and he will be born of the race of those who *come from my blood*" (*haimatos ex emei eisi*).[10] Zeus congratulates himself upon the imminent birth of Heracles, and, unwisely, he boasts of it: Zeus is a father proud of his blood. One may object that this "blood" is purely metaphorical and alludes to the generation of human beings only by analogy. But thus to reduce the importance of this *haima*, which is not declared to be immortal, does nothing much to advance the idealization of the bodies of the gods. For it simply constitutes a recognition of the fact that, among the gods, the transmission of an identity works on exactly the same model as in human reproduction. We must accept that, for a general theory of the physiology of the gods, we should do well to concentrate on what the poet himself declares when providing a very didactic ex-planation of the effects of some custom, rather than on a random re-mark made by one of his characters. For, thanks to the Muses, the poet knows what he is talking about, whereas the character he has created is prompted by his *thumos*, his heart, when he boasts of his glory before the other gods.[11] Let us trust the knowledge of the nar-rator rather than the inevitable emotions of one of his characters. Let us affirm, with him, that the gods do not have blood, so they are physically different from mortals.

But it is not just a matter of blood. Whether mortal or immortal, anthropomorphic bodies are complex and active; their parts and hu-mors and their functions and movements are immediately evident in any account of their lives. And if we observe the bodies of the gods, beyond the glosses, in the tumult of the time of the story, we are bound to admit that the divine organism as a whole is not nearly as different from the human body as *haima* is from *ikhōr*. On the contrary: *haima* constitutes an exception. Apart from the matter of blood, everything in the bodies of mortals and in those of the Immortals corresponds perfectly. The limbs are the same; the tissues are identical; the internal parts differ in no respect. The same terms are used to designate them and to refer to their functions. It is true that when the hand of Apollo is clapped upon Patroclus's shoulder from behind, it makes the latter dizzy. In the midst of the affray, the young hero lays about him, dealing death to right and to left, "just like a god." But a real god, Apollo, lies in wait for him:

"Phoibos met you in the battle's fury . . . , a terrible god. Patroclus did not see him moving through the rout. Apollo came against him hidden in thick mist, and stood behind him and struck his back and broad shoulders with the flat of his hand, so that his eyes spun round. Then Phoibos Appollo knocked the helmet from his head and . . . his long-shadowed spear . . . was shattered in his hands . . . and the strength collapsed from his bright body.¹²

One of these two bodies is invisible to the other and extraordinarily powerful; nevertheless, it operates as would be natural for a man: using its hand, *cheiri*.

It is also true that when the Olympian Poseidon leaves a scene, he is betrayed by his feet, despite all his attempts at disguise. The god leaves his marine dwelling and arrives upon the battlefield. He addresses the two Ajaxes, the son of Telamon and the son of Oileus, after assuming the aspect and voice of the diviner Calchas. Tapping them with his stick, he relaxes their limbs—first their feet, then their hands. Then, suddenly, like a predatory falcon, he takes off. Very swiftly, so swiftly that those for whom he had disguised himself realize that he cannot be a man: "Aias, this was one of the gods who hold Olympos taking the seer's form and urging us to fight by the ships—it was not Kalkhas, our prophet. . . . I could tell it well from the form of his feet and legs (*podōn ōde knēmaon*), from the back, as he left us."¹³ Footprints (*ichnia*) were left on the ground, in the dust. "It is easy to recognize the gods," as this same Ajax remarks, but for altogether banal reasons, because they leave behind them footprints that can be followed and tracked. When a god walks, placing his feet upon the ground, he is unmasked, seen to be a god. His steps leave traces as do the steps of men, a hunter, for example, whose trail can be smelled out by a lion, or even the steps of animals hunted by hounds with a heightened sense of smell.[14] *Ichnion* is the most common indication of a faded presence, of the passing of a living creature, of whatever kind, that "breathes and moves on the earth."[15] Those are the words of Apollo himself, when he warns his enemy Diomedes: "Think, son of Tydeus, and shrink back! Never think yourself the gods' equal—since there can be no likeness ever between the race of immortal gods and men who walk on the ground."[16] Walking, or even crawling (*herpein*) is a typically human way of coping with space. The gods "possess" the place where they live, they are those who "possess Olympus" (*hoi Olumpon echousi*). The eaters of bread, in contrast, are creatures who tread upon ground that does not belong to them and that, according to the *Cypria*, may not even support them. Poseidon betrays himself by the most mortal thing about him, his footprints.

Apollo's open and heavy hand is set in opposition to the hands of Patroclus, suddenly drained of their strength when Patroclus is seized by the god. Poseidon's feet, leaving their divine tracks, are balanced by the feet of the two Ajaxes, filled by the god's energy and ardor. The poet seems to delight in depicting physical confrontations between men and gods in which, however extraordinary the nature of the gods' bodies—with their distinctive *strength* or *imprints*—we are nevertheless reminded of one fundamental homology: the anatomy is identical. It is surely no mere chance that the most dazzling revelation of Aphrodite's beauty is reserved for the most beautiful of all women, Helen, the one who most resembles her. To speak to Helen, she adopts "the form of an old woman of many years, a wool-worker who, when Helen lived in Lakedaimon, used to work beautiful wool for her and was much loved by her." But Helen recognizes her from "the goddess's beautiful neck and her lovely breasts and the eyes that flashed brightness, and she was astounded and spoke out to her."[17]

Whether or not the poet seeks to emphasize the common features of the gods and mortals who confront one another, one thing seems certain: by affirming the superiority of the features of the gods, he at the same time makes the point that humans and gods are comparable. Let us now concentrate for a moment upon beauty, that divine attribute par excellence which, more than any other, can be misleading as to the nature of a being with a human appearance: Is this

an Olympian or a mortal? Let us take two goddesses—Hera and Calypso—at moments in their two lives when their most feminine attributes are brought into play, for the purpose of seduction.

Hera and the Ribbon of Aphrodite

Hera is a sovereign power. She is both the sister and the spouse of
Zeus and is constantly provoking and confronting the lord of Olympus in order to implement her own strategies. As part of the trio
composed of herself, Athena, and Aphrodite, all seeking to win the
favors of the Trojan prince, Paris, she embodies and holds out the
lure of power, while her two companions and rivals respectively offer the young man military glory and the love of the most beautiful
of women. Hera is a thinking woman, a woman of action, a bossy
woman, and charm is not her usual mode of intervention. When it
can serve her purpose and facilitate her maneuvers, however, she is
perfectly prepared to fall back upon it. When she needs to organize
an immediate diversion, to distract Zeus's attention from the spectacle of the affairs of men, "the ox-eyed queen Hera wondered how
she might fuddle the mind of Zeus who holds the aegis."[18] By behaving as a queen and speaking of power? No, the goddess with the
great eyes of a heifer decides instead to play out a masterly scene of
sexual provocation. To this end, she prepares her body. Away from
all prying eyes, having shot the bolt of a great door that no other god
knows how to open, she sets about an immaculate, carefully judged
toilette.

> First she used ambrosia to wash every stain from her lovely body, and
> then she rubbed herself richly with oil of immortal sweetness, a per-
> fumed oil she had which, if only shaken in the bronze-floored house
> of Zeus, would spread its fragrance over heaven and earth. When she
> had rubbed this over her beautiful skin, she combed her hair and
> wove it with her hands into glistening plaits to hang ambrosial and
> lovely around her deathless head.[19]

To be sure, she anoints herself with ambrosia; her plaits are divine, "ambrosian," and her brow is immortal. But her body, the external envelope of her body (*chrōs*), is apparently no different from
the *chrōs* that constitutes the "skin" of mortal beings, of a man such
as Odysseus, for example, who will likewise one day wash and purify

his salt-encrusted and dirt-caked *chrōs* when he is washed up on the shores of Phaeacia.[20] Although Hera's skin is described as "beautiful," there is nothing histologically special about it. On the other hand, we know that it is sometimes dirty, that it needs to be cleaned, scrubbed free of stains, in the same way as the skin of an exhausted soldier, filthy with dust. Such *lumata*, dirt of a very physical kind, makes mortals too sullied to communicate with the gods or to take part in ritual actions. When Agamemnon plans a sacrifice to Apollo, he orders his warriors to purify their bodies and discard whatever sullies them (*lumata*) in the sea.[21] Even a deity's epidermis is not proof against *lumata*.

After being sprayed with ambrosia, Hera's body receives a massage and is rubbed with oil. So she does not, after all, have the magical ability to keep herself spontaneously soft and fragrant. Hera's skin, like any woman's, does not look after itself: it needs to be artificially softened and scented. The fact that the cosmetic used is exclusive, made for herself alone and called *ambrotos*, immortal, simply places in the world of the Olympians an operation that, in itself, remains typically human. It is, after all, a very common form of body care, for men as well as for women, one used by all the most perfectly muscled heroes as well as by all the most coquettish girls.[22] Finally, Hera arranges her hair, unaided, with her own hands. Purified, perfumed, dazzling, the goddess's body is ready to slip into its clothes and be adorned:

> She dressed herself in an immortal robe, which Athene had made for her in fine-napped cloth and embroidered with many figures. She pinned it across her breast with golden clasps, and she fastened around her waist a belt hung with a hundred dangles. And she put earrings in the pierced lobes of her ears, pendant clusters of three drops, glittering bright with beauty. The queen among goddesses covered her head with a beautiful shawl, new-made and white as the sunlight, and bound fine sandals under her shining feet.[23]

Her grooming is methodical, studied. We become aware of new aspects to the goddess's body, ones that were not picked out as she took her bath, smoothed oil into her skin, attended to her hair. As her body is clothed, it is unveiled. It has a bosom, ears, soft lobes that must have been pierced; a slender waist, cinched in by a belt; feet that must be shod with sandals. Her whole body must be dressed in the most feminine, unshowy manner: just a veil, a gown, sandals, a belt, and then earrings made of jewels the size of blackberries. There is nothing particularly divine about all this, nothing that would be denied to a woman. On the contrary, the effect of it all is to give the goddess the body of an elegant woman. Then, "when she had clothed her body in all her finery, she set out from her room."[24]

The interlude that follows moves into the domain of magic. Before joining Zeus, the lovely goddess equips herself with a magic instrument: a ribbon–which Aphrodite herself, expert in the arts of the bedchamber, usually wears–tied around her bosom. It is "a band of elaborate embroidery, in which all her magic powers were worked. Here there was love, and desire, and the sweet allurement of whispered talk, which seduces the heart even in those of good sense."[25] All the power of seduction is concentrated in this object that Aphrodite keeps about her own person, tied round her famous bosom. Hera takes it, places it in a fold of her gown, and leaps in a single bound from the summit of Olympus to Lemnos.

However beautiful, however adorned Hera's body was, it was not, not yet, ready for the amorous meeting. Something was lacking, something that this accessory lent by another provided, namely, the power to arouse desire. Tenderness, attraction, seductive words: these things would fail to materialize naturally, simply as a consequence of the goddess's physical beauty and her careful grooming. Hera does not rely on her own attractions. In order to please her husband, she borrows this tiny object, so small that it can be concealed in her dress, which will produce sexual desire for her, albeit through none of her own doing.

All this could be given a taxonomic interpretation, so to speak: Hera is a deity of what Dumézil calls the first function, the function of sovereignty. So she is incapable of exercising a power that characterizes a completely different function, one that is embodied in the person of Aphrodite, namely, erotic power. The sovereign goddess *has* to be helped by the goddess of love, both because she is excluded from the function reserved for the latter and because she has no desire to intrude upon Aphrodite's exclusive domain. As we have seen, when Aphrodite meddled in the affairs of war, the lord of the Olympians admonished her sharply, bidding her to remember her proper function. Such an explanation, in terms of spheres of activity and modes of action, is certainly pertinent. Yet, it will not suffice. The situation in which Hera finds herself with regard to Aphrodite is not the same as the situation of Aphrodite faced with the limitation of her powers. The case of Hera borrowing Aphrodite's ribbon raises an infinitely more crucial and subtle question: Where does desire come from? What causes desire? And here, again, the Olympians and mortals turn out to be perfectly comparable.

Desire and Aphrodite

"Among the steep hills of many-fountained Ida,"[26] a young cowherd watches over his charges. Suddenly, a magnificent girl appears before him. He marvels, is ravished, and is filled with desire. It is so strong that, immediately, as soon as she has agreed, he wants to make love with her, even if it costs him his life. He wants to take her, but in truth it is he who is snared. Imperious *eros* has seized hold of the young man: *eros has taken possession of Anchises*. Aphrodite has tamed him, subjugated him, bewitched him. The goddess has filled his heart with "sweet desire."[27] And this *glukus himeros*, substantially present within him, is what now dictates "his" words and "his" actions.

Seizing, taming, overwhelming: that is how desire, taking the form of an entirely external force, acts upon the masculine body of Anchises, the Trojan prince, and that is how it acts upon the bodies of those like him, his fellow men. The beauty of the young feminine creature who presents herself to his eyes is just the starting point. "Marveling, Anchises observed her noble appearance, her figure, and the brilliance of her clothing."[28] Her cloak is brighter than a flame; necklaces and bracelets adorn her marvelous skin: "shimmering like the moon . . . her tender breasts . . . [were] a marvel to see"[29]; and her gaze is pure. Anchises's eyes are riveted to this amazing sight. But desire does not arise *in* him: it seizes hold of him, captures him, *eros eilen*, and in doing so loosens his tongue.

Subject to desire, man is passive, at its mercy. When *eros* seizes him, all that remains for him is to be automatically engaged in the procedures of seduction, or, in the world of the philosophers, in an apprenticeship to learn *enkrateia*, mastery. But man is not alone in suffering this subjection. The gods, too, suffer it, as do animals.

The girl who captures the eye of Anchises and for whom he is seized by desire turns out to be in the same state as he. She has been dazzled by the beauty of the young man's body, and she too has a heart filled with a sweet desire that has been "cast" upon her. She is subjected by the attraction that she feels and that has impelled her to adorn, bathe, perfume, and dress herself, decking herself with jewels before appearing in the sight of this mortal man. She has done all this despite her nature and her name (for this is the goddess Aphrodite in person). The seductress is seduced; she who is constantly manipulating the force of desire now feels it at work upon herself; the constraining effects of *glukus himeros*, the very weapon that she daily uses against others, is turned against her, taking her by surprise.

[handwritten margin note: urged, forced to do something or pushed, driven into motion]

Aphrodite can subject to the law of desire all creatures that are alive and that can move: the gods, mortals, and all the animals of the land and the seas. Only three individuals resist her—the three goddesses obstinately pledged to virginity: Athena, Artemis, and Hestia. All the rest, the gods in particular, experience her power: "Of all others, there is nothing among the blessed gods or among mortal men that has escaped Aphrodite. Even the heart of Zeus who delights in thunder is led astray by her; though he is the greatest of all and has the lot of highest majesty, she beguiles even his wise heart whensoever she pleases, and mates him with mortal women."[30]

Sweet desire is Aphrodite's business, the essential element in her work, her *erga*. Yet *himeros* is not a power that she actually embodies. Aphrodite remains separate from the desire that she manipulates and that she wears embroidered on the ribbon bound around her bosom. Desire is autonomous, a thing in itself. So it is possible for another god to use it; and Zeus does so, turning it on Aphrodite herself, in vengeance, to stop her boasting of holding all the Olympians in her power while she herself remains safe from *eros*. It is Zeus who "puts sweet desire in her heart." He does so because, in the midst of the Immortals, Aphrodite, with a quiet but triumphant laugh, used to flatter herself that she could unite gods with mortal women and goddesses with mortal men, just as she pleased. As Ann Bergren has skillfully shown, Aphrodite took pride in confusing the frontiers of the cosmos in this fashion. But Zeus turned the weapon of desire against her, and she herself, without realizing it and unable to escape, became the victim of what she laughingly used to inflict upon other living creatures.

Trapped by the source of her own strength and her prestige, by what, really, she ought to understand and know how to deflect, the goddess is found to be in the same position as other gods and mortals in the grip of desire. Even she, who plays with desire every day, cannot really control it.[31] Hera, even less, *a fortiori*. For seduction, fine ornaments are not enough: you need *himeros* and *philotēs*, and words of love to intervene, to arouse bodies and bring them close to each other.

Women, Whether Divine or Mortal

"Among the steep hills of many-fountained Ida," a great god, the greatest of all, surveys the armies of men joined in battle. Suddenly, a young woman appears before him. In all the beauty of her body and her ornaments, and desirable thanks to the talisman concealed in her bosom, Hera leaps before her husband, "and Zeus, the cloud-gatherer, saw her, and as he saw her, so desire enveloped (*amphikaluptō*) the thought of his heart."[32] Like the mortal prince visited by Aphrodite, the king of the Olympians is seized by *eros* and hastens to speak. Does Hera wish to leave, to visit her parents? Not yet, not yet. His desire is too much for him. He cannot wait. Zeus presses his young wife: "Come, let us go to bed now and enjoy our lovemaking. Never before has desire for goddess or woman so flooded (*periprocheomai*) the heart in my breast and enslaved (*damāō*) it . . . Nothing compares with the love I feel for you now, and the sweet desire that has its hold on me."[33] Like Anchises seized (*aireō*) by desire for Aphrodite, Zeus is gripped, overcome, flooded, enveloped in a desire to sleep with his wife. But his words are different. Anchises is dazzled by an unknown beauty whom he suspects of being a goddess. Zeus sees clearly that it is his own sister, his own wife, who is before his eyes. And his amazement at the pressing desire that nevertheless overwhelms him finds expression in a string of compliments that reflects the full degree of the strangeness and uniqueness of his feverish desire.

For a Greek, the climax of love, its most intense moment, is when the lover's gaze falls upon something never seen before. It is then, in that instant, that the total ravishment of a mortal–Odysseus or An-chises, for example–is expressed, as a suspicion or fear that this beauty is excessive, divine. As for a god, he certainly has nothing to fear from either the divine or the human nature of the one–whether woman or boy–whom he desires. Yet a god, too, is subject to the same laws of desire: its external and rapacious power, its speed and irrelevance to time. The love of gods is not eternal; it is as intermit-tent and ephemeral as that of mortals. So it is that the day when, to his amazement, he finds himself lusting so avidly for his own wife seems to Zeus to mirror another day: the one when he slept with her secretly, for the very first time. He seems so amazed that he cannot stop telling her how strong his desire is, since it is even stronger than the desire that he felt for Io, for Danae, for Europa, Semele, Al-cmene, Demeter, and even for herself, Hera, on that day when he seduced her.

Not the most tactful words of love, perhaps, but ones that make the god all the more like a mortal. At this point, Zeus closely resem-bles at least two mortal men: Paris and Odysseus. He resembles Paris, Helen's husband, who, on the day when his wife, encouraged by Aphrodite, sets up an erotic ambush for him, expresses his desire for her in the very same words as those that rise to Zeus's lips: "Come, let us enjoy the bed of love. Never before has desire so en-veloped my heart, not even on that first time when I stole you away from lovely Lakedaimon and sailed off with you in my seafaring ships, and lay with you in love's union in the island of Kranae–even that was less than the love and sweet desire for you that comes over me now."[34] He also resembles Odysseus, the lover of the goddess Ca-lypso, who, held captive on her delightful island, does not, it is true, embark on a catalogue of six former amorous encounters, but does explain to his mistress that he cannot help comparing one woman to the goddess. Calypso, who is a goddess through and through, even though she lives, not on Olympus, but alone, really does love the mortal Odysseus. But he, for his part, is thinking only of his wife, and feels no desire as he lies by the side of this mistress so full of desire for him. Calypso draws attention to her Olympian beauty. She flatters herself she is just as beautiful, just as attractive. Has there ever been a woman whose body and face could rival those of a goddess?[35] Odysseus replies that he knows that, compared to her,

Penelope is small and without beauty, and also that she is mortal and will grow old. Notwithstanding, every day he sobs as he dreams of going home, of living to see the day of his return.[36]

In the Homeric world, not only are human and divine bodies comparable, not only is great beauty enough to make one look like a god, but it is possible for a woman to surpass a goddess, even if she is less beautiful and less statuesque. Males, whether they be men or gods, are all subject to the same desire and express it with the same words.

Gods in Subjection

An attentive study of the effects of amorous desire on the bodies and words of the gods reveals them to be beings who are extremely human and every bit as susceptible as men. It might be argued that sexuality possibly represents a very particular sphere of action, one in which the protagonists of classical mythology were especially inclined to demonstrate their anthropomorphism. An understandable lapse into uncharacteristic libertinage? Just one weak point in otherwise superhuman deities? Not a bit of it. The fact is that love introduces a whole domain in which the dissimilarity between the Olympians and mortals appears to be definitely eroded, where there is nothing to indicate that the one group is better equipped to organize its existence than the other. What are in play here are humors and parts of the body—the heart (*thumos*, or *kēr*), the diaphragm (*phrēn*), the chest (*stēthos*)—that correspond to the causes and seats of affective impulses.[37] This is where the passions come into their own: anger, pity, hatred, friendship. The diet of the gods may account for their lack of blood, but in every other respect their social behavior is grounded in a "biology of passions," rooted in bodies as instantly recognizable to the Greeks as their own.

Bile, that is to say, anger, constitutes one of the most active ingredients in the plot of the *Iliad*. Within its semantic field we come across gods who are prey to rancor (*mēnis*) or fury (*menos*), Olympians who are angry (*chōomenoi*), blessed beings who are indignant (*ochthein*) and irritated (*nemessaō*).[38] Nor can these emotions be explained away as incidental manifestations of character. On the contrary, those emotions constitute dynamic factors in the narrative. If you reconstruct the day-to-day life of the Olympians, you cannot avoid the evidence that Zeus's strategic designs, which are supposed to determine and provoke events, are in truth simply secondary effects, themselves the results of a more immediate and less considered impulse: the god's immense irritation at Agamemnon.[39] His divine rage is itself the culmination of a whole chain of passionate reactions, for Agamemnon has provoked the resentful fury of Achilles, who appealed to the pity of Thetis, who, in her turn, managed to arouse the anger of Zeus. And Zeus's anger itself takes over from that of Apollo, one of whose priests was subjected to an insult by Agamemnon and then turned to Apollo, begging for vengeance. The actions of the gods are prompted by one rush of fury after another. Zeus and Apollo, Hera and Athena, Ares and Poseidon are all particularly prone to operate in this fashion. Their response to an insult tends to be a surge of bile that launches them into action. Anger turns out to be the driving force in their hectic lives and, in consequence, also in the history of mankind. For in the *Iliad*, it all comes to an end, precisely, with a truce designed to arrest all this rage and in which the Olympians, headed by Apollo and Zeus, renounce their anger against one another, the arguments that divide them, and the disagreements that have impelled them to engage in fighting and confrontation. Irritated, for once, unanimously, by Achilles' onslaught upon Hector's corpse, at one in their new and ultimate wrath directed against the hero maddened with rage, they decree a cessation to the hostilities and, by so doing, bring to a close the story that derived its energy and its staying power from all those passions.

But the gods also demonstrate the entire range of deliberative and intellectual faculties: will (*boulē*), "heart" (*thumos*), intellect (*nous*).[40] They manifest all the most active aspects of subjectivity. In particular, the *thumos*, the seat of feelings but also of the sudden surges of determination and decisiveness that assail the human ego, functions absolutely normally in the gods. For Athena, to will something is to be impelled by her great heart (*thumos*)[41]; for Zeus, to express his thoughts is to declare what his "heart" within his breast dictates[42]; for all the gods, to implement divergent decisions is to have "divided hearts,"[43] and similarly, for one of them, it means meditating within the diaphragm in order to arrive at the choice that appears best in his "heart of hearts."[44] In short, the Olympians rely on their *thumos* just as much as mortals do.

Finally, let us consider that basic sign of humanity and of the difference between social groups: language. We are told that the inhabitants of Olympus have a language of their own. The poet notes that a particular place or a particular bird is given a term of its own by the gods, a term different from that used by humans.[45] The first surprising thing about this might be that this language, supposedly reserved for the gods, is mentioned in connection with words and objects that belong entirely to the world of humans. Furthermore, all the Olympians, certainly beings who love to talk, always speak Greek amongst themselves, just as they do with mortals, without the slightest suggestion that the poet is translating a language peculiar to the gods for the benefit of his readership of mortal Hellenes. Nor do the gods who approach humans in order to talk with them ever indicate that they are bilingual. Sometimes they abandon their divine voice, *audē*, and borrow the voice of a human, but never his language. In conversation, there is no difference between the gods and mortals. The declared language problem is always overcome by a spontaneous use of Greek. Of course, some situations are exceptional. For example, when Aphrodite sets out to seduce the young Trojan, Anchises, she appears before him in the form of a Phrygian girl and, to win his love, tells him that her father plans to have her marry precisely him, the noble Anchises. To make the story more credible, she explains that, to reach him, she has undertaken a long journey and that she has learned the Trojan language, so she can speak to her Trojan betrothed: "I know your speech well beside my own, for a Trojan nurse brought me up at home . . . so . . . that I well know your tongue also."[46] So, in this case, the goddess did choose a particular language to address a mortal, but that was simply a part of the masquerade in which she plays a Phrygian girl in the land of Troy.

3 Spending the Time

In principle, the existence of the gods unfolds within horizons where death is unknown. However, the Olympians do not live in an immobile eternity, bathed in a pure light, for they enjoy their time that is untouched by black mortality within the dimension of an "ephemeral" continuity that is renewed *day after day*. Even in the most serene and idyllic evocations of Olympus, the beatitude of the Immortals is presented as happiness all day long and every day. Olympus is described as the place "where people say the gods have made their everlasting home. Shaken by no wind, drenched by no showers, and invaded by no snows, it is set in cloudless, limpid air with a white radiance playing over all. There, the blessed gods *spend their days* in pleasure."[1] Even if the season never changes, the lapse of time between the rising and the setting of the sun is the only time span that suits the Immortals.

The Deities of Time

Although it is they who model astronomical time, the Immortals respect constraints. Zeus himself, the great sovereign god, is master of chronological intervals and rhythms: he manipulates the thunderbolt and the rain, phenomena that may strike humans unexpectedly. But except when he uses them as signals to indicate his moods of the moment, the son of Cronos supervises the orderly succession of the seasons (the Hōrai), who belong to the group of the Olympian powers, and the days. Rosy-fingered Dawn is herself a goddess. The return of flushed day is caused by her rising and leaving her old, sleeping husband. She awakes and rises "to bring light to the deathless gods and mortal men."[2] Night, a primordial creature, "overpowers both gods and men."[3] Like the creatures that grow weary, the Olympians are submitted to alternating repose and wakefulness. In the evening, "they each went home to sleep, in the houses made for them in the cunning of his craft by the famous lame god Hephaistos. And Zeus the Olympian lord of the lightning went to his own bed, where he always lay down when sweet sleep came over him. He climbed to his bed and slept there, and beside him slept Hera of the golden throne."[4] Needing and wanting their sleep, the gods go off to bed–sometimes to a respectable conjugal bed–in exactly the same way as men do.[5]

Living as they do on the summit of a mountain that rises into the transparent sky, the Olympians are immersed in the fresh air of the ether, the space in which one of their number constantly revolves: "Leaving the waters of the splendid East, the Sun leapt up into the brazen firmament to bring light to the immortals and to mortal men on the fruitful earth."[6] A great deity such as Hera has the power to make the Sun speed up his ride: a day of fighting is too long for the warriors under her protection; it needs to be shortened, so the Sun must spur on his horses.[7] But that is an altogether exceptional infraction of a rule that, otherwise, all the gods are careful not to break. Hera is cunning. She loves to scheme and spy. On more than one occasion she has persuaded Sleep to overwhelm Zeus, in order to foil his plans.[8] Once, she cut short the pregnancy of a woman in its seventh month and inordinately prolonged the labor of another, Alcmene, Zeus's mistress, pregnant from his exertions, in order to delay the birth of her rival's bastard, which Zeus had imprudently announced, and to have another child born in his stead. By bringing one delivery forward and holding back the powers of childbirth, Hera presumed to distort the natural and divine timing that is normally the same for all feminine bodies.[9] In similar fashion, when Odysseus returns to Ithaca, another cunning goddess, Athena, prevents Dawn from harnessing her horses, so that the gleams of dawn, hostile to lovers, do not come too quickly to disturb the husband and wife so recently reunited.[10]

Sun and Dawn, and Night and Sleep, are all deities. Always on the move, never failing to repeat their journeys, they turn time into a succession of phases and moments, each with its own qualities, its own incomparable colors. By their toing-and-froing and their presence or absence at one or another point in space, they introduce discontinuity and repetition into the hollow heavens. For the Olympians, showing respect for them means acknowledging them as high-ranking deities endowed with autonomous and redoubtable powers. Inducing them to deviate exceptionally from their routine is part of a diplomatic game or an abuse of power that must not be allowed to upset the necessary equilibrium of the cosmos. The powers of time themselves fear the sovereign god. When Hera asks Sleep to make Zeus sink into slumber—for she wants to neutralize him while Poseidon comes to the aid of the Greeks—the brother of Death confesses his apprehension to her: "Hera, queenly goddess, daughter of the great Kronos, any other of the living gods I would readily put to Sleep, even the river-stream of Ocean, who is the creator of them all. But I would not come near Zeus, the son of Kronos, or put him to sleep, except when he himself tells me."[11] Sleep has not forgotten the day when, once before at the behest of Zeus's wife, he dared to make Zeus sink into slumber: upon waking, Zeus would probably have cast him into the sea had not Night, swift Night, whom Zeus feels bound to honor, intervened to defend him.[12] Only on one occasion had Dawn failed in her task, thereby disturbing the celestial order: it was on the day when her son Memnon, the prince of the Ethiopians, had died on the field of battle, slain by Achilles. On that day, "Those bright hues by which the morning skies flush rosy red grew dull, and the heavens were overcast with clouds."[13] Ovid tells the tale of the goddess's great grief and her journey to Olympus, to see Zeus and beg him for some mark of honor for her child. On that day, both gods and men realized how precious the work of Aurora was, for, as she reminded her sovereign, it prevented Night from overstepping his bounds.[14] The order established by Zeus after the searing quarrels that had ravaged the family of the gods was founded upon sharing and moderation: divisions in the swaths of time and mutual recognition of one another's rights, skills, and attributes.

Sun, the all-seeing one, and Aurora in her saffron gown, swift Night and gentle Sleep are all living characters, each with a biography and a memory, feelings, passions, and each confidently assured of his or her role and rank. One even wonders whether a day itself should have a mythical face; and Hesiod does include Day among the children of Night.[15] In the Homeric world, however, a day is an interval between the dawn and the night, the period of light that Aurora ushers in and that Sun keeps going as he rides through the sky. It is an empty period, cut out of the temporal expanse, ready to accommodate the events that come to settle in it. A day is a portion of Time; yet it can equally be a point in time, a date when something destined to happen does so, or some event takes place—a fated day, a day of freedom, say, or the day of one's return. Qualified as it is by whatever it carries, a day seems to be something concrete, which may be warded off, destroyed, or stolen, or which, quite literally, approaches.[16] It has a substantial reality, even a physical weight. Zeus will eventually weigh up the respective days of the Achaeans and the Trojans, of Hector and Achilles. The heavier, the day most laden with fatality, will be the day of the losers and the hero closest to death.[17] In that particular sense, a *fated* day does seem to be animated; it is the other name for *Kēr*, the power of death.

Although in a cosmological sense day is not one of the deities and has no personal identity, the segment of time that it represents provides the life of the gods with its essential reference point. There is no succession of seasons in the land of the Olympians; the passing of months and years is undifferentiated for the Immortals. There is a past—which it is possible to remember—and a future—for which one can plan—but the future and the past are made up of identical days that make one no older as they pass. The Immortals are born forever. They are conceived and born, then grow to the age that is to be theirs, at which point they stop. From then on, there are nothing but days ahead. The possibility of dying would be such a burden if aging continued ad infinitum! The Sibyl and Tithon, deified human beings, did experience that exhausting kind of immortality, the constraint of old age without end. The Sibyl was a priestess of Apollo, beloved by her god, who presented her with this poisoned gift: she was not to die until she once again set eyes on the land of her birth. For many centuries, withered and shrunken, she had been living in a vial out of which only her voice emerged. One day she begged men who had come from her native land, Troad, to consult her, to send her a sealed letter. At the sight of the seal, made from mud, she was at last delivered from her agony. As for Tithon, the husband of the youthful Aurora, he had obtained the boon of eternity through the intercession of his wife. But they both forgot to make the request specific and ask for eternal *youth*. So this Immortal was condemned to wither away forever, without hope.

The lives of genuine Immortals, from the stock of the gods, are crystallized at a particular changeless age. They lead a purely daily life, for only days begin and end with the Sun. The gods' days are never counted, but they fill them, occupy them, measure them. They mark them by their activities and their preoccupations. They attend to their internal affairs and their private distractions, but above all it is the human world that constantly claims their attention. The gods are there, everywhere, all the time. They are tacticians and strategists, aggressive and combatant; they can adopt every kind of appearance, slip into any costume, any countenance. Nothing human is beyond their ken in this war which they direct with their might, and above all their cunning, as though it were their own enterprise. They are omnipresent in the fighting and on the battlefield, just as if here, too, they were at home.

Enjoyment and Cares

The gods, who are both *masters* of cosmological time and *subject* to it, are also *responsible* for the time lived by humans, in the sense that they care and they respond to the desires of humans. On this level, too, they possess extraordinary power, but the exercise of that power is indissociable from their capacity to be *affected*. Their emotional sensitivity is the other side to their active powers, a fact that has raised doubts in some quarters as to their capacity to enjoy themselves.[18] Can Olympian beatitude, day after day the same, be compatible with commitments in the world in day-to-day history? That question prompted two lines of thought, which between them imparted a particular tang to ancient theology.[19] So let us return to the factual question: *How do the gods spend their time?* Let us see how they are said to in stories, irrespective of the theories of philosophers.

First, let us imagine the city of the gods. Consider how Ovid represented it for his Roman readers in the *Metamorphoses*:

> There is a high way, easily seen when the sky is clear. It is called the Milky Way, famed for its shining whiteness. By this way the gods fare to the halls, and the royal dwelling of the mighty Thunderer. On either side the palaces of the gods of higher rank are thronged with guests through folding doors flung wide. The lesser gods dwell apart from these. In this neighborhood the illustrious and strong heaven-dwellers have placed their household gods. This is the place which, if I may make bold to say it, I would not fear to call the Palatia of high heaven.[20]

For the Romans, the world of the gods is urban, a celestial replica of the fashionable quarters in which the aristocracy of the Augustan period could pursue their *dolce vita*. What did the gods do with their time in their *palazzi*? The only activity envisaged seems to be the service that they devote to their Penates, the household gods, gods who are responsive to domestic piety. Not a very taxing responsibility. But the setting of these *palati caeli*, presented at the beginning of the *Metamorphoses*, is not destined for scenes of peaceful religious reverence. Far from it. For the gods hurrying along the Milky Way, heading for the residence of their king, are preparing themselves for a difficult time. Jupiter, carried away by a daunting rage, such as only he can manifest, has convened an emergency assembly. If there is one place that is particularly home to the gods, it is somewhere where "political" decisions are taken, where power is exercised, where world concerns are managed.

We can also imagine Olympus as a Greek scene, a less structured, less urban space. Here, too, there are houses, one of which belongs to Zeus and is the place for assemblies and divine banquets. In this luxurious setting,[21] we can imagine the Immortals all together, the gods who, as a group, are said to be "blessed," to "lead an easy life," "free from cares."[22] As the *Odyssey* puts it: "There the blessed gods spend their days in pleasure."[23]

Let us now imagine being present at a Homeric dialogue, quite a sharp exchange, in the course of which a woman's voice, but a powerful one, is raised against her neglectful husband: "How can you intend to make empty and fruitless all my labors, and the sweat that I sweated in my exertions, and the weariness of my horses?"[24] Hard work, weary horses, sweat. This must be about the human lot, we think, or perhaps the lot of the animals whose bodies strain and suffer when they take part in the labors of men or when they flee, galloping madly, pursued by death. The blessed Immortals, free from cares, with their easy life, ought to be able to stay far away from a world where vulnerable bodies are overwhelmed with exhaustion and stink with sweat.

And yet this resentful lady complaining of being so overworked, of the exhaustion of her mares, and of the "sweat that I sweated in my exertions" turns out to be neither a beast of burden nor a mortal: "I too am a god and of the same descent as you,"[25] she declares. She is Hera, the sister and spouse of the lord of Olympus. This domestic row, with its demands for rightful recognition for exhausting work, takes place at the heart of the Olympian world, in Zeus's house, when angry words are exchanged between the god and his wife.

Just now, it was suggested that this is a world of beatitude, free from cares, where life is easy: this is the *dolce vita*. Now, we discover it to include exhausting, sweaty labor. And yet we have not left Homer, or even the *Iliad*. Let us venture a little further into the text and into the meaning of its words. It is surely not unreasonable to look closely at the language, given that the element in which the Greek gods live is poetic language. It might be thought that Hera's words are merely a figure of speech, that her "sweat" should not be taken literally, as if it were the sweat of some boxer or some ox. But then what should we make of the perspiration of Hephaestus, the blacksmith god whom Thetis found "busy at his bellows and sweating as he plied them"[26] in his forge. At this point, it is the narrator who is speaking, affirming that, to his mind, a god's skin can perfectly well be damp, indeed should be if he is working hard. In short, sweat is to be expected and is not out of place in the body of an Olympian. Furthermore, even if one is bent on reducing its importance, over and above the presence of sweat one is confronted by all that it signals and is caused by: namely, exhaustion, labor, cares. For when Hera reproaches Zeus for not appreciating her exploits, what she is actually defending is all that she is *doing* for the Greeks, all the trouble that she is going to *for the sake of* the allies of the Atridae in their struggles against Troy and the family of Paris. Fatigue is the extreme manifestation of care, *kēdos*, which ought to be so alien to the gods who are described as *akēdees* (a privative alpha + *kēdos*). "This is the fate the gods have spun for poor mortal men, that we should live in misery, but they themselves have no sorrows."[27]

The above words, pronounced by Achilles, constitute one of the general statements that you keep encountering in the *Iliad* and that you are tempted to take seriously as an expression of the overall view that the text conveys. Nothing could be more misleading, however. For even if Achilles declares that the gods are *akēdees*, the gods themselves are well acquainted with *kēdos*. Achilles' mother, Thetis, a marine goddess who is often very unhappy, worries constantly about her son,[28] is *kēdomenē* for him.[29] And Achilles himself mentions the *kaka kēdea*, "the cares that weigh upon her [Thetis's] heart," which the gods are preparing to dispel.[30]

The semantic field of *care* is certainly not off limits for the gods. Quite the contrary. Paradoxically, if one sets the instances where words connected with "cares" occur in relation to one or another god alongside occurrences of what seems to be the "definition" of the gods as beings to whom cares are unknown, it is the latter that appear to be exceptional and to call for some explanation. Might Achilles simply be criticizing the gods, not because they are indifferent to humans generally, but because they are unmoved by their "sorrows"? Might he be indicating his scorn for beings who "are uncaring," rather in the same way as fish "uncaringly" will devour human corpses?[31] It would be possible to gloss Achilles' remark in all kinds of ways. However that may be, and whatever the meaning given to the adjective *akēdees*, a tension undeniably exists between the two opposed aspects that the *Iliad* attributes to the gods: the cares by which they are burdened and their carefree nature.

At this point, it would seem fair to raise an objection on the score of the lack of continuity in the Homeric text, in its composition, in its story. And it is an objection that certainly needs to be addressed. The text's incoherence—whatever its reason—is very real and not only runs deep but also goes back a long way. It must have been noticed as early as the classical period and seen as an inherent flaw in ancient theology, a fundamental indecision on the very nature of the divine powers.[32]

The gods are thus not ignorant of cares. In fact, there is more to it than that: if there is a story at all, life to recount–for both humans and the gods–it is because the *kēdos* of the latter is constantly on the alert, ready to become attention, affection, protection, or fury, punishment, and vengeance. The concern felt by the gods is, quite literally, the motivating impulse to the whole story.

Zeus and Hera in Action

Let us consider two responsible and sovereign deities, Zeus and Hera, who adopt two different ways of acting upon their concern. Right at the beginning of the events related in the *Iliad*, Achilles, the son of Thetis, is maddened with rage. Agamemnon has offended him and Achilles wants to kill him. He seizes his sword. Will he leap into action? A goddess intervenes. The hero stops short and recovers his self-control. The murder of the king is narrowly averted. Vidal-Naquet has analyzed this scene from the point of view of temporal experience: "For the human observer, in fact, time is pure confusion. Achilles unsheathes and then replaces his sword without the onlookers' understanding this temporal sequence. Invisible to the others, Athena has conversed with him, and her speech, in the words of R. Schaerer, opens up before him the perspective of time."[33] From the point of view of intelligibility, there is a definite contrast between the human spectators and Athena, all confronted with the sight of Achilles brandishing his sword. It is a contrast that Athena herself introduces, as Vidal-Naquet points out, through her intervention, her presence, her concern at what is happening at this particular moment in the war. The goddess intervenes in what seems to be humans' time, which could quite well have unfolded autonomously. She bursts into it in order to interrupt or reverse what is about to take place, to remodel the heroes' futures. But why is Athena there? What is the reason for her presence? Literally, the care, the concern, the *kēdos* that is felt by Hera: "The white-armed goddess Hera sent me, as she loves both of you alike in her heart and *cares* (*kēdomenē*) equally."[34] That is what Athena says. At the beginning of the *Iliad* the heroes seem to be acting in response to instantaneous impulses, fixed in an immediate present: He is insulting me, I'll kill him, now, right now; you want my share of the booty? Then I'm walking out, now, right now. Their reactions are immediate, as swift as their rising humors: anger, fury, resentment. Speed is an aspect of their power, a function of their honor: it is impossible to tolerate an insult. Suddenly, a goddess infiltrates this choppy sequence of actions, desires, declarations. She is there to decree a *pause*, a waiting period, a deferred exchange of words, time to savor a cold kind of revenge. Athena teaches Achilles a different pleasure: the less burning, more effective pleasure of a *plan*, a pleasure that can be savored in anticipation, over and above the tyrannical "now" of the hero's desire. This perspective of *patience* is created as a result of the goddess's *caring* attitude, which in this instance is one of benevolent concern.

As Pucci has pointed out, it is Hera's attentive concern that shapes the temporality of the *Iliad* and rescues the story.[35] By stopping Achilles when he is on the point of eliminating Agamemnon, the *kēdos* of the goddess, in opposition to the hero's precipitation, intervenes for the express purpose of making possible and inaugurating a future that can be recounted. Nor does it flag, this concern that generates the story. It is the reason why the Argives react to the ravages of arrows that Apollo shoots into their camp,[36] the reason why Athena, and Hera herself, take risks every time the consequences of another will, that of Zeus, cause them to be concerned for the future of the mortals whom they love.

As for Zeus, he twice takes action to affect the destiny of the mortal men: once right at the beginning, once right at the end of the *Iliad*, when the god, terribly worried (*kēdetai*), takes pity on them. Those two instances of his caring concern exactly mark the start and the end of the vicissitudes that humans undergo as a result of a quarrel between heroes which becomes important only because a god decides to make it his business. At the beginning, Zeus worries and feels pity—or perhaps pretends to—for the Greek king, Agamemnon. He claims that that is why he sends him the dream that sets the whole drama in motion.[37] Whereas Apollo came down from Olympus in order to take his revenge, thereby completing a cycle of reciprocal violence, Zeus intervenes so as to engage everyone, men and gods alike, in a new cycle of murderous violence. For Zeus, as for

Hera, but in his case to promote a different strategy, *kēdos* is a primordial dynamic element capable of setting off a course of events, but also of halting one. The next time Zeus becomes worried and takes pity, it is for a different sovereign, the Trojan Priam.[38] And because of this concern, he decides to bring about a truce. It brings the *Iliad* to a close.

In not only its language but also its very structure, the *Iliad* makes it clear that it is not a matter of two independent concepts, time on the one hand, worries on the other. On the contrary: solicitude is the gods' means of making time exist, and of entering it, alongside human beings.

This means that this, our very first vision, presented in a continuous, recognized narrative, of the world in ancient Greece, postulates a connection between time and cares as essential to the experience of time. But here, clearly, the primary and distinctive attribute of the subjects is their *immortality*. Now, if being careworn is the natural state for human beings living within time, that–according to one familiar contemporary view–is because of death and people's attempts to turn away from it, so it is, of course, an inauthentic and vulgar state to be in. People occupy a preoccupied day-to-day existence in order not to have to assume the destiny *for* which every mortal being came into the world. But in the *Iliad*, men–if they are heroes–go out to meet their destiny, live constantly in anticipation of their deaths. For them, the day that counts is the day of the kind of death that they expect. Meantime, days follow one upon another, without brilliance, insignificant. In contrast, the gods live their immortality, precisely amid cares, in an everlasting sequence of similar days. So the day-to-day, the humdrum, *is the particular dimension of the life of the gods*, from which the absence of death removes all heroism. For the gods have nothing to lose. In the eyes of some, indeed, they resemble ridiculous little alienated *petits bourgeois*.[39]

Anxieties and Dangers

Yet, when they perform their exploits on the battlefield, the Olympians do go so far as to brush with death, as though it were a real risk. They are vulnerable, for they can be wounded. When slashed by a man's hand, their flesh bleeds with blood that is not human but is none the less precious for their life. They suffer, they seek medical attention: a qualified medical practitioner is permanently present on Olympus.[40] They even come close to the worst: Ares confesses that he almost remained among the corpses on the ground when Diomedes, with the aid of Athena, wounded him.[41] Like a god, the hero, with his powerful war cry, fell upon the real god. Athena, invisible in the helmet of Hades, was at his side: her hand even caught the spear hurled by Ares and tossed it aside, after which she threw all her weight behind the weapon that Diomedes launched at Ares' belly, the very spot "where the skirt-piece was belted."[42] The "fine skin" of the god of bronze was torn, and he raised his voice in a cry "loud as the shout of nine thousand or ten thousand men on a battlefield."[43] Back in Olympus, Ares displays his wound before Zeus, showing him the divine blood (*ikhōr*) that is flowing from it. Groaning, he complains, "We gods have always had to endure the most horrible suffering through each other's malice, when we do favors to men."[44] Jealous of Athena and the favors bestowed upon her by their father, he accuses her of having incited Diomedes and spurred him on. As for himself, he brazenly admits that only flight saved him from extreme danger: "My quick feet carried me away: otherwise I should be lying there suffering long in agony among the grim dead, or living on robbed of strength by the bronze spear's blow."[45]

As we have seen above, Aphrodite is also wounded by Diomedes' spear and it is by flight that she too, like Ares, escapes from her enemy. Borne back to Olympus by Iris, she collapses over the knees of her mother Dione, who clasps her in her arms, caressing and consoling her. Who has been so bold as to strike down her lovely child in this way? Aphrodite thinks that it was an ordinary mortal, a warrior who had decided to take on the Olympians. But her mother knows better: Diomedes was no more than a tool. It was Athena who spurred him on, Athena, who so detests her rival. And, like Ares, Dione bewails the fact that, for the sake of humans, the gods are fighting one another:

> Have patience, dear child, and bear with it, for all your distress. Many of us who have our homes on Olympos have suffered at men's hands, in the cruel pain that we bring on each other. Ares suffered when

Otos and powerful Ephialtes, children of Aloeos, bound him in a strong prison. He was imprisoned in a bronze jar for thirteen months–and there Ares, the war-glutton, would even have perished if their stepmother, beautiful Eeriboia, had not told Hermes of it: he stole Ares out of the jar when his strength was then failing and the cruel prison was wearing him down. And Hera suffered, when the powerful son of Amphitryon hit her in the right breast with a three-barbed arrow–then she too was seized with pain that could not be soothed. And monstrous Hades had to suffer with the others–he endured a speeding arrow when this same man, son of Zeus who holds the aegis, shot him in Pylos among the dead men and put him to agony. And he went up to Zeus's house and high Olympos sore at heart, the pains piercing him through: the arrow had been driven into his massive shoulder and was galling his spirit.[46]

As Ares and the meditative Dione see it, the origin of the grave accidents that cause the blood of the gods to flow is itself divine. These Olympians seem certain that, behind any mortal who raises a hand against one of their number, there lurks an adversary of their own race. Any man who allows himself to attack a god in full knowledge of what he is doing can only be a poor fool who does not understand the fate that already awaits him. For the sake of men, because of men, and in the world of men, the gods do sometimes encounter danger, but such adventures are, in any case, all part of Olympian history. It would appear that the ultimate reason for all this is the gods' excessive concern for humankind: they take too great an interest in the ephemeral living creatures that we are, and on that account take risks. When they interweave their lives with ours, the gods become rash. And in the end, can this be worthwhile? Is it not senseless to interfere and put their own peace and happiness at risk for the sake of beings who are so fragile and so negligible? Sometimes that very question is explicitly posed, as if the Immortals in truth dreamed of *ataraxy*. One day Ares loses his son Ascalphus, a boy born to him by a mortal woman and whom he loves dearly: the young hero has fallen on the battlefield. No sooner does the warrior god, the scourge of the mortals, learn of this than he is overcome with grief, mourning a mortal man, his son. Maddened with rage, he desires vengeance. Instantly, he seizes his weapons and dashes from the hall where the assembly is in session. His horse-drawn chariot awaits him. But Athena catches up with him, pulls off his

helmet, and wrests his spear from him. Ares has declared himself
ready to deflect the thunderbolt of Zeus, has he?—despite Zeus having forbidden all military intervention, and even if it means fetch-
ing up amid corpses in the blood and dust? This is inconceivable
madness! Ridiculous ardor! Athena seems to understand better than
Ares that men are born to die, one after the other, and that it is a
mistake to save the sons and offspring of any human being.[47] The
gray-eyed goddess is, to be sure, mindful of the consequences,
namely the brutal anger of Zeus, and simply produces an effective
argument to neutralize the seething rage of Ares. But she is not
alone in betraying a kind of lassitude in the face of all the agitation
and trouble provoked by the gods' relations with human beings.
Later, on another occasion, when almost all the Olympians are present on the battlefield, lined up against one another, two separate
voices are raised to remind them that it is simply not worthwhile
abusing one another and fighting, god against god, for the sake of
mere mortals. That is what Hera tells Hephaestus, thereby quash-
ing the fervor with which he was making Xanthos, the river god,
flame and boil.[48] On the same grounds, Apollo rejects the challenge
that his uncle Poseidon flings down before him: "Earthshaker, you
would not say I was in my right mind if I do battle with you for the
sake of wretched mortals, who are like leaves—for a time they flourish in a blaze of glory, and feed on the yield of the earth, and then
again they fade lifeless. No, let us withdraw from battle immediately,
and leave the mortals to fight on by themselves."[49]

That same theme is frequently repeated: the gods should not tear
one another apart over mere mortals. And from time to time an
Olympian does draw back, halted by the danger and realizing how
pointless it is to suffer or to make one of his peers suffer, just for the
momentary salvation of a being destined for nothingness. Perhaps
the Epicurean mistrust of those absent, indifferent, unconcerned
divine powers was not misplaced. However, the actual behavior of
those powers inclines, rather, toward commitment, involvement
with the humans whom they come across. The whole epic testifies
to that. The fact is that the gods are at once bold *and* fearful, big-
hearted and, quite frankly, cowardly. Sometimes they find it natural
to allow themselves to be mortally wounded, sometimes they prefer
to save their "fine skins." Such inconsistency is particularly notice-

able in the relations between Ares and Athena. At one moment Athena is suggesting to her brother that they should drop the fighting[50]; the next she is attacking him and sinking Diomedes' spear into his abdomen.[51] There may be some logic behind these moody swings. But essentially it would seem, rather, that the field of possibilities before the gods is vast and wide open: so vast and so rich that the desire and ability to avoid hostile blows (for the Olympians can, of course, at any moment fly away, disappear) jostles with the accepted possibility of suffering. Even the risk of death is possible.

4 Gods with a Particular Lifestyle

Earth is weary; humankind is getting her down. She asks great Zeus for some remedy to bring her relief. The sovereign of Olympus is moved and thinks of a radical one: that of decimating the whole, swarming mass of human beings. But not with an instantaneous thunderbolt. Instead, he sets in motion a long, drawn-out strategy. First, there will be a marriage between a mortal and a goddess, Peleus and Thetis, from which an extraordinary hero will be born: Achilles. Zeus himself will seduce a young princess, Leda, to father Helen, a sexual object of great beauty. Upon the lives of these two figures, Achilles and Helen, will hang the fate of the whole human race, in the Trojan War, a veritable genocide willed by a god. The scholar Proclus sums up the facts as follows:

> Zeus deliberates with Themis as to how to bring about the Trojan War. While the gods are celebrating Peleus's wedding, Eris comes upon the scene. She engineers a competition between Athena, Hera, and Aphrodite, to decide which of the three is the most beautiful. Zeus decides that Hermes must take them to Paris-Alexander, who lives on Mount Ida, for him to judge the contest. Exalted at the prospect of marrying Helen, Paris decides in favor of Aphrodite. Then, following the advice of Aphrodite, he builds himself a fleet ...; Alexander sails to Lacedaemonia, where he is received as a guest by the sons of Tyndarus; then he moves on to Sparta, where Menelaus

receives him. During the feast, Helen accepts gifts from Alexander. Then Menelaus sets sail for Crete, after bidding Helen to look after their guests until their departure. At this point Aphrodite propels Helen into Alexander's arms.

And the entire human race is unwittingly caught up in the intrigue. The narrative of the *Iliad* makes no mention of these events, which are recounted in the *Cypria*, a great epic that has been lost, and of which all that survives is the above laconic summary plus one or two fragments. In the fifth century B.C., Euripides was to use the theme in order to rewrite the story of Helen, totally exonerating the lovely woman by representing her as a tool of fate. Instead of appearing as a flighty, deliberately unfaithful wife, Helen ought–according to Euripides–to be regarded as "the all too beautiful thing" (*kallisteuma*) that the gods used to set the Greeks and the Phrygians against each other and provoke deaths, so as to relieve Earth of the countless mortals that covered her.[1] All the same, even in the *Iliad*, this marvelously beautiful object, programmed to be a scourge and propelled by Aphrodite toward her guest, certainly puts up no resistance to the forces that drive her. And nobody can escape her. Hers is–literally–a fatal beauty, impelling and irresistible, for Helen arouses desire: that is the immediate, automatic, and ineluctable effect of her presence. And the man who succumbed to this desire, carried away by *ananke* (erotic necessity) really had no choice. The Trojan elders of the *Iliad* recognize this fact when they observe Helen walking along the ramparts: "No shame that the Trojans and the Achaians should suffer agonies for long years over a woman like this–she is fearfully like the immortal goddesses to look at."[2] Helen, a divine beauty, brings about a divine destiny. "It is not you I blame," Priam tells her. "I blame the gods, who brought on me the misery of war with the Achaians."[3]

And what of the *judgment* (*krisis*) of the young man in this affair? The desire that dictates his behavior operates in complicity with Zeus's intentions. The god knows that Aphrodite's gifts are more powerful than the attractions of military power and sovereignty. If Helen is offered to a mortal man, his reaction is assured. The strategies of the gods are sometimes based on the passions of men.[4] In this particular case, it is the fate of the entire human race that is at stake.

The eaters of bread are a tiresome burden who must be dislodged from the space that they occupy. They should be reminded of their finite nature, that they are as ephemeral as the leaves of a single season and are far too sensitive to the impulses of their being.

The Reactions of the Gods

The Greek warriors slumber in their tents. Their ships lie at anchor close by. Invisible in the darkness, as black as night, the archer-god takes up his position. Nothing betrays his presence except the chinking of the arrows in his quiver. Suddenly, a sinister whistle is heard, as he lets fly the first arrow. All hell is let loose: animals and men alike are decimated. Apollo's action continues for nine days—nine days of nothing but unrelenting slaughter by the god. "On the tenth day, Achilleus called the people to an assembly."[5] About time, too! At last, some reaction on the part of the men. Apollo's treacherous and ferocious attack is met by a carefully policed initiative. However, this man who was the first to have the presence of mind to call the princes and warriors together only appeared to be using his head. In reality, it was once again a deity, the white-armed goddess Hera this time, who laid that idea upon his diaphragm.[6]

So, in reality, it is not men themselves who revolt against the scourge of Apollo, but a relative of that god, another Olympian, who knocks some sense into the victims of her rival and mobilizes them. Loyal to her alliance with the Greeks against the city of the impudent Paris, Hera will not tolerate the extermination of her allies. What might have happened if a deity from Olympus had not been concerned about their fate does not bear thinking about. However astounded we are at the inertia of the mortals, we have to try to get used to the strangeness of their role in the theater of shadows through which they pass. Now alert and swift to act, only intermittently are mortals in control of events, for these bear the mark of divine intervention.

There is only one question on the agenda of the Greeks' assembly: what offense can have triggered Apollo to take such reprisals? Has some promise been forgotten, some sacrifice overlooked? Perhaps the aroma of roasting lambs and goats will calm him down. Bewildered and worried, but convinced that they are at fault, the

Greeks turn to Calchas, the man whom Apollo himself has endowed with the capacity to know the past, the present, and the future. But Calchas sets them straight: it is not on account of a religious oversight that Apollo is so angry. It is because the *honor* of one of his priests, Chryses, has been slighted. Chryses' daughter has been taken prisoner by Agamemnon in the conquest of the town of Chryse, and he now refuses to return her. The old prelate had gone to Agamemnon, offering a ransom in exchange for his daughter, but the king insulted him by refusing to accept it. And this insult to Chryses personally affects Apollo, for it is he whom the priest serves. Now, the young woman will have to be returned to the god himself, without a ransom and, furthermore, with a great hecatomb of many sacrificial victims by way of compensation. If these conditions are met, the scourge will be lifted.[7] Agamemnon agrees. However, touchy over his own prestige, and so as not to lose face before the other princes, he decides to appropriate another female captive, Briseis, who has been allotted, as part of the booty, to Achilles: "Just as Phoibus Apollo is taking Chryseis away from me–I will send her home with my ship and my companions–, so shall I take the beautiful Briseis."[8]

Such is the initial motivation–the revenge of an angered, overwrought god, boiling over with fury. The *Iliad* opens with the scene of his ravages. Right from the start, the presence of the gods is manifested by anger. The Olympians are touchy, resentful, lethally violent, no wiser and no less passionate than human beings. Agamemnon should already have learned that lesson on the day in Aulis–a stopping place on the way to Troy–when, with the fleet at anchor and the army encamped, the king diverted himself by going hunting and, unthinking, let slip a little exclamation that would weigh heavy upon him for the rest of his days: Ha! What a lovely doe he had laid low! Artemis herself could not have done better! The king had exulted at his catch and had forgotten what no mortal should ever forget, namely that the gods, all the gods, are incapable of tolerating the idea that they can be surpassed. It was no more than a light remark but proved to be a boast to be regretted, for Apollo's sister, the huntress, never forgave him. A sudden storm arose over the sea, which Calchas, the deviner, when summoned, interpreted as anger on the part of the goddess. To win a pardon, the king would now have to sacrifice his own daughter. At this, Agamemnon agreed to kill Iphigenia—a move that was to cost him dearly—but at the precise moment when the knife was about to be plunged into the victim's breast, Artemis had slipped a doe into her place. Nobody had noticed.[9]

Thus, even before offending Apollo, Agamemnon had provoked Artemis. The response in both cases was a merciless fury that could only be appeased by a sacrifice. Yet, on the part of the mortal, it had just been a silly mistake: a wish to hold on to a captive because she was so pretty, pride at having been so successful in the hunt. Was it really so serious? Trivial though it might appear, it was enough to unleash black rage on the part of the Olympians. Humans are exposed to the gods' moods. And the gods are quick to resent the smallest mistakes that humans inevitably make. Why did such a pious king as Agamemnon not take more care not to offend the two archer deities? It would seem that, whatever elementary rules for maintaining good relations with the Olympians existed, Agamemnon had not understood them or did not know of them. Why were the gods not more tolerant toward these beings who were so little in command of their own words and actions? Therein lies the whole problem of the gods' presence on earth. Nobody was supposed to be ignorant of the law, and every infraction deserved a punishment; but was there any code of penalties?

Some transgressions were deliberate and premeditated—for example, the killing and eating of the cattle of the Sun, an act committed by Odysseus's companions, in Sicily. The animals were categorically forbidden, untouchable; the starving sailors contravened an explicit order, knowingly defied divine vengeance and anger. Eurylochus, at the end of his tether, declared: "If in anger at the loss of his straight-horned herds he chooses to wreck our ship with the support of the other gods, I would sooner drown instantly in a watery grave than waste away by slow degrees on a desert island."[10] Overcome by hunger, threatened by the worst of deaths, the wretched men decided to slaughter the sacred animals. They set up a sacrifice in which they intended to offer the gods the portion that would be their due in a correct ceremony. But, because of the circumstances, the entire procedure was inappropriate. The sailors used oak leaves in the place of barley grains, which were not available, and they made libations with water, because they had no wine.

And the supreme paradox was that the victims they shared with the gods belonged totally to one of their number anyway. Is it surprising that the slaughtered beasts, for their part, were not even properly dead? The hides walked, the pieces of raw and cooked meat lowed lugubriously as the spits turned. Predictably enough, the Sun sought revenge. He threatened to plunge into Hades and shine there, for the dead, because that Sicilian herd of cattle had been his pride and joy whenever he rose into the sky and again when he returned to earth. So Zeus promised him whatever he wanted: "Sun, . . . shine on for the immortals and for mortal men on the fruitful earth. As for the culprits, I will soon strike their ship with a blinding bolt out on the wine-dark sea, and smash it to pieces."[11]

However, that considered decision to disobey was exceptional. In Homer, cases of deliberate outrage such as that of Odysseus's companions and that, even more serious, of Penelope's suitors, are rare. The suitors systematically neglect to pay the Olympians the elementary homage that is the gods' due at meals: they never sacrifice, and on the day of the festival of Apollo they consume everything themselves, promising to burn goats' thighs for Apollo . . . the next day.[12] As we know, they too would be exterminated, during a meal, that very day. But most of the insults that drive the gods into a rage are, so to speak, involuntary; they are mistakes rather than deliberate acts. Euripides' Agamemnon sadly reflects that sometimes failure to observe the cult of the gods can overturn a man's entire life.[13] And when, under the hail of Apollo's arrows, the Greeks try to remember what frightful thing they can have done to deserve this, they think they must have forgotten to fulfill some vow. Such forgetfulness would indeed have been unpardonable, as is shown by another version of the sacrifice of Iphigenia. According to this version, when his daughter was born, Agamemnon was so rash as to promise Artemis the finest fruit of the year–without thinking of this, his own fruit–and, furthermore, without then bothering to fulfill his promise. The goddess did not forget, and later she exacted her due.[14] Since, all those years ago, the finest fruit had been the little girl born in the king's house, it was she, this priceless creature, who had to be put to death, trapped by her father's words. Only on that condition could the becalmed fleet once more put to sea.

The Greeks, decimated by Apollo's shower of arrows, thus asked themselves: Have we forgotten a vow? Or have we overlooked a sacrifice? For the latter was also a pertinent question. The story of Oineus, the vinous one, is well known. He was, in fact, an extremely pious person, but he had neglected to offer the first fruits to Artemis whilst sacrificing a whole hecatomb of victims to the other deities. The goddess (again Artemis) thereupon let loose a wild boar in his vineyards. The precious vines were ravaged and many of the hunters who had gathered to catch the beast were killed. At last, Meleager, Oineus's son, managed to kill it. But Artemis, who was still feeling slighted, then caused a quarrel to break out among the company of hunters "over the division of the boar's head and bristling hide." Instead of a fair distribution taking place, war broke out among these friends.[15]

When Apollo unleashed his fury upon the Greeks, he had not been denied a sacrificial victim, nor had any promise made to him been broken. Nor had he suffered the indignity of being unrecognized, as frequently happened to his brother Dionysus, whose sudden appearances so often gave rise to misunderstandings. Born from a Theban princess and Zeus, who carried him in his own thigh during the last months of his gestation, Dionysus was horribly insulted by his maternal family in Thebes, where he was received as a stranger and nobody would believe his divine origin. His cousin Pentheus paid dearly for this: he was hunted down by his own mother, while she was gripped by Bacchic mania, and was torn to pieces by her, as if he were a young fawn. In Attica, because his effigy was not welcomed and treated with honor as soon as it was introduced there, Dionysus inflicted a sickness upon the sexuality of all the men. He could only be appeased by the institution of a cult worthy of him and by the introduction of phallophoria (processions in which a phallus was paraded). Also in Attica, his magical beverage was spurned when the peasants, claiming that the wine was deadly, on the grounds that it made them sleepy, killed Icarius, the man who had introduced them to it. In revenge, the god taught the ungrateful boors a lesson. He appeared to them in the guise of a beautiful child in the full flower of youth, and they were all seized with desire and longed to seduce him. He thus caused a veritable erotic epidemic. But no sooner had Dionysus the ephebe provoked their desire than he disappeared, leaving the peasants stupefied and, thanks to the priapic tension of their sexual members, much over-wrought. The incident was eventually resolved by an offering of wooden statuettes.[16]

But the Apollo of the *Iliad* has not been discounted in compari-son to a rival god—as sometimes happens to Aphrodite when a girl consecrates herself to Artemis and the life of a virgin; nor has he been misunderstood, out of stupidity, as Demeter was when, for ex-ample, she had been roasting a child in order to render him immor-tal and the overcurious mother, coming upon the scene, shrieked in horror—at which the angry goddess abandoned the child to his mortal condition and ordered the institution of the cult of Eleusis.[17] Of all the virtually limitless gamut of errors likely to irritate the gods, in Apollo's case it was an offense done—in the blindness of de-sire—to one of his priests. His vengeance may seem ill-judged—for Agamemnon is not affected personally, whereas his subjects die by the dozens—and excessive—since, had nobody intervened, the scourge would have continued indefinitely. But there are no set cri-teria to determine the scale of punishments meted out by the gods. For "a word that slips out through clenched teeth" the gods may de-cree death, just as they do for the most premeditated sacrilege. Those who deliberately slaughtered the cattle of the Sun and those whose only fault is to belong to Agamemnon's army thus both per-ish, with no distinction made between the two groups.

Metamorphoses and Punishments

Apollo demands a sumptuous sacrifice, for sacrifice is the most usual means of effecting reconciliation between the Olympians and the mortals. But there are many notable exceptions, for some faults are considered by the gods to be inexpiable, and these are marked out by a definitive punishment, as the whole of the later tradition of metamorphoses testifies. If you commit a crime, you become some-thing else—an animal, a plant, a star—taking a form that will forever, either through its permanence or its reproduction, signify the event that provoked the change. For example, the weasel gives birth through her mouth—or so the Ancients said—because she represents and repeats the action once perpetrated by Galinthias, the young woman whose lying *mouth* (*ore mendaci*) announced the *delivery* of

Alcmene and the birth of Heracles, thereby contravening the will of Hera.[18] The spider, endlessly respinning her web, perpetuates the work of Arachne, the conceited weaver who one day declared herself more skillful than Athena. The goddess's reaction was: well, if she weaves better than the goddess, let her get on with it![19] Such cruel ironies turn a body and its repeated gestures or its natural qualities into a living transcription of a bad memory. Sometimes, as in the story of Niobe, death and metamorphosis coincide. Niobe, the mother of six boys and six girls, had rejoiced in her offspring and boasted of them, saying that "Leto had two children only, but she herself had borne many"[20]: regrettable pride for which Niobe's children paid with their lives, as Artemis and Apollo–Leto's children– fairly divided between them the task of picking them all off, down to the very last one. With arrow after arrow, Apollo massacred the males, Artemis the females, while Niobe herself was changed into a stone. And all because Niobe ventured to compare herself to the beautiful Leto."[21]

As well as death and metamorphosis, the gods have other ways of taking revenge upon those who offend them. There are eternal tortures in Hades, which are the lot of individuals who have been particularly insolent. Odysseus meets three of these: Tityus, Tantalus, and Sisyphus. Tityus, a son of Earth, is stretched, helpless, on the ground. His huge body covers nine stades, but his imposing size is of no avail to him now against the two vultures which, perched on either side of him, devour his liver. The giant is expiating his former presumptuousness, for once, long ago, he tried to seduce Leto, the mistress of Zeus.[22] He transgressed the rules of amorous behavior, as did Ixion, a figure who, according to other accounts,[23] was received personally into the house of the master of Olympus. He was thus highly favored since, having shed the blood of his own father-in-law, he had been banished and was an outcast among men; only the great Zeus had the generosity to welcome him in, so as to purify him. But Ixion repaid that fine gesture by pressing his suit upon Hera, the wife of the very master of the house. To provide an abject lesson, he was punished by being nailed to a perpetually whirling wheel. Tantalus, for his part, was subjected to a different torture: standing in water, he could see refreshment approaching his lips, but as soon as he tried to drink, the water all drained away into the earth. Just above his head hung boughs laden with fruit–pears, pomegranates, apples, figs–but as soon as he lifted a hand to pick one, a gust of wind blew them all away.[24] Thirsty, famished, and condemned to a powerless longing to eat and drink, Tantalus suffered the consequences of a "Promethean" act. As a guest of honor at the gods' table, for Zeus used to like to confide in him, he had ruined his chances as a favorite by stealing the Immortals' nectar and ambrosia, the divine nourishment to which he owed his own immortality, planning to make mankind a gift of them.[25] As for Sisyphus, a modern symbol of the human condition, with the stone that he indefatigably pushed up a hill to the point where it repeatedly rolled back down to the bottom, he was paying for an indiscretion that had offended Zeus.[26]

But alongside such definitive sentences to torture, there did exist the possibility of sacrifice, that royal means of compensation and intercommunication between the gods and mortal men.

5 Savoring the Sweetness of Life

Can there be any society where nourishment is simply a means of filling one's stomach, quenching one's thirst, satisfying a natural need? The Greeks were extremely sensitive to the symbolic and social functions of actions connected with nourishment, and in their meals, banquets, and symposia they brought into play all the techniques of etiquette that are associated with moments of intense conviviality, conversation, and sociability. From philosophic dialogues entitled "Symposium" or "Banquet of the Seven Sages," down to voluble, erudite discussions known as "Table Talk," Greek scholars regarded a meal as an opportunity par excellence to put on a cultural performance.[1] Because a dining table implies fair distribution, invitations, and an alternation of roles, it is a place where symbolism is rampant, where men talk and reveal themselves, and where the cooked fare introduces an aesthetic that satisfies a hankering rather than an appetite.

In both the Greek city and the Homeric world, pleasure and social intercourse are the two most striking aspects of conviviality. To be sure, there is also the body's visceral, compelling hunger to be considered, for it makes men "yield to the cursed need for food"[2] and forces human beings to eat because they are so pathetic, unable to labor for a single day without sustenance. They need bread and wine, for "this gives strength and courage. A man will not be able to stand and fight all day long to the setting of the sun if he has gone without food: his heart may be eager for the fight but, without his knowing, his body grows heavy, and thirst and hunger come over him, and his legs weaken as he goes on."[3] Eating is a matter of necessity. But dining or lunching is above all a matter of organizing agreeable pauses in the long days of hard work.[4] At meals, human beings enjoy the sweetness of life, be they ever so humble. Eumaeus, Odysseus's swineherd, tells him that despite the hardships of life, the gods are benevolent when they allow a mortal the pleasure of food and drink and the leisure to entertain friends.[5]

Now, the gods, like humans, or even more so, also relish the shared pleasures of a celebration. They do so in a number of ways, savoring the aromas that rise up to them from the altars upon which men lay their sacrifices, sharing their ambrosia and nectar at the banquets that they organize among themselves, and also, more often than one might think, frequenting the dining tables set up by mortals.

Appetizing Aromas

"Hear me, lord of the silver bow, protector of Chryse and holy Killa, and mighty lord of Tenedos . . . "[6] The priest insulted by Agamemnon has finally received full satisfaction. His daughter has been restored to him, and he has been provided with victims for a sacred hecatomb. Already, he is preparing for the great ritual of the expiatory sacrifice. All those present have washed their hands, then picked up a handful of barley grains. They listen to Chryses appealing to the god, beseeching him to halt the scourge that is decimating the Argives. Lifting his arms to heaven, the old man presents his request to the lord of Chryse; before laying a hand on the beasts assembled around the altar, speech must establish contact between the mortals and the god. Apollo listens to the words of his priest, from afar.

But once this verbal prelude is over, actions speedily take over: barley is sprinkled on the brows of the oxen; then, "first they pulled back the victims' heads and slaughtered them and flayed them; and then they cut out the thigh bones and covered them with fat, folding it twice over, and placed pieces of raw meat on top."[7] The god's share–the first fruits–is prepared for him, to be served in the form of smoke from the sacrifice. The entire mass of bones and raw meat is burned: "The old man burnt them on cut firewood, and poured libations of gleaming wine."[8] Only after offering the god his ethereal nourishment do the sacrificers spare thought for themselves: "Then, when the thighs were burnt up and they had tasted the innards, they chopped the rest into pieces and threaded them on spits, roasted them carefully, and then drew all the meat off."[9] As quickly as possible, they embark on the cooking for the mortals' banquet. Then, as soon as "they have put away their desire for eating and drinking," the young men draw and distribute the wine for the libations, each of them offering it up to Apollo. "So all day long the young men of the Achaians appeased the god with music, singing a lovely hymn and dancing for the god who works from afar."[10] Apollo is grateful and "listens with delight in his heart."[11]

In the remainder of the ceremony, the meat is roasted, distributed, and eaten by the assembled mortals; then follow the two moments that represent the end purpose of the sacrifice: the moments of speaking to the god and of appeasing his wrath. Apollo is involved, offered a sacrifice, then praised. From this point of view, the solemn liturgy of this sacrifice to Apollo constitutes a model: the feasting of the sacrificers goes hand in hand with the homage—both poetic and in the form of nourishment—offered to an Immortal. There are many ways of demonstrating one's liberality and zeal: one can offer thanks, flatter, seek favors, ward off anger. Before a battle, upon returning from an ambush, when hoping to obtain a special alliance or to avoid a punishment, men are careful to invite the Olympians to the imaginary reception that is constituted by the ceremony of a sacrifice. For that reason, the most ceremonious of Homeric sacrifices are essentially religious acts and only coincidentally occasions for feasting on the part of the celebrants.[12] Alongside this dominant model of sacrifice, however, one also comes across rather different situations.

Sometimes a share is offered to a deity in the course of a banquet held primarily in honor of a human guest. Eumaeus, Odysseus's loyal swineherd, slaughters the finest beast in his herd for the stranger who is his guest. He does not realize that this is Odysseus, his master, in person, but his sensitivity and country courtesy prompt him to treat the stranger handsomely. In this case, the Immortals are quite rightly remembered. Eumaeus flings into the fire the bristles from the pig's great head, then the first fruits plucked from the victim's body, burning the limbs that are now covered in grease. Of the portions grilled for his guests, he offers the first to Hermes and the Nymphs, not taking his own share until he has poured out a cup of dark wine for the gods as a whole. Not to forget the gods in the course of a meal the pretext of which is purely human hospitality really is tantamount to paying them constant attention. Eumaeus certainly reserves two slices of pork for the noble stranger for whom he has killed the beast, but he still begins by paying homage to the Immortals. His guest receives the best portion, but the gods take precedence and are the first to be served.[13]

At meals the gods are usually the principal interlocutors, or, more rarely, they are absent guests who are never forgotten. In any event, they are involved in a distribution of food that obeys the rule of the offering of first fruits or, according to some authors, the fiction of an offering of the entire sacrifice: the morsels set aside for them are said to represent the whole body of the victim (but, of course, this makes no difference to the distribution of the meal that in reality takes place). However, the idea of a sharing does not coincide totally with the notion of a sacrifice. For there are also, on the one hand, holocausts, and, on the other, meals shared by human beings, for which animals are killed for their meat and then consumed, with no attention at all paid to the Olympians.

According to Asclepiades, a historian from Cyprus cited by Porphyry, a neo-Platonic philosopher of the third century A.D., the total sacrifice, or holocaust, in which the victim is totally consumed by the flames, provided the original model of a sacrifice. In the very earliest times, men never killed, either for the gods or for themselves. Then, one day they introduced the practice of killing a sheep as an oblation for the gods. Ordinary mortal men were kept away from this. But on one occasion a priest allowed himself to be tempted by a morsel of roasted fat that had fallen from the altar. He picked it up, then licked his fingers. That was the initial transgression, and it led to the inauguration of a diet for mortals that included meat. The holocaust was thus replaced by a sharing.[14] In the Homeric world, a total offering to the gods, leaving nothing for men, requires a situation out of the common run. Entire animals are burned on the pyre of Patroclus, over which the excessively grieving, distraught Achilles presides. And on two occasions the entire slaughtered animal is disposed of by being buried or cast into the sea. These are sacrifices that consecrate a vow or a pact. We might have expected that, in such circumstances, where it is a matter of sealing an inviolable agreement between mortals, commensality would take precedence over offerings. But, on the contrary, it is precisely in those cases that the sacrificers do not touch the meat of the slaughtered victims. The rite has no connection at all with food, but does carry a threat of violence, the murderous violence that will be unleashed if the undertaking is broken. The act of pouring a libation–spilling some wine onto the ground, for the gods–assumes a macabre meaning: if anyone violates the pact, his brains and those of his children are to be dashed onto the ground, just like the drink spilled there. Those are the terms of the curse that accompanies the gesture: they prefigure vengeance, anticipate reprisals. The gods are invoked not only as witnesses, but also as those to be responsible if it ever comes to a settling of accounts: "If any of this is falsely sworn, may the gods heap on me the misery they give to a man who offends them with his oath."[15]

In total contrast to sacrifices in which no portions of food are left for men, it does sometimes happen that the gods are totally ignored in a meal shared by mortals. Such is the case when Priam and Achilles come face to face, when the old king comes to beg for the corpse of his son to be returned to him. The two men can think of nothing but the truce between them and regard each other with mutual respect and admiration. Both behave like divine creatures and there is nothing sacrilegious about their meeting. Far from it: Hermes himself has been detailed by Zeus to conduct Priam to Achilles' hut. Yet the warrior invites his guest to share a spitted lamb with him, and sets aside no portion for any of the gods.[16] Nor does anybody spare a thought for the gods at another dinner that appears in no way out of the ordinary and for which the Achaeans kill oxen in their stalls and procure themselves an excellent "lemnos."[17]

The Sacrificial Relationship

However, in a model sacrifice, nourishment in the form of meat is shared between the mortals and the Immortals–offered by the former to the latter, but also shared by them. An authoritative version of the origin of this custom exists, recorded by the other great theologian of Greece, Hesiod. Once upon a time, he sings, there was a Golden Age. Men and gods lived together, in the same place, and there, to their unanimous stupefaction, the very first woman was presented to them all as soon as she was created. Here, the men and the gods all ate together, until one day it fell to Prometheus to prepare the large ox for their banquet: "Prometheus was forward to cut up a great ox and set portions before them, trying to befool the mind of Zeus. Before the rest he set flesh and inner parts thick with fat upon the hide, covering them with an ox paunch; but for Zeus he put the white bones dressed up with cunning art and covered with shining fat."[18]

By trying to favor the men, the Titan put an end to the shared meals that had brought the Olympians and the mortals together. Stirred to anger, Zeus deprived men of fire—which Prometheus then, through a cunning ruse, stole back from him—and then sent them an assuredly much overrated evil, woman. The unfair division of the ox ushered in a new era: from that point on mortals were ritually to repeat Prometheus's insolent behavior, burning on their altars the bare bones of their victims, covered in fat, for the gods, and keeping for themselves the red meat and the entrails.

In this form, sacrifice established a moment of communication and contact between the inhabitants of the earth and the masters of Olympus. The recipient of a sacrifice would be solicited, hailed by those who were offering up a victim. Apollo heard and listened to the prayer from Chryses, and he was pleased by the paeans sung for him and by the libations of wine spilled on the ground. Silently, he approved of the ceremony and accepted the prayers formally addressed to him. The following day, when Agamemnon's emissaries left Chryse, Apollo called up favorable winds to speed them on their way. A deity did not necessarily use visible signs to manifest his response—consent or rejection—to the request that accompanied the ritual. On such matters, the gods were secretive. Agamemnon would never know, when Zeus accepted a sacrifice, whether the god intended to heed his prayers.[19] Nor did the women of Troy receive any explicit response when they promised a virgin heifer to Athena if she would break Diomedes' spear,[20] for they did not hear her quiet "No." The postulants never knew whether the Olympians would do as they were asked. Human beings would express their desires, send up their messages, then have to wait and see.

When addressed through sacrifice, the gods responded more or less secretly to the mortal hopes that were expressed, but when the victim's thighs were roasted, the gods were no longer present. The cult betokened this distance between the two groups, even as it made it possible to restore communications through the ritual. That was all that remained of their lost commensality. However, it did sometimes happen that an Immortal would come in person to be present at a ceremony held in his or her honor. One case in point is that of Athena, who accompanies Telemachus when he goes to Nestor's manor house to ask after the fate of his father. Assuming the appearance of a wise counselor, Mentor, the goddess has already taken an active part in a sacrifice for Poseidon. It was she who, at nightfall, interrupted the admittedly prolix reminiscences of the master of the house.[21] It is Poseidon's own niece, a true-bred Olympian, who organizes the sacrifice for her father's brother before making her farewells amid general amazement. For, although she says her goodbyes to her hosts with the voice of Mentor, she then suddenly flies away, just like an osprey. Nestor has recognized her: "Of all that live on Olympus, this was no other than the Daughter of Zeus, the august Lady of Triton," he exclaims, and immediately promises her a heifer "broad in the brow, whom noone yet has broken in."[22] Athena is delighted and accepts the prayer and the promise. The next day, at dawn, "Athene . . . came, to accept the sacrifice."[23]

The Gods' Share

For the gods of the Homeric world, the sacrifice of an animal victim represented an opportunity to communicate with men and share meat with them, even if only in the form of an aroma. Although by and large in conformity with the model of the trick that Prometheus played on Zeus, the ritual of sacrifice differed in one crucial respect. Let us assume that the "thighs" (*mēria*) burned on the altar were in fact femurs—that is to say, the thigh bones—rather than whole thighs (although we cannot be absolutely certain about this). At any rate, we have to recognize that Homer's gods were never offered completely "white bones" (*ostea leuka*), as Zeus was when he was fooled by the Titan. For, on top of the fat used to surround the *mēria*, there was a layer of raw meat, designed to go up in flames and produce a

smoky aroma *for the gods.* In at least one passage of the text, such
morsels are the first to be cut from the victim's limbs; and one com-
mentator of a later period notes that the purpose of this thin layer
of meat was to signify that the Ancients wished symbolically to offer
the gods the entire animal.[24] This would explain the enthusiasm
with which the gods received sacrifices offered by the men of
Homer's world. Zeus may have been right to show his resentment
when he discovered bare bones beneath the fat that concealed them;
on the other hand, he had good reason to delight in the altars
heaped with the bones, fat, and red meat that the Trojans and
Greeks presented as burnt offerings.

The Greek gods were carnivorous. Ambrosia and nectar were, of
course, their special, Olympian forms of nourishment, but they
were by no means averse to the meat of animals, provided it was
served up to them in the form of an *odor.* That is a presumption of
even Hesiod's account: Why should Zeus have been angry if he did
not feel *offended* at having been denied meat? It is only Hesiod, that
embittered peasant who seems to have regarded absolutely everything on earth as wearisome, starting with women, who failed to see
that the sacrifices to which the Immortals were so partial were not
mere repetitions of Prometheus's harmful trick.

This aspect of the gods' dietary behavior is made particularly explicit in the insistence on the need to abstain from meat and reject
sacrifice that is expressed by the pagan theologian, Porphyry. To
murder living creatures in order to offer a share of them to the gods
was to ascribe to those superior beings the very lowest tastes of impious men. On those who practice blood sacrifice, Porphyry comments: "It would make more sense to say that they were perverted
than that the gods were, since they regarded the gods as evil beings,
bereft of any natural superiority over ourselves."[25] He intended,
thereby, to condemn the fact that sacrifice rested upon false theology and a totally vulgar conception of divinity. Porphyry was a neo-
Platonist, who attacked the Christians for believing in the incarnation because of the incompatibility of the nature of a deity and the
baseness of everything carnal. In his eyes, the gods had to be conceived as vegetarians. Only sacrifices of fruits, oils, and herbs ought
to be made as burnt offerings. That was how men in ancient times
used to manifest their piety and gratitude, before the introduction

of blood sacrifices. And blood sacrifices themselves were, according to Porphyry, a relatively recent product of various natural disasters involving "hunger and all the injustices that stem from it."[26]

The very first pig to be slaughtered was killed by a woman, by mistake. "At this, her husband prudently, and thinking that she may have committed an illegitimate act," went to Delphi, to consult the Pythia. Apollo "accepted what had happened," ratified the error, and thereby authorized its repetition. The first sheep was offered up to a god as a first fruit after that same oracle had laid down one condition, namely, that the candidate "should acquiesce by bowing its head in the direction of the lustral water." As for the first goat and the first ox to be slaughtered, they were killed for having been greedy: the goat because it had eaten the leaves of a vine, the ox because it had consumed a sacred cake left, with other vegetable offerings, for Zeus Poleius. In each case, whether the animal was killed by mistake or as a result of a surge of anger, the first sacrifice was an unfortunate accident caused by the imperfection of the control that human beings exercise over their actions. All the god did was accept what had happened. In the case of the sheep, a man's desire to kill it preceded the animal's acquiescence to its slaughter. The god who was consulted does not appear to have wanted to make any decision. He left open the question of whether or not to kill, a matter to be resolved case by case, between the executioner and his victim.

Clearly, the behavior of the gods poses a delicate problem for a theologian. If the gods were really as ascetic and pro-animal as Porphyry suggests, should not Apollo have punished the animals' killers or at the very least forbidden any repetition of the occurrence? There was nothing to prevent the Immortals from punishing human faults, however accidental, as we have seen. To show that the sole justification for blood sacrifice is the combination of an accident and the injustice of men, Porphyry appeals to tales in which, as he puts it, the death of living creatures is caused by ignorance, anger, or fear. But those same tales also involve an Olympian god, and by no means one of the least important. Apollo is presented as an accomplice, albeit a reluctant one, in the founding of the ritual persistently condemned as illegitimate by this philosopher.

The thinking of Porphyry the theologian on the nourishment that is worthy of the gods oscillates between two arguments. According to one, to ascribe a taste for meat to the Immortals constitutes a typical human mistake: this argument presupposes that no god could possibly accept flesh-and-blood victims. According to the other argument, it has to be admitted that some divine powers do relish the savor of roast meat; however, those beings are not gods, but harmful demons: "It is they who delight in libations and the smell of meat," declares Porphyry, citing the *Iliad* (9.500). For the soft and corporeal part of their beings "lives on vapours and whiffs, on a life nourished by various effluvia; it derives its strength from aromas that arise from blood and burning flesh."[27] In short, if the Homeric gods delight in the smell of blood and red meat, they cannot possibly be real gods. It is the kind of inductive argument in which the Church Fathers were to delight. If Apollo chose as priestess a woman who, with straddled legs, took in vapors through her sexual orifices, the lord of Delphi can have been no god, but rather an evil demon. Such were the arguments used by, for example, Origen (third century A.D.) and John Chrysostomum (fourth century A.D.) in their bids to destroy the prestige of the Pythian oracle. Somatic and carnal elements were extremely operative criteria for precursors of the history of religions such as these, whether or not they were Christian. On the pleasures of "the table of demons," Celsus and Origen were essentially at one. The pagan polemicist recognized that "perhaps we should not refuse to believe the sages: they say that most terrestrial demons, absorbed in generation, *riveted to blood and the savors of fat* . . . , can do nothing better than cure *bodies*, predicting the destinies of individuals and cities, for their knowledge and power extends no further than *mortal* activities."[28] Origen, for his part, added that, faced with such greedy demons, the best thing to do was to entrust oneself, body and soul, to the supreme God, through Jesus Christ.

Nectar and Ambrosia

"The whole day long till sunset we sat and feasted on our rich supply of meat and mellow wine"[29] (Odysseus's reminiscences of his famous stay with Circe, the magician). "When they had finished their work and prepared the meal, they set to eating and no man's desire went without an equal share in the feast"[30] (the sacrificial banquet on the Chryse seashore, for a group of Greeks). The recipe for a successful feast is to take plenty of time—a whole day, if necessary—organizing a fair distribution, so that everybody is contented and nobody lacks for anything.

Similarly, "They feasted all day long till the setting of the sun, and noone's desire went without an equal share in the feast."[31] Spend a good, long time, and let there be plenty to enjoy: the concept of perfection is the same, yet this is a different kind of feast, an Olympian one.

The gods eat and drink: their daily bread and wine is ambrosia and nectar and has been ever since childhood. When Leto, given a welcome by the islanders of Delos, gives birth to Apollo there, the infant is not suckled by his mother, even though she is a goddess. Instead, the immortal hands of Themis ply him with nectar and delicious ambrosia. The effects of this diet are soon manifest: the baby kicks and wriggles so actively that his swaddling bands cannot hold him. He casts aside those constraints and begins to speak. He immediately calls for his lyre and his bow, announces his plan to found an oracle, and, leaping from his cradle, sets off to roam the highways.[32] Hermes first sees the light of day in a cave that contains "three closets full of nectar and lovely ambrosia" locked by a great golden key. In these three cupboards the food of the gods was placed alongside many garments "such as one kept in the sacred houses of the blessed gods."[33]

Ambrosia and nectar, the food of and for the gods, can also be used to deify and immortalize a child born to be mortal. Demeter tries to infuse immortality into one baby boy by smearing his skin with these active substances and rubbing them in. The great goddess, in mourning since the disappearance of her daughter Persephone, got herself taken on as a nurse in the home of a man of Eleusis: "So the goddess nursed in the palace Demophoon, wise Celeus's goodly son whom well-guided Metaneira bare. And the child grew like some immortal being, not fed with food nor nourished at the breast, for by day rich-crowned Demeter would anoint him with ambrosia as if he were the offspring of a god and breathe sweetly upon him."[34] But immortality can also be administered orally. The Hours distill nectar and ambrosia between the lips of Aristeus, the son of Apollo and Cyrene, a mortal woman, to save him from death.[35]

By smearing the body and massaging it with the substances that can cure mortality, or by gently pouring them into a mortal's mouth, the nature of a human body can be changed. They nourish it, eliminating hunger and thirst, and they ward off the processes of corruption.

One day Achilles, a failed Immortal who, more tragically than any other hero, was destined to die before his time, refuses to lift bread or wine to his lips. Immersed in his grief, he wants to remain, to the last, undivided from his friend slain in battle, his other self, who took up his arms and died in his place. He refuses to heed the pressing advice of his comrades-in-arms. They tell him that the war cannot be won on an empty stomach, that men cannot last out their days without taking nourishment. But Achilles is adamant: he will touch no food. High on Olympus, however, Zeus is watching, and he too knows that the knees of men buckle and tremble when assailed by hunger. He bids Athena go and comfort Achilles without him realizing, and the goddess flies off, eager to be of help. She does not make him eat, though, but instead pours upon his chest wonderful ambrosia and nectar, "so that hunger does not come over him."[36] A body weakened by fasting can be restored to all its strength and vitality in this way. And even a dead body, an already stiffened corpse, can be treated by these divine panacea—if it is a special body, that is, such as that of Patroclus. He is to be burned on a pyre and his remains—the whitened bones and the ashes—are to be buried. But before the solemn funeral rituals can take place, a number of days must elapse, and the flesh of humans soon rots. Vermin, the foul product of the race of flies, threaten to invade Patroclus's body. So, to preserve it, Thetis instills ambrosia and red nectar in Patroclus's nostrils. She tells her son, who is anxious that the body should not decompose, "I shall make sure to keep away from him the cruel swarms of flies that feed on the bodies of men killed in war. Even if he lies here for a year's full circle, his flesh will always remain as it is, or even firmer than now."[37] Ambrosia and nectar can be used to feed a newborn god, to change a mortal into an Immortal, or even to keep a corpse from rotting; and they can revitalize a hero's body when it is weakened by hunger and thirst. But they do not have the power to bring a dead body back to life. Bringing back the dead would be more a matter of retrieving from Hades whatever remained of the identity of a mortal, his double, without his physical substance, that is to say his *eidolon*. Ambrosia and nectar could thus be said to be a treatment for immortality, substances that give a body the ability to resist time and defy death. On immortal bodies, a regular application of them sustains beauty, brilliance, and energy. As we have seen, Hera rubbed herself with ambrosia before her erotic meeting with Zeus. But first and foremost, ambrosia and nectar are the daily nourishment of the Olympians. As such, they constitute a particularly important element in the life of the gods.

A Taste for Happiness

To say that the gods eat and drink is really not enough from the point of view adopted here. To be sure, eating and drinking number among the many activities pursued by the gods. But more needs to be said. If we thought about the gods as much as people used to, before what Heine calls their exile, we might have added that *the gods are always engaged* in drinking and eating. They do so in a continuous present. At any moment, one of them–possibly Themis–will be offering a bowl of dark red nectar to Apollo, who has just arrived, or to Hera, who is approaching. For there is no particular fixed time for feasting, no special, rare occasions. "They feasted all day long till the setting of the sun."[38] If Apollo arrives unexpectedly, "His father offers his son nectar, greeting him holding a golden cup."[39] When the august Hera reaches steep Olympus, she finds all the other immortal gods gathered together in Zeus's palace. "When they saw her they all rose to their feet and offered their cups in greeting. She ignored the others and accepted a cup from beautiful Themis."[40]

A feast lasts *all day long* (*propan ēmar*), as can be seen from the way in which, at any moment, in any part of Olympus, a cup may be proffered to whoever has just arrived. Feasting fills every last bit of time. That is how the gods fill their days in the places that belong exclusively to them.

The feasting of the gods: in the High Renaissance, Raphael, Giulio Romano, and Tintoretto all painted pictures of such scenes. Classical painting would be sadly diminished if the gods were not portrayed eternally at table, grouped around opulent *natures mortes*, complete with tablecloths, crockery, and sophisticated dishes, and constituting such a contrast to the frugal last supper of the dual-natured Christian God, distributing bread and wine with death fast approaching. The dwellings of the Olympians were to become the setting for banquets and garden parties reproduced ad infinitum in the most realistic of landscapes, in the theater, and in paintings produced for the courts of Europe, all competing in the reinvention of the life of the gods.

Perhaps this endless feasting symbolized the whole of a contented existence in which happiness consisted in convivial enjoyment in which all cares were forgotten. Perhaps this is the key to Olympian beatitude. Perhaps we have at last laid bare the secret of those words: "without cares," "an easy life," "blessed." Perhaps the moments of tension, effort, and anxiety were exceptional crises set against a background of continuous leisure enjoyed with a cup in hand, whilst savoring ambrosia. An everlasting banquet certainly provided one model of perfect contentment. Plato was to make fun of the Orphics, who could only imagine the condition of the Blessed in the Beyond as that of a gathering of companions forever seated round a table.[41] In contrast, the punishments of the Underworld consist of the torture of eternally thwarted desire: plaiting a rope that always comes apart, stretching out hands to proffered fruits that are snatched away, trying to fill a jar that leaks, pushing a stone that always rolls back. They are all variants of the same experience, the impossibility of fulfilling a wish. Ocnus, Tantalus, the Danaids, and Sisyphus all suffer from the intolerable insistence of their desires.[42] Their daily lives are passed in perpetual tension. Meanwhile, the Blessed pass their time in perpetual enjoyment, riveted to a table laden with all they could possibly desire.

The Philosophers' Critique

When Lucretius compares men who have dissipated their time in the pursuit of useless things, hence in dissatisfaction, to men who have lived a worthwhile existence, he draws a contrast between the Danaids, obsessed with their jar, and a guest who rises from the table, contented and replete. But the Blessed whom Plato mocks never do leave the table, however much the philosopher despises their debauchery. However, the gods are not, in fact, riveted to their golden thrones, to their plates laden with ambrosia, and to the crater from which Hebe or Hephaestus serves brimming cups of ruby nectar. As we have seen, their tasks and their concerns frequently tear them away from the delights of Olympus. The Greek gods are not lazy. Even Plato acknowledges that. In response to those who, even before Epicurus, said that they existed but took no notice of men, the author of the *Laws* pointed out that "the gods, being good with all goodness, possess such care of the whole as is most proper to themselves."[43] What are the various characteristics of goodness? Temperance, intelligence, courage, virtue: concepts that are opposed to selfishness, laziness, and self-indulgence. And if that is true for humans, and even for animals, it must also hold true for the gods. Could the Olympians be drones and parasites? Not conceivably. If they are good—and that is the postulate—they cannot be lazy or indulge in *truphē*, luxury without moderation.

For Plato, the gods can do anything that mortals can do, and do it better, going so far as to attend carefully to the last details of their enterprises. They excel at finishing touches, work perfectly completed, and hold laziness in horror. However, another philosopher, Aristotle, modifies the confidence and certainty of his master. He declares that the whole of mythology, centered on the representation of the gods in human form, is a late tradition grafted on to a more ancient belief according to which "the heavenly bodies are gods, and . . . the Divine pervades the whole of nature."[44] The anthropomorphic gods, with their histories and their mode of life, are, Aristotle thinks, pedagogical inventions useful "to influence the vulgar and as a constitutional and utilitarian expedient."[45] When he himself ponders upon human ethics and the ideal style of life that is worthy of humankind, Aristotle compares the life of mortals to that of the Olympians. Indeed, he goes further, and suggests that it is on the basis of what one can conjecture about the daily life of the gods that one can understand wherein lies happiness for men.

The life that becomes man the most is the life of the intellect. And such a life is also the happiest. That is blindingly obvious to Aristotle. All the same, he feels obliged to argue his case:

The following considerations also will show that perfect happiness is some form of contemplative activity. The gods, as we conceive them, enjoy supreme felicity and happiness. But what sort of actions can we attribute to them? Just actions? But will it not seem ridiculous to think of them as making contracts, restoring deposits and the like? Then brave actions—enduring terrors and running risks for the nobility of so doing? Or liberal actions? But to whom will they give? Besides, it would be absurd to suppose that they actually have a coinage or currency of some sort! And temperate actions—what will these mean in their case? Surely it would be derogatory to praise them for having no evil desires! If we go through the list, we shall find that all forms of virtuous conduct seem trifling and unworthy of the gods. Yet nevertheless they have always been conceived as, at all events, living and therefore living actively, for we cannot suppose they are always asleep like Endymion. But for a living being, if we eliminate action, and *a fortiori* creative action, what remains save contemplation? It follows that the activity of God, which is transcendent in blessedness, is the activity of contemplation; and therefore among human activities that which is most akin to the divine activity of contemplation will be the greatest source of happiness.[46]

Aristotle thus denies the gods any active life, arguing that their sole mode of life is thought. And that kind of life, which is the only kind that is not ridiculous for a god, is also the most worthy for a man. A few centuries later, in Rome, Seneca repeated that a philosopher lives as happily as a god, except that his happiness is brief, for he makes a *vita* of the *tempus* at his disposal, turning time into a life that belongs to him and that incorporates the past, the present, and the future, as he contemplates it. He is as happy as an Immortal because, instead of wasting his days, frittering them away in a thousand and one occupations, he truly possesses each one, as he does his whole life, and can pass them in review. Choosing *otium*, "the wise man's life spreads out to him over as large a surface as does eternity to a god."[47]

This theme of the immobility and expanse of time in the eyes of a god who encompasses the whole of its duration in an *eternal today* (*sempiternum hodie*) was to be very dear to Christian theology. It answers the need to think of the time lived by a divine being as consecrated to the continuous exercise of contemplation and knowledge.

The gods are not lazy, Plato protests; they busy themselves in the service of the world. The gods are not lazy, Aristotle corrects him, but they can only give themselves to a contemplative life, the kind of existence that Seneca was to call *otium*. Certainly no philosopher speaks of the sweetness of their life in terms of feasting.

The Sweetness of Life

And yet, it is in those very terms that Homer tells of their beatitude. On the day when a quarrel erupts between Zeus and his wife, Hephaestus does not conceal the fact that his sole worry is lest this discord should interrupt "the excellent feast." He urges his powerful mother, despite her anger, to "make her peace with our dear father Zeus, so that the father does not scold her again and spoil our feasting."[48] Hephaestus is concerned, quite literally, for sweetness (*ēdos*) and leisure when he fervently hopes that Zeus will not decide to trouble (*tarassein*) the party. And what he so much fears is not, it seems, the interruption of a mere meal, but the disruption of a whole day of leisure.

Or, you might say, the disruption of a whole life of leisure if, instead of being drawn into the tumult of the Homeric epic, you envisaged the Olympian existence as Hesiod depicts it, ever unchanging and immobile. In the past, throughout the Golden Age, men lived like gods. What does that mean? Without cares, without fatigue, without old age: "With legs and arms never failing they made merry with feasting beyond the reach of all evils."[49] So the gods are permanently engaged in a *thaleia*, a joyful, convivial, "sympotic" banquet, which, among men, is placed under the aegis of a Muse, Thalia, who civilizes the inhuman, bestial desire for drink and food,[50] the same Muse who was later credited with disclosing to mortals the *komikos bios*, the comic life, or comedy.[51]

On another day when, for the very first time in his life, the very young Apollo climbs up to Olympus, what meets his eyes is a scene of the ordinary existence of his fellow gods. His father, feeling very happy, hands him a cup of nectar, as if the gods gathered there had absolutely nothing else to do. And "then straightway the undying gods think only of the lyre and song, and all the Muses together, voice sweetly answering voice, hymn the unending gifts the gods enjoy and the sufferings of men, all that they endure at the hands of the deathless gods, and how they live witless and helpless and cannot find healing for death or defense against old age."[52] Drinking and enjoying their privileges: that is what makes the Olympians happy! The cunning Hermes realizes this at once, even as a tiny child, when he chafes and rebels against his mother's boring plans. What? Live a modest life, deep in a cave, far from Olympus? "Better to live in fellowship with the deathless gods continually (*ēmata panta*), rich, wealthy and enjoying stores of grain, than to sit always in a gloomy cave!"[53] And the kind of richness he has in mind is certainly that of food–not ambrosia and nectar, but rather the offerings of sacrifices.

Comic Life

The gods are not just assiduous banqueters in their own homes and in those of anyone who invites them down to dine. As we have seen, they also receive the aromas of meat that is roasted on the altars of mortals. They are ferociously attached to this, insisting upon it with a greed that was to be ridiculed in one famous comedy, Aristophanes' *Birds*, and also in the dialogues of Lucian.

When the birds of the sky decide to intercept and keep for themselves the appetizing smells produced by sacrifices, the gods are obliged to beg from these creatures and to negotiate a deal: they will give up sovereignty in exchange for their allowance of aromas. It seems that ambrosia and nectar are inadequate nourishment for a god. By deviating the smoke rising from roasting thighs, the Birds plan to have the gods die of a proverbial hunger.[54] The gods have no choice but to elect, democratically, three delegates–Poseidon, Heracles, and a Triballian, who represents the barbarian gods. The mission of these three is to set up talks to negotiate a peace with the Birds. As Prometheus, acting as a spy, reveals, since the city of the Birds colonized the air, smoke from the altars has no longer been rising to the gods. The consequence is fasting, famine.[55] The barbarian gods demand that Zeus get the supplies of chopped entrails reestablished. Meanwhile, the Birds, who proclaim themselves to be immortal gods, the ancestors of the very Olympians, promise the ephemeral human beings that they will keep a vigilant lookout on

their behalf, which will bring them prosperity and ease. Their chorus leader tells the mortals that the Birds will keep an eye on the me-
teorological outlook and keep them informed when changes occur.
Instead of living a retired life in the Sky, majestically enthroned like
Zeus, they will be present to bring the mortals riches, health, life,
peace, youth, laughter, dancing, celebrations, and the milk of the
birds. The mortals' wealth will be such that they will have more than
they can cope with.[56]

Humans will even be able to come and live in the city of the bird-
gods, where happiness awaits them. "Is there anyone amongst you,
o spectators, who would lead with the birds a life of pleasure, let him
come to us with speed"[57]: in the play, this is the generous invitation
proffered to the assembled Athenians seated on the tiered steps of
the theater. And soon a great sacrifice, a grill of dissident birds, will
be prepared and arranged by the new gods for . . . themselves. The
three Olympians arrive as ambassadors just in time to see the poul-
try, sprinkled with grated cheese, silphium, and oil, ready for roasting, and to express their passionate nostalgia for such a delicious
dinner.

In comedy, happiness is above all satiety, an excess of material satisfaction, both for men and for the gods. The only difference is that
the gods get what they want more quickly and more easily. Faced
with the Birds, who are the new gods, since it is they who control access to the sacrificial aromas, the Olympians, condemned to lan-
guish, are reduced to indigent dependents. Obsessed with a desire
that they can no longer satisfy, they experience the dereliction of
human beings. They beg, hope, and wait. Infinite feasting, for which
they had never before had to prepare, since it was always ready for
them in inexhaustible profusion, becomes their goal, to be recovered by negotiating an exchange.

In a similar vein, but in a different situation–an emergency assembly convened to settle an extremely serious matter (how to react
to the criticisms of the philosophers)–the Olympians show that even
the gravest of circumstances cannot force them to forego what Lucian (third century A.D.) calls "their usual daily shouts" as they think
about their food: "Give us our shares! Where is the nectar? The ambrosia is all gone! Where are the hecatombs? Victims in common!"[58] When frustrated, the gods wail about their hunger and

thirst, as if even meeting for a short assembly without refreshment and tempting nibbles is intolerable to them. And, as it happens, the subject to be debated is of crucial importance, precisely because it affects their way of life: do they or do they not take an interest in human beings? How do they spend their time? The philosophers are spreading doubt. What do the gods, the interested parties here, have to say about it? Many of them bay for vengeance or say nothing at all. But there is one who does take things seriously: Momus. He declares that Epicurus is right: "If you would have me speak the truth, we sit here considering just one question, whether anybody is slaying victims and burning incense at our altars; everything else drifts with the current, swept aimlessly along."[59] This does not amount to total transparency, for such things are only said behind closed doors, between gods, when "there is no man in our gathering."[60] All the same, it is an astonishing confession. However, Zeus does not altogether agree.

Business Dinners

Plague take all philosophers who say that bliss is to be found only among the gods! If they but knew all that we endure for the sake of men, they would not envy us our nectar and ambrosia, putting their trust in Homer, a blind man and a fraud, who called us blissful and told about what is in heaven when he could not even see what is on earth. Here is an example, right at hand: Helius puts his team to his chariot and traverses the sky all day long, clad in a garment of fire and resplendent with rays, not even getting leisure enough to scratch his ear, as they say; for if he unconsciously relaxes the least bit, his horses run away, turn out of the road, and burn everything up. Selene too goes about without a wink of sleep, giving light to night-roisterers and people returning late from dinners. Apollo, again, has taken up a very active profession, and has been deafened almost completely by people besetting him with requests for prophecies. One moment he has to be in Delphi; the next he runs to Colophon; from there he crosses to Xanthus, and again at full speed to Delos or Branchidae. In a word, wherever his prophetess, after drinking from the holy well and chewing laurel and setting the tripod ashake, bids him appear, there is no delaying—he must be present himself immediately to reel off his prophecies, or else it is all up with his reputation in the profession. I say nothing of the devices they get up to test his powers of divination, cooking mutton and turtle together so that, if he had not a good nose, that Lydian would have gone off laughing at him. As for Asclepius, he is pestered by the sick: "Dire sights he sees and touches what he loathes, and in the woes of others finds a crop of sorrow for himself." Why should I refer either to the Winds that aid the crops and speed the ships on their courses and blow upon the winnowers, or to Sleep, that wings his way to everyone, or to Jack-of-dreams, that keeps vigil all night long with Sleep and serves as his interpreter? All this work the gods do out of love of man, each contributing to life on earth.

And yet the others are not so badly off in comparison to myself. I am the monarch and father of all; but how many discomforts I put up with and how many bothers I have, distracted as I am by such a number of things to think of! First, I must oversee the work of all the other gods who help me in any way in administering my sovereignty, in order that they might not be remiss in it. Then I myself have to do any number of tasks that are almost impossible to carry out on account of their minuteness; for it is not to be supposed that I simply manage and direct in person the principal features of my administration, such as rain, hail, wind and lightning, and that then I am through, being dispensed from thinking about details. No, not only must I do all that, but I must look in all directions at the same time, and keep an eye on everybody, just like the herdsman at Nemea, to see who is stealing, who is committing perjury, who is offering sacrifice, whether anybody has poured a drink-offering, from what quarter the steam and the smoke of burnt-offerings rise, who has called upon me in sickness or at sea. What is most laborious of all, at one and the same moment I must attend the great sacrifice at Olympia, keep an eye on the armies at war near Babylon, send hail in the country of the Getae, and attend a banquet among the Ethiopians.

At that, it is not easy to escape criticism. It often appears that the others, "the gods and the warriors crested with horse-tails," sleep all through the night, while I, though Zeus, am not "held in the sweetness of slumber," for if I drowse off, even for an instant, Epicurus is instantly confirmed in his assertion that we exercise no providence over what happens on earth. And we cannot make light of the danger if men are going to take his word for this: our temples will have no wreathes, our wayside shrines no savory steam, our wine-bowls no drink-offerings, our altars will be cold, in short there will be a general dearth of sacrifices and oblations, and famine will be rife. For that reason, like the master of a ship, I stand by myself high up on the stern with the tiller in my hands, and everybody else aboard gets drunk, perhaps, and goes to sleep, whereas I, without closing my eyes

or eating, "ponder in heart and in soul" for the benefit of all, re-
warded only by being considered captain.

So I should like to ask the philosophers, who say that only the gods
are happy, when they suppose we really find leisure for our nectar and
our ambrosia in the midst of our countless bothers.[61]

It is only fair that Zeus should have his say, for he knows what he is
talking about when it comes to the matter of the happiness of the
Olympians. Every time anyone tries to imagine how the time of the
gods, presumed to be happy, is filled, a picture of them consuming
ambrosia and nectar, relaxed and joyful, at a banquet is produced.
Yet the Olympians simply do not have the time to spend on such
happiness. Without respite, they are occupied by other things.
Worse still, far from devoting themselves to the sole, unique experience of convivial celebration, they are obliged to do a thousand
things at once. Not only is their time constantly taken up by one task
after another, but at every moment they are torn. They have to split
themselves in two, do everything at the same time. Moreover, nourishment itself, when it is a matter of aromas given off by sacrifices, is
another cause for concern, for two reasons: first, given that their
nourishment depends on an exchange agreed upon with humans,
the gods are obliged to take care of earthly matters *in order to* receive their share of victims; and second, because presiding over
these rituals performed at the altars is itself a considerable chore.
Kēdos and *hēdos*–cares and pleasure–are inseparable, the more
so given that on the Olympus of the *Iliad* the banquets are almost
invariably used as opportunities for discussions, deliberation, and
decision-taking. The assembly convened by Zeus in Lucian's dialogue cannot proceed until the voices clamoring for ambrosia, nectar, and aromas are hushed; in other words, it is held in absolute abstinence and sobriety. But the plenary sessions held in the home of
the lord of the gods frequently take the form of *symposia*, in which
the nectar flows. Unlike men, who *follow* their political work by dinners and celebrations, the gods speak with their mouths full. The
taste of nectar mingles with that of the words–sometimes bitter and
bilious, sometimes full of sweetness–that make it possible to manage the affairs of the world.

6 Divine Interference

Let us return to a decisive moment, the point when one goddess, bearing a concerned message from another, first comes to set in a temporal perspective, before an impatient mortal, the matter of a plan and the expectations produced by it. When deities erupt into the mortals' world, how do they set about getting what they want and changing the behavior of the mortals? What methods do they choose to exert their power over them?

Between Achilles and Athena communication is verbal and face to face. The paladin, eager to fall upon the king, has drawn his sword. Behind him, invisible to all, a hand touches his hair. Achilles starts, and turns. His astounded eyes meet those, dauntingly glittering, of the virgin Athena. Surprised but unintimidated, the hero, who is used to dealing with the gods, is the first to speak: "Why have you come this time, daughter of Zeus? Is it to witness the insult done me by Agamemnon, son of Atreus? Well, I tell you something which I think will certainly be done as I say: for this arrogance of his at some time soon he will lose his life."[1] He shows all the vanity of a soldier convinced of his mastery over the future, just as if a deity were someone to be told of his own intentions and given orders. Nevertheless, attentive and angelic, the emissary from Olympus replies gently: "I have come from heaven to stop your fury, if you will obey me. The white-armed goddess Hera sent me, as she loves both of you alike in her heart and cares for you equally. Come then, leave your quarreling, and do not let your hand draw the sword. But use your tongue to bring shame on him, telling him how it will be. I tell you this, and it will certainly be as I say. There will be a day when three times these splendid gifts will be laid before you because of this insult. Restrain yourself, and do as we ask."[2]

The man who allows himself to be carried away by passionate anger is taught self-control by the goddess, taught how to develop a subjective attitude in conformity with reason. But by the same token he is invited to obey, to submit himself to her authority. Her "control yourself" really means "obey me." The deity teaches the man to be himself, to rid himself of the tyranny of the humors and the impulses of his body. The rising bile, the heart palpitating in his chest, his clouding eyes—all the symptoms of violent rage, to which heroic temperaments are particularly prone, must be overcome in a gesture of power and submission combined, as if, with all his strength, the man is nevertheless incapable of controlling the extreme responses of his body. The goddess comes to the aid of Achilles, to save him from his impulsive reactions, and the pious paladin surrenders to her: "A man should heed your words, goddess, however angry he is at heart. That will be better for him. Obey the gods, and they will hear you well."[3] He does not renounce his anger for, as Apollo's prophet Calchas remarks, bile can certainly be swallowed for a day, but the rancor persists: "Even if he holds down his anger for a day, he still keeps resentment in his breast, until he can give effect to it at some later time."[4] Obedient to Athena's will, the warrior "makes do with words." Instead of shedding the king's blood, he lets fly a stream of insults against him. He does not satisfy his thirst for vengeance there and then, but bides his time, nursing his bitterness at the offense done to him.

When Athena prevents Achilles from satisfying his desire for revenge in an instantaneous attack, she opens up before him the prospect of future revenge, more carefully planned compensation, calculated patience. By agreeing to temporize and to wait for the presents three times as precious that he will one day be begged to accept, the impulsive prince opts for an agreement with the gods in

which he goes so far as to accept the strategy of Hera, who has intervened because she loves him and his opponent "equally." For
Achilles does recognize his alliance with that goddess, even though
her favor is to be shared by the man whom, just a moment earlier, he
had been about to kill. Agamemnon had accused him of being a military oaf who derived all his pleasure from quarrels, war, and fighting[5]; but now it is Achilles who gives his sovereign a lesson in wisdom. When the king's messengers come to his hut, demanding
Briseis–for now Agamemnon is as set on having her as he was on
keeping Chriseis, and thereby slighting Apollo–Achilles pro-
nounces the following carefully meditated, pious words:

> Welcome, heralds, messengers of Zeus and of men. Come closer. It
> is not you I blame, but Agamemnon, who has sent you here for the
> girl Briseis. Come lord Patroclus, bring the girl out and give her to
> them for the taking. And these two themselves can be my witnesses
> before the blessed gods and mortal men, and before that heartless
> king, if ever in time to come there arises a need for me to protect the
> others from shameful destruction. His mind's madness is set on dis-
> aster, and he will not take thought for the future as well as the past, to
> preserve the Achaians as they fight by the ships.[6]

Overcome by his anger, the king fails to see the danger into which
he is leading his army. But the warrior enlightened by Athena swears
by the blessed gods and savors his own clairvoyance.

The Gods' Power over Men

Athena's calming power over Achilles immediately raises an essential question. How do the gods work on men, how do they manage
to direct their behavior, and how far does their power over mortal
souls extend?

The gods are certainly extremely overbearing. They have not the
slightest respect for the subjective dignity of these beings, whom
they manipulate without compunction, by taking them over, im-
pairing their faculties, tampering with their feelings, neutralizing
their gestures, and, finally, through engaging in persuasion and in-
timidation. They will draw the line at no form of meddling, even the
most underhanded, provided it serves their own ends. They would
appear to be deterred by no principles, and the intellectual, affec-

tive, and somatic functioning of mortals is subjected to every kind of dislocation imaginable.

To a sleeping man, what could be more credible than a dream in which he sees a wise friend offering him advice? Yet the dream image is really a god in disguise, who has in this way insinuated himself into a mortal's innermost being in order to mislead him.[7] Even while awake, a man may, all of a sudden, become just the disguise or mask of a god who takes him over completely, as a temporary likeness.[8] Does Achilles have any inkling that he himself *did not* produce the idea that Hera deposited, like an object, upon his diaphragm?[9] And all those heroes in whom Zeus inspires new ardor,[10] whom Athena fills with courage,[11] whose terror Zeus dissipates,[12] do they realize that some god or other is making them act differently? Sometimes it would seem that they do. Poseidon fills the two Ajaxes with a sudden spurt of energy, and the two paladins do detect a divine presence, but only when, suddenly shedding the voice and countenance that he had adopted, the god turns himself into a bird and disappears.[13] Afterwards, one Ajax claims that the gods are easy to recognize,[14] and he senses the *thymos* that the god has exalted in him. All the same, at the actual moment when they were filled with ardor, and before seeing the miracle with their own eyes, the two Ajaxes had no idea that they were being controlled by a god. Nor does the idea of Poseidon's influence occur to the Achaean kings when he fills them with energy.[15] The gods take over mens' dreams and clothe themselves in mens' identities and bodies. They give men thoughts and are constantly affecting both their limbs and their minds. They make themselves unrecognizable and insinuate themselves into the very sources of mens' actions and being. And the changes that they bring about are complete, leaving the men affected totally blind to them, as if these very men who know full well, in general, that they are always at the mercy of the gods, now have no perception of or control over even the most profound of epiphanies.

Sometimes, however, the gods act upon mortals in a more visible and honest way, remaining outside them, beyond the frontiers of their being. But even then, it is not always easy to recognize them. All the same, even if they do adopt a disguise, at least they keep a certain distance from the mortal they are meeting. They exert their influence through advice, suggestions, or orders,[16] in short, through speech–an exchange of words which, despite the interference, the pressure, and the despotism, at least preserves the integrity of the mortal who is addressed.

Humans are malleable. But at the same time they remain responsible for themselves. Though at the mercy of the gods when the latter take a hand, they have to manage on their own as soon as the Immortals decide to ignore them. When Zeus forbids his fellow gods to involve themselves in the war, the Greeks and the Trojans still go on fighting and taking tactical decisions. Now autonomous, now predetermined, they live in uncertainty as to their own subjectivity. Thus, when Agamemnon offends Achilles, he acts spontaneously: it is *his* resentment, *his* anger that dictate his words. Achilles himself regards this simply as impious behavior. But later, when the king reflects upon his actions, he seems to be repentant–or, rather, he regrets them, so he attributes them to the will of Zeus.[17] This shows how very much confusion exists between self-awareness and awareness of the absolute and elusive power of the deity. Although the narrative does not explicitly declare that Agamemnon's fury was inspired by Zeus, when Agamemnon reflects upon his actions, all he can see is the god's mark upon them. Paris represents the inception of his amorous desire for Helen in similar fashion. That irresistible passion does not seem to the young prince to be a feeling initiated within himself: no, it was a gift of the gods, a present that he could not refuse, and one that he had not chosen.[18]

Whether they are really directed by some divine power, as Paris is, or whether–as in the case of Agamemnon–they are objectively responsible for their reactions, the Homeric heroes regard the gods as the source of the emotions that erupt within them and dominate them. The case of Agamemnon is particularly significant, for a divine etiology to his anger gradually comes to seem the only plausible explanation for it. Even Achilles ends up believing that "Zeus the counselor has robbed him of his wits."[19] The passionate nature of rage and of love may, to us, seem to justify the idea of a completely external force with which, after the event, it seems ludicrous to identify oneself. But in the world of the epic, no human faculty is beyond manipulation, certainly not reason or will. Yet there is one character who does not seem to believe that, namely Peleus, Achilles' father. On the day of his son's departure for Troy, he is said to have reminded the young warrior that it is Hera who decides on the victory and Athena who arranges it, if they so wish. On the other hand, the control of one's passions—or, to be more precise, the *thymos*, the seat of the great impulses of the emotions—is one's own responsibility.[20] That seems a reasonable division, which leaves room for self-awareness and self-control; but it is illusory, for Achilles, of all men, appears quite incapable of overcoming his fury and has to be calmed by Athena. If ever there was an impulsive, touchy hero, unable to control his own heart, it is Achilles. Locked in his resentment over the loss of Briseis, the captive with whom he claims to be in love,[21] he only decides to emerge from his stubborn reclusion on the day that he loses his dearest friend. From start to finish, the son of Peleus acts passionately, pulled this way and that by divine influences.

Really Responsible Gods?

However, the division of attributes that the intervention of Athena implies is no less illusory, namely that mortals are characterized by imperious and blinding desires, the gods by pedagogy and reason. One might be tempted to see in the poem's two opening lines an emblematic image of both the separation and the relationship between the human beings and the Olympians, and hence also an archaic Greek portrait of a human being as subject—a subject that does not really exist, since it is cleft in two, pulled apart by passions and by the gods, and thus doubly determined by powers other than itself. Snell tells us that Homeric man is totally fragmented, both as to his body and as to the opposed forces that clash within him, as in an empty space, to determine actions and words that cannot be considered as "his." The whole of Achilles' behavior certainly testifies to the faltering nature of his control over whatever moves him and his inability both to overcome his anger and to disobey a god. Suddenly, the melancholy grief that assails him over the departure of Briseis finds expression in a rush of tears. The hero weeps. He turns his back on his friends and looks out to sea, as Odysseus was to do when his nostalgia became unbearable, despite the love of the beautiful Calypso. Those awesome eyes that can blaze right through an enemy, so hard is their brilliance, are now swimming in tears. The great man wants his mama. And his august mother hears him, even in the depths of the sea, where she is seated by her old father. Swiftly, she emerges, like a mist from the white sea. She sits facing her tearful son, strokes his hand, and speaks to him, addressing him by all his names: "Why are you weeping, my child?"[22]

It is well known that Plato, despite his admiration for Homer, dismissed such scenes, in which the most virile of warriors so lack self-control as to burst into tears. He found them unbecoming. He was in favor of censoring all the passages in which the ancient knights set a bad example to the young soldiers of his own day, all of whom were readers of the *Iliad*.[23] However, in the epic world, the manifestation of one's feelings and the overflowing of the emotions was an essential aspect of the nature of a hero, of a sensitivity—no doubt excessive in the eyes of a philosopher who was also an educator—proportional to the greatness of a past age. All those characters, who are so outstanding in their beauty and courage, and their strength and endurance, are *also* terribly passionate. The philosopher's knife had not yet dissected the soul into three parts: a desiring part, an irascible part, and an intellectual and morally conscious part. The intellect had not yet become the driver who controls the other two components of the soul, likened, for their part, to bucking horses. A hero was not so much a metaphorical driver of the harnessed pair that drew his soul along, but rather an anarchical amalgam of desires, intelligence, anger, and virtue.

The gods are there, then, to help these great desiring machines not to succumb to their emotions, but to become immune to the violent impulses that take possession of them. In the case of Achilles, fury gives way to despair. No sooner has he been restrained by Athena than he needs Thetis, partly as a consoling mother but also as a goddess who is on good terms with Zeus. Similarly, later on, his rancor against Agamemnon is replaced by hatred of the assassins of his dearest friend. Blown from one passion to another and from one deity to another, the hero truly is as flighty as a leaf.

All this is undeniable, but the gods do not invariably play the role that Athena adopts at that one particular moment of the war. On the contrary, it has to be said that her behavior then is in no way typical; rather, it is unusual and misleading: unusual in relation to the entire variety of possible situations in encounters between men and gods; and misleading if considered as an example. The basic, indeed primordial reason for this is that the gods do not all act in the same way either in relation to one another (each has his or her own style and mode of action) or in all circumstances, for despite possessing a particular style of his or her own, a god is not invariably the same. This versatility is one of the aspects of the day-to-day time, that is to say, ephemeral time, in which the gods live: for them, as for mortals, one day is not identical to another. Each day is full of its own concerns—concerns that very often relate to the mortals—and besides, each day brings its own moods.

For *like* men (and this is the reason why the encounter between Athena and Achilles is not typical), the gods are assailed by moods—desire, pain, joy, anger: in other words, erections, tears, laughter, and black bile. These so-called Blessed Ones are neither indifferent nor impassive. They are changeable, reacting to whatever affects them on a register of sensitivity that is not theirs alone. The life of the Olympians is animated and oriented by all kinds of emotions. It is true that Ate, the goddess who brings blindness, making it impossible to discern what is extremely clear, and who leads us into error and mistakes, now assaults only mortals. She is no longer allowed into Olympus. But that makes no difference to the fallibility of the gods as such. On the contrary. The reason why Ate can no longer show her face in the gods' fiefdom is that Zeus threw her out, furious at having fallen victim to her on the day when his heart (*thumos*) put boastful words in his chest, words that were the undoing of his son Heracles.[24]

Thirdly, even if Athena goes to Achilles to reason with him, plenty of other gods, and by no means the least of them, such as Dionysus, Hera, and Zeus, are liable to foist upon mortals madness and the most destructive kinds of frenzy.

Thetis—to get back to the story—leaves her marine home and emerges from the waters. There, on the beach, mother and son, goddess and hero, speak tenderly together. As she caresses him, Thetis urges her big boy to tell her all about it, to tell her the whole story of what has happened. To be sure, the goddess already knows what is making her son unhappy; nevertheless, she persuades him to tell her everything, starting right at the beginning. Obediently, Achilles pours out his heart to her; he begins the story with the insult done to Apollo, stressing his own role in defending the rights of the god against the thuggish Agamemnon: "I was the first to urge the appeasement of the god."[25] Omitting mention of his burst of rage and Athena's diplomatic intervention, he presents himself as a most sensible paladin of the archer-god, Apollo: he was faced by a miscreant king, behaving wrongly because he was possessed, seized by an anger that he could not control.[26]

In the self-portrait that the most bloodthirsty of the Achaeans paints for his mama, he appears as a wronged child, loyal, responsible, and chivalrous. Tactfully, he reminds her of the favor that she enjoys from the lord of the Olympians. Did she not put Zeus in her debt when she saved him from the plot hatched by Hera, Poseidon, and Athena? They had wanted to cast him, the sovereign god, into chains, but Thetis had called upon the help of a hundred-armed monster, which, seating itself beside the Father, deterred the conspirators by its very presence. In effect, what Achilles is asking his mother to do is intercede with Zeus so that Agamemnon suffers a defeat and is taught a lesson for offending the bravest of the Achaeans.

7 Scenes of Sovereignty

On the day when Thetis, the sea goddess who lives beneath the waves, flies off to Olympus to solicit the vengeance of Zeus, the reader of the *Iliad*, for the first time, leaves the terrestrial theater of the war and enters the corridors of divine diplomacy, on another stage, the space inhabited by the gods. The home of the Olympians, a place of revelry, is also, indeed primarily, a place where power—the half-despotic, half-collegiate power of Zeus and his fellow deities—is exercised, albeit in an ambiguous fashion.

A long wait seems inevitable, for the Olympian court is absent. The whole company of the gods has accompanied Zeus to the Ocean's edge, on a visit to the Ethiopians, who are particularly highly esteemed mortals. The goal of their journey is a banquet. Thetis is thus kept waiting for twelve days.

> But when the twelfth dawn came round from that first day, the ever-living gods returned to Olympos all in a body, with Zeus at their head. And Thetis did not forget her son's demand, but she rose through the swell of the sea at early morning, and went up to the vast sky and Olympos. She found the wide-seeing son of Kronos sitting away from the others, on the highest peak of ridged Olympos. She crouched in front of him and reached with her right hand to hold him under the chin. Then she spoke in entreaty to Lord Zeus, son of Kronos.[1]

This sequence of journeys and happenings affords us one of our glimpses of the life led by the gods, in which the realism of their au-

tonomous existence is skillfully handled. First, the journey to
Ethiopia: Why now, and why does it take twelve days? One might
think that it was a trick on the part of the narrator, who needs to fit
in, between Achilles' tears and Thetis's ambassadorial mission, the
episode of Chryseis's restitution to her father and the great sacrifice
to Apollo by which it is followed, and which does indeed effect a reconciliation between the Achaeans and the god. But, in truth, that
would be an inadequate rationalization, for the expedition to Chryse
takes up no more than two days and one night, and that includes the
two-way journey by boat and the monumental hecatomb offered up
to the god, on the beach, in the evening. So the gods' journey has
another purpose, namely that of introducing an event, whether ordinary or exceptional, into a life which, as the reader needs to ap-
preciate, goes on anyway, whatever else is happening. It alerts the
reader or listener to the fact that the gods do not exist simply for the
sake of men, that they have other things to do and may be otherwise
engaged when a mortal has need of them. In short, this is a useless
detail that is nevertheless precious, for it establishes a respectful
distance between the time of the adventures that the gods share with
men and the private sphere of the customary pursuits to which they
devote themselves.

You cannot count on meeting the sovereign god by crossing the
threshold to Olympus on the off-chance, even if you are a deity.
Thetis cannot speed up the Olympians' return, so she waits pa-
tiently. But as soon as Zeus returns home to the loftiest peak of his
mountain, Thetis pays him a visit. The etiquette for royal audiences
is very simple on Olympus. Dispensing with a master of ceremonies
and even ordinary attendants, Zeus receives his visitors in person.
If Thetis adopts the position of a suppliant, that is because of the
contingent purpose of her visit, for she is seeking a favor. In other
circumstances, she would have had the right to address her king
standing erectly before him.

It was a pure coincidence that the interview between Zeus and
Thetis could not take place immediately. In themselves, the relations between the gods are remarkably informal. The sovereign's
prestige is manifested by a number of external signs: Zeus leads the
procession of gods when they all go somewhere together.[2] At home,
he receives a number of marks of homage: when he returns to his

palace, the other gods rise and go to greet him[3]; frequently, he holds himself apart from them in haughty solitude, seated on a rock that crowns Mount Olympus.[4] Like any celestial and paternal deity, he is fond of mountain peaks, which befit his majesty and also afford him a good view of the world below.

One day, for example, Zeus is furious at the Greeks and even more so at the gods who support and protect them, in particular, his wife and his daughter Athena. He convenes an early assembly, not in the palace, as is customary, but out in the open, on the very highest summit of Olympus of the countless peaks. He thus forces the other gods to climb up to his mountain hermitage, the aerie that is his own particular space. Up there, before his subjects, he is the first to speak: "Listen to me, all you gods and all you goddesses, so I can tell you what my heart within me urges. Now let no female god or male either attempt to frustrate my stated will, but I want agreement from all of you, so I can bring the business to a speedy end."[5] *Primus inter pares*, Zeus forthrightly declares his supremacy over the entire society of gods. It is a supremacy which, like that of Agamemnon over the other kings and paladin princes, is not necessarily taken for granted, so the sovereign judiciously backs up the announcement of his wishes with a threat: "And any of you I find prepared to flout the gods and go bringing help to either Trojans or Danaans, he will be blasted without regard and sent running back to Olympos. Or I will take him and throw him into murky Tartaros, far down, into the deepest abyss below the earth, where the gate is iron and the threshold bronze, as far below Hades as the heaven is above earth—*then he will realize how much I am the strongest of all the gods.*"[6]

Zeus sounds off against all possible flouters of his orders, as if his status as sovereign was not assured, certain, and unchallengeable, as if his position as leader might be questioned and repudiated. The violence of his words, to which he appends a terrible threat, is a response to his need to reconfirm a power that the other gods do not necessarily recognize to be absolutely legitimate and unshakeable and that it is, on the contrary, necessary to manifest, demonstrate, even occasionally defend, in the face of serious attempts at subversion. In other words, the divine royalty is exposed to the risk of collapse, and, in the jockeying for position, in the course of which the gods size one another up, the sovereign must make a show of his strength in order to retain his position. Hence, Zeus's extreme ferocity and the flashy show of his predominance at a moment when, as we shall see, the many strategies of the other gods are conflicting with his own plans. Having made an amazingly paternalistic concession to his daughter Athena, the only Olympian who dares to open her mouth, the king withdraws majestically to another mountain:

> So speaking, he harnessed a pair of bronze-hoofed horses to his chariot–wing-swift horses with flowing manes of gold–and dressed himself in gold and took up his whip which was finely made of gold, and mounted his chariot. He whipped the horses on, and they flew eagerly on their way between earth and the starry heaven. He came to Ida with the many springs, the mother of wild creatures, to Gargaron, where he has his precinct and his altar, fragrant with sacrifice. There the father of men and gods reined in his horses, unyoked them from the chariot, and rolled thick mist over them. He then sat down on the peak of the mountain, glorying in his splendor, and looking out over the Trojans' city and the ships of the Achaians.[7]

Moving from one summit to another in this way, the father of the gods manifests his fragile omnipotence and looks down from on high at the bloody spectacle of the savagely rent human world.

Zeus Commits Himself

On the day that Thetis visits him on the highest peak of Olympus, the sovereign does not convene an assembly of his fellows up there. Instead, he returns to his palace. He has, reluctantly, listened to the request made by the suppliant goddess and has promised to punish the Greeks by making them aware of the full extent to which their salvation depends upon Achilles. He will force them to the brink of defeat in order to make their king beg the insulted hero to return to the battlefield.

Zeus is uneasy about having agreed to Thetis's pleas. This promise that he could not withhold from a formerly precious ally will upset the equilibrium. He himself, the king, will have to side with one or another of these two armies of men, despite the fact that the strategic position that he has favored is one of distant neutrality, a haughty indifference in the face of the respective interests of these mortals bent on killing one another.

Some of the gods have already taken the part of one or the other set of mortals, committing themselves to demanding alliances, first and foremost among them the three goddesses made rivals by the judgment passed by Paris. Aphrodite is fighting on the side of the Trojans, even risking her own lovely skin for them, while Hera and Athena are constantly to be found alongside the Greeks. Both of them have made a promise to Menelaus, and neither has forgotten it. For his part, Menalaus, the deceived husband and insulted king, has vowed not to return to his own land until Troy is destroyed.[8] Of the male gods, Apollo will fight with the Trojans, despite having accepted the hecatomb offered him by the Greeks to expiate the offense done to his priest, Chryses, and will frequently be personally involved in the fighting. Poseidon, Zeus's younger brother and Hera's brother and brother-in-law, will, under pressure from her, side with the Greeks, only too pleased to have a chance to frustrate his elder brother, whose supremacy he finds hard to bear.

Each of the deities pursues his or her own ends, affection or pity for the mortals being but one of the motivations for actions that stem, above all, from a personal desire to settle old scores with their rival siblings and fellows. But there are some deities who do not choose between the two factions of mortals. These are the powers that personify war itself, discord in all its own disruptive force. First and foremost among these is Ares, a son of Zeus and Hera, who is the warrior god *par excellence*. His sovereign father is not very fond of him on account of his bellicose nature, supposed to be inherited from his pugnacious and quarrelsome mother, Hera: "You are the most hateful to me of all the gods that hold Olympos; always your delight is in strife and war and fighting. Your mother Hera has an ungovernable spirit in her, loath to give way, and it is hard for me to bend her."[9] Zeus's criticisms of Ares are almost word for word the same as Agamemnon's complaints of Achilles: "Of all the kings whom Zeus sustains you are the most hateful to me—always your delight is in quarreling and wars and battle."[10] We all by now know how serious friction between a sovereign and one of his paladins can become. But, unlike Achilles, Ares does not enter into a personal feud with his father. In contrast to Zeus, he is the embodiment of absolute and indiscriminate violence. His passion for war is so blind that he seems incapable of maintaining any strategy of alliances for

any length of time. Indifferent to either cause, Ares is not so much
neutral as on both sides at once, in disorder. He dispenses his aid
without thinking.[11] Forgetting a promise to stand with Athena and
Hera, he joins the Trojans as soon as Apollo tells him to.[12]

Another power who does not take sides is Eris, Strife. When all
the other Olympians withdraw temporarily from the struggle–to fall
in with Zeus's orders for the time being–Eris has free rein on her
own between the two armies.[13] No sooner do the other gods suspend
their tactical interventions than Strife, for her part, blossoms, for
she rejoices in any massacre that falls into her lap and that degener-
ates into pure slaughter. At such a time, all that takes place on the
battlefield is a balanced, virtually infinite interchange of mortal
blows.

Zeus's position prior to his decision to heed Achilles' mother is
quite unlike that of the other gods. Basically, the sovereign respects
the diplomatic choices of his peers, but he holds himself apart.
There is nothing personally at stake for him in this war, except–if
we are to believe the *Cypria*–the mutual extermination of the two
sides, that is to say, the auto-destruction of the human race. In
themselves, both the Greeks and the Trojans are dear to him.[14] But
he has promised the Argives that they will capture Troy. If he now
compromises his position, it is for the sake of the honor of a member
of his own race. Once committed, he follows a tortuous line of conduct. It seems as though, despite his decision to teach the Greeks a
lesson, he is still concerned to conceal his partiality. So his behavior bears comparison with that of Ares or Eris, except that, whereas
Strife immerses herself in the turmoil of the warriors killing one another and keeps a close eye on the battle, it is from afar that Zeus
contemplates "men killing and being killed."[15] He can see both the
city of the Trojans and the ships of the Greeks.[16] Whereas Ares
switches thoughtlessly from one alliance to another, the king medi-
tates a complicated strategy, thanks to which the Greeks will be under the illusion that he is on their side, only to find that he has
tricked them.

In other words, the sovereign god enters into the diplomatic game
without showing his hand. Neither side can ever be sure of him.
Even at the moment of the greatest success for the Trojans, one of
them, the wise Polydamus, makes no secret of his perplexity: "Now

if Zeus the high-thunderer is planning misery for them and their utter destruction . . . , then of course I would want that to happen immediately."[17] But as that supposition may be totally hypothetical, he counsels extreme prudence in the maneuvers of encirclement. On the Greek side mistrust is expressed by Nestor, an old man without illusions. He suspects Zeus of having sided with the Trojans, and his words about the king are bitter. Addressing the impetuous Diomedes, he exclaims: "Can you not see that Zeus's aid to victory is not with you? Now Zeus . . . is granting Hektor the glory for today—another time he will give it to us, if that is his will."[18] The thinking of this god is inaccessible even to the wisest of men, for his power is greater than that of any hero. His ability to change his plans from one day to the next stems from an *intelligence* that knows no bounds or constraints.

The Scrutiny of Hera

The reason why Zeus's actions seem arbitrary to mortals is that the latter do not understand the motives behind them. But the king of the gods does act in conformity with a courtly code of honor and shows a relative degree of respect for the decisions of his peers. When he returns to the palace after pledging his word to Thetis, he has to face the scrutiny of Hera. No sooner is he seated upon his throne than the sharp eyes of his wife fix upon him, probing, drilling into him. Her jealousy erupts and recriminations are poured upon the sovereign in the presence of his entire court.

Hera takes umbrage at every decision, every thought that her husband does not share with her. She wants to know everything and, indeed, has a knack of finding out all that Zeus does or wants to do. As we have seen, a detailed list of his amorous infidelities does not bother her. It is with a smile on her lips that she listens to the—to be honest, quite short—catalogue of her seducer-husband's seven conquests. But when Zeus hides his military complicity with Thetis from her, she cannot bear it. And the sovereign seems unable to elude the extraordinary insight of his wife. "No action of mine can escape you,"[19] he complains, as if his thinking—so daunting and mysterious to mortals—were an open book to her.

Worn down by her suffocating perspicacity, Zeus's reaction is to lash out at her: she is becoming hateful to him; he will hit her if she does not immediately take her seat in silence. His wife obeys, furious with him, her angry lips sealed. But for the court of the Immortals, this quarrel is a bore. Why get so angry between gods, over an affair that concerns mere mortals? Why spoil the pleasure of a party in which they can drink sweet nectar together on Olympus? It is Hephaestus who begs his mother to calm Zeus down. He fills up the drinking cups and all the gods smile to see him limping round so busily. So, yet again, "They feasted till the setting of the sun, and noone's desire went without an equal share in the feast, nor did they lack the beautiful music of the lyre in Apollo's hands, and the lovely singing of the Muses, voice answering voice."[20]

The rest of the day is thus spent in the harmony of a symposium, to the sound of voices raised in song. For Zeus, the morning had been difficult, but the other gods had nothing to do all day but enjoy themselves at a very lengthy banquet. In the evening, feeling sleepy, they all repair to their own homes, to rest. Only Zeus spends a sleepless night.

Zeus's Lie . . .

The king of the gods mulls things over. With a nod of his head, he has committed himself vis-à-vis his charming ally, but without thinking the details through. Now what should he do? The night brings him inspiration. He will send a dream to that other king, the leader of the Greeks, a false dream that will set everything in motion. While asleep, Agamemnon must receive the news that he will definitely be victorious. That will force him into action and precipitate his downfall. And to prevent any hesitation, all ambiguous, enigmatic omens must be avoided. Agamemnon is to receive an absolutely clear but totally false message.

Zeus calls for Dream, the nocturnal messenger, and tells him of the lie to be fed to the sleeping king. The memory of his trying tiff with Hera has given him the idea of a terribly ironic trick to play on his wife. Although it was he who overrode her and reduced her to silence, he wants to make Agamemnon think that it was she, the queen goddess, who won the argument and imposed her will upon the Olympians: "Hera's entreaties have turned them all."[21] Nestor, in his extreme wisdom, distrusts this unlikely dream, for the old king of Pylos holds no illusions on the score of Zeus. Agamemnon, however, is convinced by it. With no misgivings, he leaps toward the punishment that awaits him. "Poor fool, he knew nothing of Zeus's design."[22]

So Zeus is a cheating god. Although he feels obliged to act chivalrously toward a deity who has done him a service, he is prepared to act in totally cavalier fashion toward this human king to whom he has pledged his word of honor. It is true that the king of the gods only betrays his human counterpart temporarily, in order to teach him a lesson. So it might be argued that he is merely applying a sanction that falls within heroic law. However, he does it in a way that smacks more of insidious vengeance than of equitable arbitration. In other words, the son of Cronos deals dishonestly with the son of Atreus, despite the special relationship between them that is based on the scepter, the symbol of sovereignty that has been passed on from one king to the other.[23] This object was passed from Hephaestus to Zeus, from Zeus to Hermes, then moving from divine hands to human ones, from Hermes to Pelops, then from Pelops to his son Atreus, from Atreus to Thyestes, and finally from Thyestes to his heir Agamemnon; and the effect of its transmission was to forge a direct link between the dynasty of the Atridae and the king of the gods.[24] One might have expected to find a fundamental solidarity within the "lineage" created by transmission of the symbol. But no. Agamemnon does not belong to an elect lineage. There will be no stanching his tears when he realizes the trick played upon him by the cunning god.

Zeus is a lying god. Deliberately and cynically, he devises a false message to mislead the thoughtless Agamemnon. Clement of Alexandria had a point when he exclaimed that "this prophet Zeus, the protector of guests and suppliants, full of gentleness, the source of all oracles, the avenger of crimes" concealed another Zeus, one who was "unjust, criminal, lawless, impious, inhumane, violent, corrupting, adulterous, and passionate."[25] The offhand manner in which the king of the Olympians handles lying is all the more striking in view of the fact that Zeus is endowed with the power of truth, in his capacity of the oracular god *par excellence*, not only in sanctuaries specifically dedicated to him, such as Dodona, but also wherever Apollo delivers mantic messages through the mouths of his prophets. The young god thinks and transmits as his father wills. But for Homer's public, Zeus's insouciance and the liberties that he takes with the truth are perceived as aspects of his power, power that oscillates between guaranteeing, on the one hand, an order that is somehow "legal," and on the other, absolute arbitrariness. Can any action or attitude inconceivable on the part of the father of gods and men even be imagined? Is anything at all truly incompatible with his character and status? A reader of the *Iliad* gets the feeling that nothing is alien to this god, except perhaps dishonor. But all that that means is that this is a character who is terribly touchy and jealous where his primacy over all that surrounds him is concerned.

For that reason, the cult of truth does not figure in his concept of honor, for constant sincerity is a form of submission to a categorical imperative. Zeus is not always a liar, not always truthful, but he is always the master of his own speech. The arbitrary aspect of Zeus evokes an extraordinary lack of respect from men. They are at the mercy of the discretion of the king of Olympus, but they certainly find it hard to tolerate his despotism. Agamemnon blasphemes against "the pleasure of Zeus the almighty, who has already shattered the crowns of many cities, and will break yet more,"[26] when condemning the deception to which he has been subjected.[27] And one of the Trojans, finding himself in great danger when faced by fiercely resisting Greeks, cries out, "So, father Zeus, even you too are turned utter liar!"[28] But Zeus, to whom these reproaches are addressed, seems not to take offense; he simply carries on with his own plans.

However, even if the heroes of the *Iliad* greeted the flagrant lies of their god/father merely with disrespect, acknowledging the all-powerful nature of this speech that deceives them, there was at least one ancient reader who found these exchanges of lies and blasphemies intolerable: Plato. The philosopher who composed the *Republic* had a far more moral and coherent concept of the deity. Whatever is divine is incompatible with evil, and so with falsehood; consequently, "There is no motive for God to deceive." On the contrary, "God is altogether simple and true in deed and word, and neither changes himself nor deceives others by visions or words or the sending of signs in waking or in dreams."[29] It follows that, in a well-organized city, stories like that of the dream sent to Agamemnon should be censored and banned. On this point, as on the representation of heroes in tears, Plato was openly critical of Homer.

But according to this same criterion, in the Homeric text the dream invented by Zeus is not the only thing to be condemned, for throughout the *Iliad* the gods constantly cheat and lie and ambush their opponents and lead them astray, manifesting a total lack of trustworthiness.

. . . and Agamemnon's

As soon as Dream leaves Agamemnon, allowing his divine voice to continue to echo in his ears, the king awakens, full of hope. Zeus is handing him victory. Strangely enough, though, he decides, in his turn, to lay a trap for his men, wanting to test them, to see how they will react. And without knowing it, even as he thinks he is distorting Zeus's message, he is close to the truth concealed there. Rather like Oedipus setting off for Thebes, convinced that he will prove the oracle's predictions wrong yet confirming them despite himself, Agamemnon tells his assembled warriors that Zeus has sent him a dream and that they must depart in their ships without capturing the town. To test their courage, he tells them of defeat: "My friends, Danaan heroes, Ares' men-at-arms, Zeus the son of Kronos has snared me wholly in grievous delusion. Cruel god–in the beginning he promised me, with solemn assent, that I would sack well-walled Ilios before my return; *but now he has planned a vile deception.*"[30] Blind clairvoyance worthy of the best of tragic heroes! Agamemnon does not yet know that his words are true–except that Zeus's trickery lies in the dream, not in his former promise. Later, those very words rise to his lips when he understands the magnitude of his defeat and Zeus's deception.[31]

For the moment, he knows nothing of the catastrophe. He tells his men to leave and, to his surprise, the whole army is filled with delight by the heady idea of no more war, of returning home, of peace. Rejoicing, they rush to the ships. And just as if Zeus's opening gambit was not fated to lead to certain necessary consequences, for a moment there is a risk that this will indeed be the end of the war: "Then the Argives would have made a homecoming beyond what was fated,"[32] had not one deity intervened. But that deity is not

Zeus, anxious to set things back on the course that he had determined; it is Hera.

Angry at having lost the argument with her husband, the goddess recovers her combativeness. The Greeks cannot possibly depart, leaving that bitch Helen in the hands of the Trojans, an emblem of their triumph. They must at least recapture the woman, if not the town. Thus, although she is at loggerheads with Zeus, Hera at this point promotes his plans—namely, that the war should continue—so that her protégés may carry off the victory.

The web of human and divine interests is never more complex and tragic than at this juncture. Zeus lies to Agamemnon, who then lies to his men. To them—this exhausted band of fighters who know nothing of all that is at stake in the war—there suddenly seems, through a mistake, to be a chance of escape from this theater of heroic battle, a chance to put an end to the massacre. Then the vise closes even tighter around them. The camp is again under surveillance; and the soldiers are sent back to their posts, like mutineers. Hera dispatches Athena to encourage Odysseus to busy himself persuading the men to stay.[33] The illusion is over. Even Nestor—who had distrusted the dream sent to his king—now favors resuming the conflict. Zeus's earlier promise that they would take Troy makes him forget the strangeness of the dream. Clearly, it is Zeus's will: they must take the town.

Zeus has not lost sight of the commitment he first made to the Greeks. As we know, Troy was indeed to fall. First, though, the honor of Achilles and his mother was to be restored. However, up to book 15, the final perspective remains completely obscure. Throughout most of the narrative, it seems as though neither mortals nor gods understand the chain of circumstances and events as conceived by Zeus. The men fight on blindly, and the gods all play their own, individual games, unaware of the overall plan determined by the only true strategist, namely, their king. Thus, Hera, by impelling the Argives to attack and capture the town, sends them straight into the initial defeat prepared for them by Zeus. The woman who is so skilled at catching out her husband, when she sets her mind to it, in this case does nothing to prevent the carnage of her protégés. Is that because of her indifference to the fate of the cannon-fodder, or because she is incapable of clearly evaluating the plans of Cronos's son? The goddess really does seem to have a very imperfect understanding of those plans: all she can see is that her husband wants the Argives to die in their thousands. It is he, in person, who eventually enlightens her as to the coming phases of the war. Zeus tells her that the Achaeans will be put to flight before Troy, thanks to Apollo, who will fill them with cowardice. In their flight, they will approach the ships of Achilles, the hero still musing over his resentment. This will rouse his friend Patroclus, who will be killed by Hector. Then, at last, Achilles will make a move and, in a rage even more irrepressible than his rancor, he will kill Hector. "And from that time on I shall make a turn in the battle, driving it constantly back from the ships, until the Achaians capture steep Ilios through the designs of Athene."[34]

The *Iliad*'s entire plot is summed up in Zeus's confidential explanation to his wife. The king of the gods is the only one who knows how first one army, then the other, will act and how the chain of heroic exploits is to be linked up, with one death paying for another. The arrangement makes it possible for him to keep both his promises–to make Troy fall and also to honor Achilles and Thetis– and that seems to be the only logic behind it all. The plan for the war, conceived by Zeus without consulting anyone else, is thus a secret, both from the Olympians and, above all, from the human troops. The wretched Agamemnon, blinded by the certain prospect of capturing Troy before sunset,[35] is unaware that he knows nothing. He is totally fooled, the more so because Zeus pretends to accept the propitiatory sacrifice that precedes the attack and also, on this day, procures the king an extraordinary allure. For Agamemnon suddenly resembles Zeus himself, Ares, and Poseidon, all at the same time. His eyes and brow suggest those of the king of Olympus, his belt is like that of the warrior god, and his powerful chest puts one in mind of the sovereign of the waters.[36] But this glorious likeness of his triply theomorphic body is no more than a misleading adornment, misleading, above all, for the very man who is graced by it, since it is the better to dupe him that Zeus has bestowed upon him the mask of a sovereign destined for victory.[37]

Hera and Poseidon

To obtain a closer view of the interplay of powers and cunning ploys, and of the gods' plans and their failures, let us follow the conflict between the two brothers, Poseidon and Zeus. In the course of the Trojan War the king has his distractions, in fact is willfully distracted from keeping an eye on the battlefield. A moment's inattention can spoil his whole plan. Hera lures him into the trap of an erotic siesta. Sleep closes his eyes. Now his brother Poseidon, who is lord of the sea, is free to direct the war and lead the Greeks against the Trojan army in a battle the like of which has never been seen before. Brandishing a terrible sword, like a flash of lightning the god leaps into the front line, to confront Hector and his knights. It is not long before he makes the battle swing in favor of the Greeks. The routed Trojans are terrified. But suddenly Zeus awakes. He opens his eyes, sees the spectacular battle organized by his brother and also sees his wife at his brother's side. He realizes that he was deliberately distracted from the war, that a plot was hatched to confound his plans and challenge his power.

His rage boils over and his fury is unleashed upon his cunning wife. He threatens to beat her, reminds her of the punishments meted out in the past. But Hera defends herself, lies, falsely swearing that she had nothing to do with Poseidon's exploit: "It is not my doing that Poseidon the earth-shaker is afflicting Hektor and the Trojans and helping the Achaians, but it must be his own heart that prompts him: he must have seen the Achaians suffering by their ships and felt pity for them."[38] The goddess implies that Poseidon was guided by his own *thumos*. She is careful not to mention her own heart, which Zeus has terrified and Poseidon has filled with joy–her heart which prompted her to set up her whole plan of seduction.[39] In a switch that looks like a positive betrayal, Poseidon's ally now declares herself ready to distract him from the war, and, without hesitation, she crosses over to stand with Zeus. At this, Zeus begins to fantasize about how it would be if his wife would always act like this, in agreement with himself, as they sit enthroned in the assembly of the Olympians. Poseidon's will would soon be broken against such solidarity between their two hearts.

All the same, Zeus is still suspicious. "If what you say is truly so, go now to the company of the gods,"[40] he tells her, as if he truly cannot spot the lie, as if his power of knowledge fails to penetrate the absolute opacity of his wife's words. Just as Hera has to nag at him to get him to confess the plans he has made for Thetis, Zeus likewise now has no foreknowledge, no hold on what remains unsaid. The gods cannot read one another's thoughts, nor can they detect the presence of one of their fellows if the latter is bent on concealment. With his eyelids closed, Zeus is held prisoner by the sleep that prevents him from seeing Poseidon. At the very moment when he believes that he is in hiding himself, with Hera, within a golden cloud that protects him from the prying eyes of the other gods, it is in truth from him that someone, his brother, is hiding.[41]

As for Hera, she is certainly not one to act with open honesty: after disowning Poseidon, she knuckles under to Zeus out of fear, but is still stubborn in her resentment. When she returns to the assembly of the gods gathered on Mount Olympus, she confides to Themis what she really thinks of Zeus, saying, "You know yourself how overbearing and cruel his nature is"; and throughout that day's feasting her angry brow belies her smiling lips.[42] Momentarily submissive, she will help to realize Zeus's promises: Poseidon will be made to see reason and will leave the battlefield. But Hera will not give up what she wants.

Poseidon is almost a heroic god. His sincere and impetuous nature makes him a bad diplomat. At an assembly in which the gods have to decide what they will do in the face of the well-known accusations of the philosophers, he blurts out that his words "smell of tunny-fish,"[43] so hasty and forthright is he when it comes to defending the honor of the Olympian race. When he clashes with Apollo, he is ready to fight, whereas his more knowing nephew reminds him that it is pointless for the gods to fight among themselves for the sake of mere mortals. Poseidon is the only one who lays himself open to the anger of his brother, in order to help the Greeks. He is also the only one who, as a matter of principle, questions the legitimacy of the despotism of his elder brother. Hera calls Zeus arrogant, Athena condemns his arbitrary decisions, Ares irritates him; but all of them, from Apollo down to Hermes, take care not to disobey their father or husband, as the case may be. Power being a forceful argument, Zeus always predominates, with his threats to repeat former demonstrations of his strength; and the other gods, in fear, and calculating what the cost of defying him would be, end up by backing down, possibly still grumbling, but without an argument. Poseidon, however, stands up to him and argues.

When Zeus sends Iris to tell him that he must immediately stop the fighting and that the only means to persuade him available to the lord of Olympus are violent ones, Poseidon is annoyed but perfectly reasonable: "Oh, this is presumption, great god though he is, to talk of curbing me by force against my will, when I hold equal honor with him." The god of the sea has a sense of rights and of a fair distribution of honors. He counters the argument of brute force with that of fair shares for all. "There are three of us brothers borne to Kronos by Rhea, Zeus and I and the third is Hades, lord over the dead. All the world was divided into three parts, and each of us received his portion. When the lots were cast, I drew the sea as my domain for ever, and Hades drew the murky darkness below, and Zeus drew the broad sky among the clouds and the upper air; but the earth and high Olympos were left common to us all."[44]

When Poseidon recalls the historical division of the world–in which the earth figures not as the place inhabited and possessed by men, but as the common property of all the gods, on the same grounds as Olympus–and thus sets himself up as a champion of the Olympian order in virtually legal terms, it is not solely to claim passing recognition of his own dignity as a god.

That, as we have seen, is more in Hera's style, when she rebels against Zeus in order to win recognition and appreciation for all the trouble that she goes to on behalf of the mortals whom she protects. "I too am a god!"[45] she exclaims, pointing out that she was produced by the same parents as her brother and husband. To extract respect, Hera reminds Zeus of her consanguinity, their common origins, but she uses a rather different mode of argument from Poseidon's. Hera appeals to the aristocratic criterion of birth, exactly as she does later, on other occasions, every time she justifies the attention that she lavishes upon Achilles. She does so, for instance, when Zeus–despite having himself foreseen and included the event in his own program–angrily accuses his wife of having provoked Achilles' return to the battlefield in order to further her own ends,[46] to which Hera retorts that of course she was determined to get her way. What could be more suitable for her in her position as first lady, "the greatest of goddesses," literally *ariste theoan*, a title that befits her on two counts, both her birth and her marriage with the lord of all the Immortals?[47] And later, the goddess projects on to Achilles himself the shadow of her own dignity. At the point when almost all the Olympians are ready to put a stop to the indignities that Achilles is inflicting upon Hector's corpse, Hera speaks out against Apollo's proposal: "Yes, there could be truth even in what you say, lord of the silver bow—if you gods mean to hold Hektor in equal honor with Achilleus. Hektor is a mortal and sucked at a woman's breast. But Achilleus is child of a goddess whom I myself brought up and reared and gave as wife to a man, Peleus, who of all men was dearest to the hearts of the immortals."[48] Arguing against Apollo, who points out how well Hector has behaved and what a generous and deserving sacrificer he always was, Hera introduces a different criterion of evaluation: birth, the divine origin that sets Achilles above his victim. She does, it is true, also refer to the feasting delights that the gods owe to Achilles, but what she has in mind is the wedding banquet on the occasion of the marriage of Peleus and Thetis, which all the Olympians attended: food shared at the table of a particularly privileged mortal, to celebrate his union with a goddess, not—as in Hector's case—aromas regularly offered to the gods by a pious devotee.

Hera marshals her arguments based on class consciousness extremely coherently: birth, origins, privileges. Poseidon, in contrast, opposes Zeus in the name of other values: equal rights, sharing, abiding by the luck of the draw. But Zeus wins every time, for his power obeys a whole variety of principles. Now authoritarian, now conciliatory, frequently devious, Zeus juggles with the desires and rights of others, gods and mortals alike. On the issue of Hector's corpse, he imposes his own view upon Hera, after making a concession to her: namely, that Achilles will receive different honors from those due to ordinary mortals. He then goes on to remind her that Hector was very dear to Zeus himself, for the sake of all the gods, since the heavy smoke arising from the thighs that he sacrificed to them had, after all, been enjoyed by all of them, up on Olympus.[49] Zeus cleverly associates his own interests with those of the other gods, beginning with his argumentative wife, who is soon won over. When dealing with Poseidon, in contrast, Zeus gets the upper hand through a legalistic argument. Poseidon appeals for equality between brothers, does he? Well, he should remember another law, the one that establishes the right of elder siblings, who take priority over their youngers! Faced with this, Poseidon wisely backs down.⁵⁰

After the cunning ruse of the amorous siesta, the father of gods and men thus soon regains control. The erotic subterfuges of his wife and the high-minded outbursts from his brother are all soon foiled. And the not very cunning Poseidon is likely to remember his prank when Zeus, in the future, takes advantage of him in similar fashion. One day, when Poseidon is distracted, attending a banquet given by the Ethiopians, Zeus will make the most of his absence to get Odysseus away from the goddess Calypso. It is Poseidon who holds him prisoner, far from his own island, in the house of a mistress whom he no longer desires: a terrible ordeal through which the all too cunning mortal Odysseus is made to pay for the dreadful injury he inflicted upon Poseidon's son, the Cyclops. While the sea-god is away enjoying himself, abandoning Odysseus to the mercy of the other Olympians, Zeus seizes his chance: a messenger is dispatched to Calypso, and the prisoner sets to sea, homeward bound. The only way for Poseidon to revenge himself is constantly to send storms to disrupt a return journey willed by his burdensome elder brother. It is the start of the *Odyssey*.

A Power of Which Many a Tale Is Told

Poseidon capitulates, Hera is forced into submission, and Zeus is the winner. Really, the only failure that he acknowledges is the bungled birth of Heracles. On that occasion, his wife was more cunning than he. But after that, he banished Error (Ate) to earth, and now Zeus can no longer be deceived. However, it would be foolish to conclude that the father of the Olympians is omnipotent. For the effective exercise of power by the lord of Olympus on the contrary depends upon the continued cut and thrust of contradictory and dangerous forces.

Zeus is certainly the sovereign strategist in this whole story. It is he who fashions the ongoing saga, he who decides how men and gods shall spend their time. His plan for the Trojan War is a perfect example of his "providential" power. However, the realization of his project, once launched, is not assured by the force of a necessity that stems ineluctably from the will of the god, that is to say, from his absolute efficacious power. The chain of events devised by Zeus turns out to be fragile: it is constantly disrupted by chance, by contingencies. Zeus's plans keep clashing with other plans, other desires: both those of gods and those of men. And when such clashes occur, victory is not a foregone conclusion. On the contrary, at every turn, the outcome is chancy. Sometimes, it is as if Zeus's will is satisfied fortuitously, thanks to a combination of circumstances.

As we have seen, the story of the *Iliad* is set in motion by a decision to mobilize the Greek army and send it to besiege Troy, only to suffer a *defeat*. But the dream that Zeus sent in order to bring this about produced a contradictory and unpredictable result: the recipient of the dream pulled his army out! The trouble was that Zeus did not determine every aspect of the project, but left Agamemnon free to react to the dream. And Agamemnon acted on his own initiative, thereby threatening promptly to subvert the will of Zeus. However, Zeus is not even affected by all this. For Athena, dispatched by Hera, saves Zeus's plan . . . acting against him, since she too wants the Greeks to attack, but in order to win! The upshot of Hera continuing to play her own game, in opposition to Zeus's, is that she manages to salvage the plan that he had devised, in open conflict to her. And in all of this, Hera has in no way been manipulated. She makes all her own decisions.

As we have also seen, it was Zeus who decided that after the death of Patroclus, Achilles would kill Hector. He solemnly declared this to Hera. But, in practice, to realize the chain of events that Zeus has virtually put together, it is Hera who again takes a hand. It is she who sends Iris to Achilles to persuade him to reenter the war; and had she not done so, Hector would not have been killed . . . in accordance with Zeus's plan. Furthermore, not only does she do this on her own initiative and to further her own strategy, but she also does it without Zeus's knowing; subsequently, he reproaches her for having implemented a plan that he no longer recognizes as his own. Achilles' return to the fighting becomes well and truly determined by Zeus's wife's will.

Amnesia on the part of the god, laziness, negligence in his supervision of the world . . . : a reader of the *Iliad* soon finds himself raising the same questions as the ancient philosophers. Spontaneous rationalism? Not if you listen to the story as told. Just think, for a moment: if Zeus was really all-powerful and his plans had the force of destiny, if his will encountered no obstacles, what would be the point of the rest of the gods? Would he not be, as it were, on his own? And besides, what would there be to say? For in a single instant everything would be done, accomplished, completed. Everything would be known in advance and would amount to nothing, or to very little. For is not the narrative of the *Iliad* an epic about desires that clash, recover, and grow ever stronger? A story, above all a novel, surely derives its strength from the perception of whatever is contingent, whatever would be possible otherwise. The epic is symptomatic of God's imperfection: only if there is something that resists him is there a story to be told. Even the God of Genesis seems to manifest a weakness by creating the world in six days, instead of doing it instantaneously, all in one go.

In short, if there is a story, there have to be "weak" gods, whose power is limited, multiple, and relative. The tyrannical absolute belongs to a bygone age, when a father fearful of forfeiting his scepter would devour his own children. That father, Cronos, wanted all the power for himself alone, forever, never to be shared, never to be passed on. One of his children, saved by his wife Rhea, survived and dethroned the despot. This was Zeus, and he inaugurated a time of power that was less totalitarian but more real and more widely deployed. Obsessed with the sole aim of preserving his own reign, Cronos did nothing but make his wife pregnant and then swallow her children. Zeus, in contrast, who is forced to impose his own anything-but-absolute power, and who needs so often to do so through cunning, acting against and in spite of the other beings whom he involves in his operations, is a god who is very much alive, very active, a god whose days are brimming over with energy and enterprises.

8   The Gods and Their Days

If we are to believe the witnesses to a number of very scholarly debates–witnesses who, because their names were Cicero, Lucian, and Seneca, were at once judges and debaters–in their eyes the major difficulty that the gods of their day raised was eminently practical: What do they do? or, more to the point, "Do they do anything at all? For, as Cicero remarks, much is said about what they look like and the places where they live, and about their houses and the exploits of their lives, but the question that above all underlies any difference of opinion as to their nature is whether or not they do nothing, meddle in nothing, abstain from all concern and all cares.[1] So any reflection *de natura deorum* is bound to encounter this first reef, the problem of what they do, whether they act, whether they bother. That is the very first question since what is at stake here is the very existence of the Immortals. Whatever would one do with carefree and passive gods of leisure? The very idea is inconceivable: useless, so impossible; unjustifiable, because pointless. The opponents of Epicurus insisted that this boiled down to a timid atheism that did not dare to come clean. Such was, at least, the frame of mind in which they questioned the existence of the gods in Greece and Rome before the Christian era: the question of their *activity* was the touchstone for their presence in the world. The next postulate was that, obviously, there must be a connection between being there and doing something, so simply to be in the world without occupying oneself with the world would be absurd–particularly for a god.

This way of thinking of the divine as an active, busy, preoccupied presence can be conceived in two perspectives. The first is that of a constant in religious thought, something to which it obstinately clings; the second is that of a key idea, a distinctive trait of Greek thought.

To attribute to the gods a desire and an ability to be active may seem to be the most common way of giving a form to the very superiority and excellence of the superhuman powers.[2] Whether through an original creative vocation or through a constant commitment to watch over the world, to govern men, to regulate nature, countless deities have forever and in all parts of the world manifested their majesty by accomplishing an undertaking, by fulfilling tasks. Whether as supreme beings or as ordinary members of polytheist groups, how many gods have ever cultivated indifference and total inertia? Some certainly have: the gods of Daoism.

Here, the supreme being is neither a creator nor a judge who takes an interest in men. Neither is he an idle god, work-shy or asleep, as some are elsewhere, in Greece and in Sumer, for instance. The supreme power is, rather, an extremely abstract figure of the order of the world or, as Granet puts it, "a Reality characterized by its logical necessity and considered under the aspect of *a Power of Realization*, prime, permanent, omnipresent."[3] When a sage attains to contemplation of this figure, he can exclaim: "Oh my Master! Oh my Master! thou who destroyest all beings and who art not cruel! thou who spreadest thy benefactions throughout the ages and who art not good! thou who art older than the highest antiquity and who art ageless! thou who, bearing all as Heaven and Earth, art *the author of all things and who art not industrious!*"[4] Indefinable, impossible to slot into unequivocal categories, the Dao is a principle of cyclical time capable of introducing order and differentiation into the original chaos. It is the cause of the cosmos, but not its demiurge. In the fourth century, when a theory of immortality was being elaborated as a reward for human behavior and it became necessary to attribute to God the vigilant attention of a judge, another power appeared, the Governor of Destinies, assisted by a whole adminis-

trative personnel. For, as Granet notes, "the task of the Supreme
Unity could not be concerned with the doings of the living."[5]

If a god is believed to watch the lives of mortals, he will probably
also be believed to model his own life on theirs, devote his time to
them, be there for them. But Daoism resists this, so that even the
Immortals, men who have become "gods" following a violent death
and thanks to their virtues, form a society apart, ethereal and re-
fined, and are as powerful as they are unmoved by the demands addressed to them by mortals.

> In the faraway mountains of Kou-ye, divine beings live. Their skin is
> as fresh as frosty snow and they are as delicate and discreet as virgins.
> They eat no cereals, but breathe in the wind and drink the dew. They
> sit on the clouds and the winds and ride flying dragons to go and
> amuse themselves beyond the four seas [the frontiers of the world].
> By concentrating their minds, they can protect beings from plague
> and make the harvests ripen. . . . Those men! What power! They can
> take in the ten thousand beings and make them one.

They possess great powers, these Immortals, and could use them to
help their former peers, who grow weak and fragile from sickness
and famine. But they do not care to be useful. "The men of this
world beg them to come and put things in order, but *why should
they weary themselves with matters of the world below*?" The
Zhuangze strikes Epicurean chords: "Nothing can hurt these men.
Even if a flood comes, with water right up to the sky, they will not
perish. If heat comes that is so great that it melts stones and burns
the land and the mountains, they will not even feel warm."[6]

In Greece, Epicurus is the philosopher who was the most critical
of representations of the divine that centered on its caring nature.
He noted all their incoherences. For the spectacle of the world in all
its imperfection set alongside the belief in the existence of extraordinary beings who are tender toward our virtues, severe toward our
weakness, and who regulate the universe with infallible justice
forces one to draw disillusioned conclusions.

> God, he says, either wants to suppress evil and cannot; or can do so
> but does not want to; or else he neither wants to nor can; or does want
> to and can. If he wants to and cannot, he is weak, and a god cannot be

weak; if he can and does not want to, he is jealous, which, likewise, a
god cannot be; if he neither wants to nor can, he is both jealous and
weak, and therefore is not a god; if he wants to and can, which alone
befits a god, what is the cause of all the evil, or why cannot he do away
with it?[7]

If you assume that the gods are concerned about the world and that
they have the ability to act for our good, then you are forced to ask
why they do not do so, why they leave us to ourselves, in disorder,
injustice, and evil. How can we fail to see that to attribute to a god
the task of taking care of men is to provide an opportunity to find
him lacking, to discover him to be *imbecillis*, *invidus*, negligent?
Epicurus, accordingly, denies that the gods are in any way concerned with us. They exist, in their own space and their own time,
enjoying constant happiness, in a beatitude that no event can ever
upset. Like the Daoist Immortals, "Why should they weary themselves with matters of the world below?"

In contrast to the countless religious traditions that combine the
existence of gods with a commitment toward the age on their part,
Daoism and Epicureanism try to maintain a radical position, to as-
sert that what makes a god different or distinct from us is the fact
that he has nothing to do. What could be more alien to the spirit of
turbulent ancient polytheism or to that of the Jewish and Christian
traditions?

Genesis: Daily Toil?

Christianity, which adopts the inductive proof of the existence of God
(since the world is there, it must have been made by someone), and
which defines God as being in the first instance the Creator, the Father, the Sovereign, thereby makes the equivalence between existing
and taking action the hub of its doctrine. In Genesis, the Old Testament tells of the creative work of God the Father and the perfect attention that he pays to the continuing evolution of his work: watching, observing, spying, listening, fathoming secrets, detecting lies;
and finally and above all, to provide a purpose for this perpetual vig-
ilance, punishing and rewarding, selecting those to be saved and
those to be damned. It is because of the product of his creative enterprise that the God of Israel is the Greatest: "For the Lord is great and

greatly to be praised: he is to be feared above all gods. For all the gods of the nations are idols; but the Lord made the heavens."[28]

The Psalms pay unceasing homage to the hand of God, to his ears, his mouth, and above all his eyes. But it is Genesis in particular that, by recounting the Beginning, and because it *recounts* it, ascribes a way of using his time to the deity and by doing so raises considerable problems for the exegesis of centuries to come–problems concerning what the body, time, and the world are for God.

In a duration of time that was a succession of days, God worked, creating the world. On the seventh day he rested. Out of first nothingness, then confusion, Elohim introduced the differentiation of beings. He fashioned things and separated them. First he brought about light and then, immediately, divided day from night. No sooner was the space set out–with the earth distinct from the sky–than he introduced time: time into which, in the alternation of light and darkness, all God's works would fit. In the beginning there was one God who, wanting to make the world, invented the day-to-day. He invented it as if there were no other way to complete a task, as if, right from the start, it had to be set in time measured on that particular scale. The beginning of the Scriptures consecrates the idea that the time in which the world began was originally the time of a desire to create, the time for a task that provoked fatigue and that was filled with cares: the day-to-day that we all know so well. Then humankind had to imitate the one who, one day, had created them. They would labor for a period equal to that of the creation; then they would abstain from all tasks on the day which, as it returned cyclically, brought the *shābbath*, the Lord's rest. In other words, their life was to be shaped as the cycle of weeks passed, by that segment of daily life that God had fashioned so that everything could begin. Human beings were faithful to a model and also exemplary of that model. If they can and must live in time in the manner of God, it means that God, while not renouncing eternity, is wedded to the time that he intended for mortals. He has subjected himself to the cosmological order that he established. He has presented himself with instants upon which he himself imposed a measure.

Before history began, the world's time was created in a daily form. To be sure, the story of the Book of Genesis was fated not to be taken literally. We know how much was at stake in the choice of reading made for the Jewish tradition and for the various brands of Christianity. But what lay at the root of even the most scholarly debates? Was it not a story? Because of that, all attempts at exegesis–however scholarly in intention–measure themselves and constantly come up against a story. Let us concentrate on three episodes, three debates that will give some idea of the questions that arise when time is reconfigured,[9] as it is in Genesis. The first debate is the extremely animated exchange that took place between Origen and Celsus in the third century B.C. Their argument is over the pertinence of a story that ascribes to the Creator a contradictory and unseemly use of *time*. The second is the dispute between the Catholics and the Protestants that erupted in the sixteenth century over the legitimacy of anthropomorphic images of God. The bone of contention is the *body* of God that seems to be presupposed in the biblical text. The third episode is that in which, in the mid-nineteenth century, the champions of Pasteurian microbiology clashed with a naturalist who was convinced of the truth of spontaneous generation. What resurfaced in this debate was a theological question: What are the limits to God's work?

Celsus, an extremely cultivated man in the tradition of the Greek philosophers, particularly Plato, refutes and pours scorn upon the notion of divinity that emerges from both the Old and the New Testaments. He stresses the paradoxical nature of a story that refers to the omnipotence of a god whom it also describes as a figure who works and, what is more, does so day after day. This god must live in the same element of time as mortals, in fact needs to in order to make the world, and he accomplishes his exploit in such a human fashion that he becomes tired and has to rest. "The scripture story of the origin of men is a fine naivety," writes Celsus, "but the most stupid thing about it is that it divides the fashioning of the world into several days before there was any such thing as days! For if the sky was not yet created, nor the earth established, nor the sun revolving round it, how could there have been days?" In the first place he picks upon the inconsequentiality of time that is already daily, since it is counted in days, when no night or day yet exists. It is the movement of the sun that constitutes these periods of time. And the sun is not created until the fourth day. So this is clearly nonsense. "And besides," he goes on, "looking at things from a more elevated viewpoint, let us see whether it is not absurd that the first and very great God orders that such and such a thing be done, or such and such other thing, yet on the first day produces no more than one thing, then one more on the second day, and so on through the third, fourth, fifth, and sixth days." If a god has to space out his work over a week, as if he needed to mete out his strength, he must be extraordinarily weak! If he is, then no wonder he is exhausted after creating a being in his own image, who reflects all his own weakness. "Then, after this work, like a very bad workman, he was overcome with exhaustion and needed a rest in order to recover. It cannot be said that the First God gets tired, nor that he works with his hands, nor that he issues commands. God has neither mouth, nor voice. . . . Nor did God make man in his own image; for he is not like a man and resembles no other form at all."[10]

In short, Celsus stigmatizes all the incoherence that creation, presented as an ongoing labor, implies, that is to say, everything that is incompatible with the fact that the subject here is a god. Furthermore, he points out a very serious irrefutable problem when he ridicules the idea of days when day did not yet exist. For as soon as any subject acts, measurable time must already be there; it is a condition for all action, since an action necessarily takes up time, time that lasts and that can be measured. Unless it is instantaneous, any creation takes minutes, hours, days. Consequently, as soon as the origin of the world is conceived as the work of a subject, measured time becomes both the *a priori* and the product of that work. Hence, the very real ambiguity of the biblical text. But, to be more precise, Celsus argues like a Greek.

The Greeks never ceased to conceive of time as being "something to do with movement," that is to say, an effect of the movement of objects in space, of celestial bodies, in particular, the sun, in the sky. For a Greek, time was thus a cosmological phenomenon that by definition presupposed the universe and its movements. So when Celsus asks "how could there have been days" before the creation of the firmament (second day) and that of the sun (fourth day), he is asking a Greek question. Philo of Alexandria had answered that question, saying that it was totally impossible to believe that the world was made in six days or, more generally, within time. For time is a succession of days and nights determined by the rising and setting of the sun in the sky. Therefore, time necessarily came after the world and owes its existence to it.[11] Centuries earlier, Plato had already led the way in his account of the birth of the world. He had presented a demiurge who first made the sky, and only then thought of "that which we have named Time [*chronos*]. For simultaneously with the construction of the Heaven, He contrived the production of days and nights and months and years, which existed not before the Heaven came into being."[12] Plato is not affected by Celsus's critique, since he makes no mention of "days" in which to situate such works of the demiurge as preceded the Sky.

Genesis: Work Worthy of a God?

The sixteenth century presents us with another facet to the questioning that we are considering (for the Creator of the Sistine Chapel, that emblem of the Roman Catholic Church, should not cause us to forget the quarrels on the score of images that were then dividing Christianity[13]). In the beginning was the text, the source represented by the Scriptures. On the one hand, in Exodus 20:4, Iahve forbids any image of himself. On the other, plenty of narrative passages tell of God appearing to men, for instance, to David. Which should one go by, the commandment or the example? This is not a mere aesthetic dilemma, but a decision of fundamental importance that confronts Christians with a point that is crucial for all religious thought: Is a god representable? How does he become present?

For the Christians it was historically difficult to come to a clear decision, confronted as they were by the conflicting testimony of the Scriptures. When making their choices, both the Protestants and the Catholics claimed to have the *auctoritas* of the Bible behind them. The Protestants more or less, although with modifications, held to the declaration of the rule: "Thou shalt not make unto thee any graven image or any likeness of anything that is in heaven above." In the Roman Catechism produced by the Council of Trent in 1566, the Roman Catholic Church, in contrast, confirmed the priority given, ever since the Council of Nicea in 787, to respect for the paradigm created by the recounted scenes of, for example, the Creation. If the Bible told the story of Genesis and later also that of the

Redemption, and if it itself presented God as a speaking, acting figure, then to condemn images of God would be to censure the Old Testament. Paintings of the Almighty were therefore authorized, provided they imitated the iconographical models already inserted into the Holy Book.

In reaction to the intransigence of the Reformation, the Catholicism represented by the Council of Trent approved the anthropomorphism suggested by the Bible. Whether or not it was all a matter of pure pedagogy, the fact was recognized–and God received a body. But there was more to it. The Council encouraged images of God in action, seized upon as he did something, accomplishing the exploits credited to him; and in this way his body was placed in time. The story of his life tells of a succession of moments.

Our last example of the problems raised by the narrative nature of the Bible concerns the extent of God's activities. In the nineteenth century, three hundred years after Francesco Redi discovered the sexed nature of the reproduction of insects, spontaneous generation was a notion that was still alive and that could count on its zealous defenders. One of these, the eminent biologist Félix Archimède Pouchet, had no hesitation in backing it up with an attentive reading of Genesis. The creation of the animals and plants is indeed recounted in such a way that it could legitimately be understood as "a veritable spontaneous generation brought about through divine inspiration."[14] Does not Elohim say: "Let the earth bring forth living animals, each according to their species," bidding the ground to engender what he has created for the first time, in default of any transmission? But Pouchet went further, for he wanted to show that the reproduction of certain living creatures at the bottom of the scale was still the same: spontaneous and divine, through the earth and through God. To this end, he tried to convince the reader that God had never stopped in his work, that the Eternal One spent his time in "incessant activity," "a labor that continues through every instant."[15] Genesis certainly declares that after the sixth day God took a rest, he wrote, "but where is there a verse in the Sacred Book that tells us that he decides never to re-engage in his work? Where is it said that after that rest he broke up his molds and annihilated his creative faculty?"[16] Against those who claimed that "to have the supreme majesty producing new works day in day out is to belittle it,"[17] Pouchet retorted that, on the contrary, to immobilize that creative genius for all eternity would be to deny its omnipotence. And with the backing of many biblical quotations, he went on to praise the perpetual and indefatigable industry of the Almighty.

This summarized sample of different opinions has been briefly introduced to give full weight to a question that might otherwise have rung somewhat false, namely: What do the gods do with their time? It is a question that all of them, from the most transcendent down to those closest to human beings, need to answer since, for them, it truly is a matter of life or death.

The Life of the Gods and the Life of Men

As I have pointed out above, the second perspective that provides a framework to the ancient way of thinking about divinity in terms of an active life is basically classical. It is thinking about *la vita*, first and foremost, the life of human beings. The philosophers who concern themselves with the nature of the gods, concentrating primarily on what their occupations are likely to be, are the very ones for whom the essential function of philosophy is to provide rules according to which to live a good life. All the pronouncements of philosophy refer to life. That is how Cicero introduces the debate *de natura deorum*. For the life of human beings is the yardstick and counterpart to the life of the gods.

If you deny the activity of the gods and their concern for mankind, you strip the *vita hominum* of its meaning. For if the gods do nothing for men, the *raison d'être* of all ritual practices disappears. Why should we devote a cult to beings who are unconcerned, unmoved by prayers and incapable of gratitude? There would then be no justification for *pietas*. And along with *pietas*, many other values would lose their point: *fides*, mutual trust, *societas*, and, finally, justice.[18] In short, the social bond, with all its rules, collapses as soon as you cease to believe that the gods are responsible for it, that they are concerned about it or at least feel some interest in it. In other words, the morality of relations between human beings depends solely upon the attentive gaze that the gods keep fixed upon them. If the Immortals are believed to ignore us, we shall turn away from them and, by the same token, away from our respect for our fellows. The gods are the model of somebody else who is concerned about our life, whose eyes follow us, and to whom we are responsible for our conduct. Perhaps Hellenistic philosophy is more of a life philosophy than a subjective philosophy: life in the sense of time in which the links that bind an individual to the world are forged.

This discourse, so conscious of the dangers that would beset the social edifice were the gods believed to be utterly impassive, was, of course, directed against the Epicureans. For it was they who were spreading that suspicion. But, in truth, for the philosophers of the Garden it was more a matter of rigorous thinking: if the gods are blessed, they must necessarily abstain from all that causes trouble, and hence concern, the *cura* that is the lot of mortal beings busy with the age in which they live. To deny the gods any interest in the world–whether it be in creation, in judgment, or in predestination– is simply to conceive of them in a logical fashion and to restore to them the *beatitas* that has constantly been attributed to them ever since Homer but that is at the same time obstinately denied them, given that they are claimed to be involved, enmeshed in our affairs. The poets are principally responsible for this absurd theology, full of Olympians burning with anger, driven mad by desire, committed to wars, battles, and conflicts in which they even go so far as to get themselves wounded; Olympians with feuds, quarrels, disagreements; births, deaths; altercations, complaints; and desires that impel them into all kinds of intemperate behavior: adulteries, amorous liaisons, fornication even with representatives of the human race, to the point where mortals come to be engendered by gods.[19] Power, war, love affairs: we know all too well that an active life means constant agitation involving a multitude of gestures and passions, tensions and endeavors amid which we are torn apart by hostilities and attractions. All this is so unworthy of the gods that the Immortals take to reproducing themselves in mortals. How can one subscribe to such vain beliefs when, albeit indistinctly, all men think of the gods as enjoying eternal beatitude? Coherence demands that a blessed and eternal being "should himself be uninvolved in any affair and expect nobody to go to any trouble since nobody can excite his anger, nor win his favor, such sentiments being marks of weakness" (*imbecilla essent omnia*).[20]

In contrast to the Homeric religion, for an Epicurean the existence of the gods is defined by negative characteristics. They exist in the perfection of time that is always identical and that no happening ever comes to disrupt, since no desire ever penetrates there. There is no trace of anything that would lead to *action*; no suggestion of adventure; no desire, which leads to cares. On the contrary, without this being paradoxical, there is simply a great deal of pleasure, a flow of *voluptates*. This life away from all *libidines*, all desires, is a life filled with enjoyment. But how is that possible? How can your gods possibly enjoy it?[21] That is the question that the detractors of Epicureanism would insistently pose; and it was parried by another, which the Epicureans addressed to the religion of others: Why do your gods have desires?[22] It is an exchange that encompasses the whole problem of divine time.

What is so intriguing in the Epicurean notion of happy gods are the following questions: What life do the gods lead (*Quae vita deorum sit*)? How do they spend their time (*Quaeque ab iis degatur aetas*)?[23] Once it is admitted that they do nothing, the question remains is what happens in this empty, dead time, this holiday. *Quae ergo vita*? What kind of life do they have?[24] The question reflects an impatience with time that is not occupied, filled, brimming with things done and things to do. Just as the Epicureans are asked what is the point of their gods having bodies if they never use them, they are also bombarded with that finalist question. Not that they lack an answer. They do have one, but it is one that begs the question:

> You Stoics are also fond of asking us, Balbus, what is the mode of life of the gods and how they pass their days. The answer is, theirs is the happiest conceivable, and the one most bountifully furnished with all good things. God is entirely inactive and free from all ties of occupation; he toils not neither does he labor, but he takes delight in his own wisdom and virtue and knows with absolute certainty that he will always enjoy pleasures at once consummate and everlasting.[25]

A god enjoys himself. Sated by his own virtue, which he does not need to acquire, filled with knowledge that he does not need to seek, he lets time wash over him, flooding him with pleasure. Showered with blessings forever, he foresees delights that could not be more intense or more numerous. And above all, he has no need to look forward to that future with ambitions or expectations. For the happiness of tomorrow is already there today, just as it was yesterday: it is always present, so he neither wants it, resents it, nor wants more of it.

So that is the life of an Epicurean god. He exists within time, but without the cares and tasks that crowd upon the *laboriosissimi* gods who are believed to create or govern the world. To those who believe that a divine being is first and foremost a vigilant creator, an Epicurean responds with a question of his own: Why suddenly want to make a world?[26] Why abruptly (*repente*) awaken from an eternal slumber? The question to ask gods who are supposed to give meaning to their lives through action is not "How do they spend their time?" but "Why did they fashion the time that they spend? Why this break in the continuum of eternity that preceded the division into days? What desire impelled them at a stroke to change the scene of space?" Whereas the day-to-day life of the gods presents no mystery, that moment of the very first spark of a desire seems inexplicable. On the one hand, the Epicureans posit a totally sufficient and interminable delight that is judged to be impossible; on the other, their opponents posit an unpremeditated will that opens time up to beings, which is dismissed as incoherent thinking.

In Epicurean ethics, the primary concern is the treatment or modulation of desire. Besieged by passions, and exposed to everything around them that attracts or repels them, delights or frightens them, men and women—for the Garden is open to women, too—have a choice between two alternatives: either they say yes to all that the world offers them and stretch out for things, or else they hold back, keeping themselves in reserve. It is not that to desire pleasure is bad in itself. But what may hold one back is the knowledge that there is a danger that it may be a lure. For Greek philosophy, desire and enjoyment are not necessarily complementary, for desire proceeds from a sense of lack and likewise engenders it. But for Epicurus, the important thing is not to overcome desires (*epithumiai*). Rather, it is to know how to deal with them, to investigate them. "This question should be applied to all desires: what will happen to me if the object of my desire is achieved and what if it is not?"[27] One should establish a dialogue with nature, using persuasion without violence: satisfy natural and necessary desires, and listen to the voice of the flesh when it speaks of not being hungry, not being thirsty, not being cold.[28] In these dialogues, the sage learns to know what he should grant his body and what, given that it is not indispensable, is a mere illusion of his. Contrary to the general view, Epicurus maintains that the stomach, in itself, is not insatiable: it is more one's own idea of it that makes it seem limitlessly avid.[29] Nature has its limits. Only to those deceived by their own hollow opinions does what is sufficient seem too little rather than all that should be desired.[30] Only a churlish soul regards a living man as a being "endlessly avid for all the variety of day-to-day existence,"[31] through either greed, ambition, or sensuality.

From this point of view, one can see how stupid it is to attribute to a god supposed to be "blessed" the strange desire to succeed in an undertaking that is so unnecessary to his enjoyment: to make a world to which, furthermore, he will then have to devote his attention. If man acquires serenity in *ataraxia* (an absence of troubles), in *aponia* (an absence of fatigue), and in apathy (an absence of passions), why should a god, who is under no obligations at all, turn away from these things? A sage, a man whose life unfolds day after day, night after night, far from troubles, "lives like a god among men."[32] So why should anyone suppose that a god does not live just like that, amongst other gods?

One's idea of the daily life of men—both of what it is and what it ought to be—corresponds to that which one attributes to the gods within time. The Epicureans are very lucid on this point, both when they infer the content of divine beatitude from human felicity and also when they analyze the harmful consequences, for mortals, of a particular representation of the gods.

To be fearful of the Immortals, afraid of their rages, and to grovel for their pardon is, to the minds of these philosophers, the purest form of religious stupidity. The Greeks had a word for that kind of excessive terror: *deisidaimonia*, which we translate as superstition, via the Latin *superstitio*. *Deisidaimonia* is an attitude of perpetual terror vis-à-vis the divine powers. It stems from a sense of permanent menace, and it determines a pattern of behavior that becomes a veritable way of life. The feeling of danger makes people watch out for signs, for the slightest indications of what the gods want them to do, not to do, to say. Fear commits them to constant ritual, for always, all the time, without respite, it is essential to face up to the anger of Zeus or the vengeance of Hecate. Living in such trepidation, superstitious people live immersed in religion. It takes up all their time. Both Theophrastus and Plutarch considered such people to be sick.[33]

But in Epicurus's view, *deisdaimonia* is by no means exceptional. It reveals the basic defect of ordinary religion. A measured fear is one of the mainsprings of religious devotion as it is practiced. But wherever there is fear, there is immediately superstition. So all religious devotion is already superstitious. How could it be otherwise? Who would not fear beings supposed to govern the world and keep us under constant surveillance? It is the idea that the gods are concerned with us that necessarily makes them our persecutors. "You have saddled us with an eternal master, whom day and night we are to fear; for who would not fear a prying busybody of a god, who foresees and thinks of and notices all things, and deems that everything is his concern?"[34] If human beings imagine a god whose whole time, whole life is saturated with concern, concern about them, then their days and nights will, in their turn, be entirely occupied by his gaze, his presence. One version of such a god had the following fine psalm addressed to him: "Thine eyes did see my [days] and in thy book all my [days] were written."[35] Epicureanism rejects those written days.

II The Gods at the Service of the City

9 When the Olympians Donned the Citizen's Costume

One very windy day, the god Boreas became a citizen of the town of Thurii, the new Sybaris in Magna Graecia. In more concrete terms, in 397 B.C. Dionysius of Syracuse, at war with the Carthaginians, launched an expedition of three hundred ships crammed with armed men–hoplites, men of bronze–against Thurii. The North Wind was blowing against them, and Boreas wrecked the ships. It was a disaster for Dionysius, but the citizens of Thurii, saved by the god Boreas, passed a decree granting citizenship to the wind. They gave him a house, as they would any new citizen, allotted him a plot of land, and each year held a festival in his honor.[1] Not to be outdone, the Athenians, who had played a key role in the founding of the new Sybaris, decided to make Boreas "a kinsman by alliance."[2] On the banks of the Ilissus River there was already a sanctuary dedicated to the North Wind, who had come to their aid on an earlier occasion, in 480 B.C., against the Persion fleet, off Cape Artemision.[3] Honored by a sacrifice and a decree by the assembly, a god was thus granted citizenship, a house like those in which human beings live, and an allotment of land to ensure his subsistence, or rather an income for his cult. The North Wind was not really a typical Olympian, but this episode does testify in detail to the degree to which a Greek city felt itself to be in sovereign charge when it decided to naturalize a divine power.

But let us now take a god whose credentials are above all suspicion: Dionysus. In Arcadia, on the banks of the Alpheus River, there
was a little city called Heraia, after Hera, Dionysus's stubborn stepmother, who had her own temple there, as did the god Pan.[4] Dionysus, for his part, had two temples: in the first, as Auxitēs, the one
who makes things grow and flourish, he was the god of sap, the god
of the fecund humors rising from the earth, the god who could make
a vine grow in a single day.[5] In his other temple he was enthroned as
Dionysus Politēs, Citizen Dionysus. His position here was not the
same as that of the Dionysus of Teos, who was the latter city's major
deity, or that of the Dionysus called "public" in Tralles, or that of
the Dionysus "of the whole people" in Kyme, in Aeolis.[6] In a totally
unprecedented fashion for an Olympian, here Dionysus held the position of an ordinary citizen, a citizen in the abstract, without reference to any city in particular, as in the case of, for instance, Heracles, who happened to be Thasian, or Zeus, who would claim to be
Spartan. The Dionysus of Arcadia was there in the guise of a citizen;
but he was still the same god as he was in his native Thebes, where
he was constantly being told by the descendants of Cadmus, the
city's founder, what a very great god he was. In the outskirts of his
city, this Theban Dionysus delighted in turning himself into a deity
to whom a whole twelve altars were dedicated,[7] for to refer to the altars of the Twelve Gods was usually to refer to the whole of Olympus, given that the major pantheon consisted of twelve deities in all.
Here, all twelve altars were dedicated to one god, who was acknowl-
edged as the greatest of the Olympians. And, to provoke his family
even more–his family who owned the vast sky, where his uncles and
cousins all lived in their Olympian residences–Dionysus announced
that he was reserving three of his altars for his mother, Semele, one
of Cadmus's daughters, a mortal woman who had become immortal
and who, under the divine and Dionysiac name of the Delirious
One, Thyōne, was Semele the Maenad, ever manically leaping in ec-
stasy in the highest heavens.

Of all the Olympians, only Dionysus was both a citizen and a god
of Olympus: this constituted an extra feather in the cap of the master of the mask, who had such a taste for paradox. But that double
title of his was indicative of a process that was to become very much
a feature of the history of the Olympians. It brought about an im-

portant change for the society of the gods, one of whose consequences may not have been immediately appreciated by those who
did not keep a sharp eye on what was going on but must certainly
have been taken in at a glance by the more alert members of the
Olympian family.

One day, then, the Olympians, gathered together in an assembly,
decided to choose the cities in which each of them would receive
particular honors.[8] We can tell that this was definitely an assembly
from the vocabulary used ("It has pleased the gods," the same formula as appeared in decrees passed by the cities), not simply a family
council or meeting. Already for some time the Olympians had been
making no secret of the interest that they took in the cities of their
protégés. They would talk of it openly up there on their mountaintop, sometimes with voices raised in anger. The incensed Hera
wanted to rush the gates of Troy and devour Priam and his sons
alive, along with all the other Trojans. Then came a threat from
Zeus: "Whenever I in my turn am eager to destroy a city peopled by
men who are dear to you, do not seek to thwart my anger," followed
by a riposte from Hera: "There are three cities of all dearest to me,
Argos and Sparta and wide-wayed Mykene. Sack these, whenever
your heart feels strong hatred for them."[9] The decibels would in-
crease, and indiscretions would reach the ears of idle listeners. But
never before had anyone suggested distributing the cities among the
gods. They all had their favorites. Zeus swore by the altars of Priam,
with their unforgettable aromas. Apollo could deny his priest Chryses nothing and was attached to the city of Tenedos as well as that of
Chryse.

It was not the first time that things had been shared out between
the gods. The universe had been divided between the three sons of
Cronos and Rhea, and each had received his own fiefdom, his *timē*,
his particular field of operations. Poseidon was to live in the white-
foamed sea; to Hades went the shadows and mists of the kingdom of
death; and Zeus received the vast sky with its ether and clouds.
There had been a drawing of lots, "but the earth and high Olympos
were left common to us all [i.e., common to all the gods]."[10] There
had also been a division of authority when Zeus, who held the thunderbolt and the fiery lightning, overcame his father, Cronos. The
god who reigned in the sky then "distributed fairly to the immortals

their portions and declared their privileges."[11] But the sovereignty of Zeus was forged through other conflicts, longer confrontations, particularly with the Titans, the rivals of the descendants of Cronos. Zeus promised the gods who took his side that he would allow them to continue to enjoy their privileges if they already had some, or would give them their just dues if so far they had none.[12] What was at stake between the sons of Cronos and the Titans was power and the distribution of particular areas of authority. And "when the blessed gods had finished their toil, and settled by force their struggle for honors with the Titans, they pressed far-seeing Olympian Zeus to reign and rule over them, by Earth's prompting. So he divided their dignities (*timai*) amongst them."[13]

One great god thus made the distribution, and there were to be adjustments in the future. Hermes, who arrived late upon the scene, nevertheless won his place on Olympus, received his allotment of special powers, and at the same time enriched that of his elder brother Apollo, who was already well endowed. Then, at the time of the Eleusinian crisis, the powers of Hades, Demeter, and Persephone were redistributed.[14] But all distributions were always made on the authority of Zeus, the sovereign of Olympus.

Choosing a City

In contrast, when the time came for the gods to choose the cities in which each was to receive particular honors, there was a general rush to get in there first. To be sure, a decision would be taken in the assembly and possibly passed by an absolute majority. Nevertheless, as in the good old days of the Trojan War, the gods disagreed, defied one another, came to blows–sometimes over several generations– dragging mortals, the citizens of Athens or of Argos, into what were frequently very disagreeable clashes. The order of the day was strife, *eris*. The gods quarreled in black anger and took the law into their own hands. Emergency juries and courts of arbitration had to be convened, and on more than one occasion, their decisions were resented. The bickering resumed, worse than before. In Argolis, for example, Hera considered that the land of Argos belonged to her: had she not always been Hera of Argos?[15] Poseidon took a very different view: Argos, so rich in water, was a natural province of his empire of sweet waters, whether they ran underground or flowed forth from springs. He therefore claimed his rights over the powerful city of Argos. The only way to settle the dispute was to appeal to the local powers, the river gods who had been passing their peaceful days watching Phoroneus, the First Man, building sandcastles and dreaming of impossible cities on the banks of the Inachus River. Since the time of Ocean, the father of the gods from whom all rivers came, there had never been such excitement. The Three Rivers came together, deliberated, and agreed with their brother Inachus when he declared that the land of Argos did indeed belong to the sister-wife of Zeus. The disloyalty of his river-cousins incensed Poseidon: not a drop more water for them; they would run dry. Argos so rich in water became parched Argos. That was the state in which it was found by the daughters of Danaus, fleeing from their predatory cousins in Egypt when Poseidon, still intractable, took up position on the borders of the Argive territory, on the seashore where the Danaids were to land.

In Attica, in the land originally called Akte ("Cape," or "Rocky Coast"), then known as the Cecropian coast (after Cecrops, the creature who was half-snake, half-man), there was another violent dispute.[16] Once again, Poseidon was involved, this time in a head-on clash with Athena. Each produced evidence of their power in the territory. Poseidon struck a rock with his trident, and the sea water gushed forth right there in the middle of the Acropolis: irrefutable proof that the Lord of the Sea reigned over the highest part of the city. However, Athena knew the value of evidence vouchsafed by a witness from the earliest times. She contacted Cecrops, who had certainly not been wasting his time: hardly was he born from the Earth than he set about establishing the rudiments of civilization. He was even credited with the discovery of monogamy, to put an end to the confused unions that resulted from general promiscuity. He had introduced civilized sexuality, between a couple, one woman and one man, so that everyone knew who his/her father was, as well as his/her mother.[17] The excellent Cecrops was to hand. Athena, for her part, made an olive tree grow from the disputed land. It was the first of the sacred olive trees that flourished in the Pandroseion, named after one of the daughters of Erechtheus, the second autochthonous man (for autochthony was something that took some

time to establish, over several generations). Cecrops came forward
to testify that Athena had indeed brought forth the first olive tree,
the dazzling glory of the land of Attica.[18] The evidence provided by
the man on the spot made an extremely favorable impression upon
the jury, which consisted sometimes of arbiters dispatched by Zeus
but usually of the entire array of Olympians, the Twelve Gods. When
they were fully represented, the gods were always considered to be
twelve in number, however many of them were actually present.
Sometimes the entire city in question would be summoned to decide
the issue with its vote. In this case, gathered together in the assembly, the men voted one way, for Poseidon, the women the other, for
Athena, the motherless virgin, born solely from her father. The
women, who were in the majority–possibly by a single vote–gave the
victory to Athena. The goddess would now be representing them all,
for, thanks to Poseidon's resentment, they found themselves deprived of the vote, a measure that elicited no opposition whatever
from "the goddess who dwelt on the Acropolis," for she had no compunction in declaring that she was "entirely on the male side."[19] Nor
did she want any talk of marriage, which was anathema to her. And
leave women's wombs out of it too, she warned. All that kind of
thing was Earth's business, after all.

In truth, though, the anger of Poseidon was seldom political. By
temperament, he liked to express himself through earthquakes or
cataclysms. At this juncture, he made the sea rush in, right up to
Eleusis. Later, under Erechtheus, there was Eumolpus, the Fair
Singer who was hostile to Athens, the war between the Eleusinians
and the Athenians, and the Thracian mercenaries and Poseidon's
battle against Erechtheus. That was an unforgettable confrontation,
in which a murderer gave his name to his victim, thenceforward
known as Poseidon-Erechtheus, even in the Erechtheion itself. A
tragedy by Euripides, presented between the years 423 and 422, was
to set on stage Poseidon's hatred for Athena, from the time of Cecrops down to that of the daughters of Erechtheus and their mother,
Praxithea, the Athenian woman who was Athena's autochthonous
protégée and who, with boldness and courage, reestablished the
foundations of the city.[20]

Poseidon was engaged in litigations in seven or eight places: with
Dionysus in Naxos, with Zeus in Aegina, again with Athena in

Troezen, with Sun in Corinth. In most cases, his claims were dismissed. In Corinth, the case went to arbitration and the giant Briareus decided that he should share the territory with Sun.[21] Only in Troezen did Poseidon at last receive the coveted title of the god "who possesses the city" (*poliouchos*).[22] But every time he found himself in opposition to his nephew Apollo, the confrontation gave way to an amicable exchange: Apollo received the sanctuary-towns of Delos and Delphi from Poseidon when he recognized his uncle's sovereignty over Cape Tenarus and Calauria.[23] Already in the *Iliad*, at the height of the "war between the gods," when the gods of the two camps faced one another in single combat, Poseidon and Apollo had by common consent avoided a duel.[24]

When Plato wrote his account of Atlantis, he had no trouble imagining a different version: a drawing of lots for the whole earth, organized by Justice, in which each god received exactly what suited him/her best and, so that there would be no surprises, the gods in person then set up their own cults and sacrifices before engendering the human race that was to populate each new city. This was a distribution that was certainly not marred by quarrelling[25] and was, furthermore, totally in keeping with the image of the gods proposed by Platonic theology. But it was only achieved at the price of a radical distortion of the tradition: in the *Critias*, the cities come into being *after* the drawing of lots, whereas according to popular tradition Poseidon and Hera, or Athena and Poseidon, competed for territories that were already inhabited and more or less cultivated, that is to say, cities already founded and inaugurated by human beings, without any help at all from the gods. One fine day, men, the mortals whom the gods had kept away from the common banqueting table to differentiate them from the company of the Immortals—these men, who in truth were extremely inventive, had set about building towns and devising a way of living together that was called a city. In the Mesopotamian world, the town was an invention of the gods. The king, who built the temple and the town, was proud to reproduce the plan or model designed by a great god, from whom he also learned the art of drawing signs, ideographs and others, on an unbaked clay tablet, just as they are written in the sky. But no inhabitant of Olympus ever imagined an ideal or even an ordinary city for the delight of the gods.[26] Only one god, exiled from the sky, was to win a certain renown in the building or architectural profession, but always more or less overshadowed by a mortal, a city-founder who belonged to the human race.[27]

The surprise felt by the Olympian gods when they suddenly discovered the fine, big cities built by living creatures so deficient in "vital force" (aiōn)[28] is rather like our own when faced with the polytheistic landscape of Greece between 800 and 700 B.C. To a bird's-eye or panoptic view, the world of the gods seems to be divided into two very different blocks. On the one hand, boldly etched, the company of highly individual gods living in their houses on Olympus–the Olympians, those luminous gods of the *Iliad*, who own the vast sky, savoring their nectar and ambrosia, far removed from the earth; on the other, far below, in bas-relief, the first religious sites, set up by the descendants of that same, weakly human species, their first offerings at first sparsely scattered here and there, then becoming denser, but manifesting certain signs that are novel in comparison to the world of Homer's Olympians–who were, by and large, remote from human religious services. They are signs that indicate that now the gods are also down there on the ground, in the midst of the mortal beings who walk upon the earth. There are built-up, permanent altars, temples that shelter and are indeed designed to house the statue of the god; and precincts surrounded by low stone walls that mark out the *temenos*, the area reserved for the gods. Our surprise is certainly partly provoked by the great material distance that separates the formal perfection of the gods of Homer's text from the clumsy artifacts exhumed by the archaeologists who discovered these roughly shaped, obscure deities that seem to be rising out of clefts in the earth rather than descending from the heavens, ready armed. These are powers that are dispersed among widely scattered groups of dwellings, in contrast to the residents of Olympus, who have the air of a unified family group.

There is both fiction and, quite by chance, also history to establish links between Homer's gods and the beginnings of polytheism in the eighth-century cities. According to the local evidence, it would appear that, by the seventh century, Homer's epic with its Olympians constituted an indispensable reference for any discourse on the gods, whether they were the gods of a single city or were regarded as Pan-Hellenic deities. The plain synchronism is irrefutable.

The eighth century witnessed the beginnings of the city more or less at the very moment when the gods were noticing the cities and talking about them among themselves. All over the place the Greeks were founding cities, and the phenomenon is the more visible since it was in Sicily and Magna Graecia that most of the new cities were appearing. For over three centuries the land of colonization, southern Italy, was to serve as a laboratory for the creators of cities. And there certainly was something of a creator in a city-founder, that is to say, a man who, acting as leader, cleared the ground and opened up the way ahead for a small band of followers. Founding a city involved elaborating an ideal of a city, with all its essential components, projecting an abstract model of citizenship on to the surface of the land–and foreign land, what is more. It meant creating something out of the *tabula rasa* of a place that was not yet even a site.

Making a Territory,
Creating Gods for Each City

In this very Greek activity of repeatedly creating cities, the gods were not forgotten. They had a place; they had *their* place. The *Odyssey* provides us with on-the-spot, concomitant information about this. The Phaeacians were such great navigators that their ships, reading the minds of the sailors, could guide themselves over the high seas.[29] At home in their cities, between the port and the agora, the Greeks told themselves the emblematic story of the founder of a city–the city of Alcinoos–the king of the Phaeacians who was Odysseus's host on the last lap of his journey home to Ithaca. The founder's name was Nausithoos, and he was a really not too obscure contemporary of the creation of the new city of Megara Hyblaea in Sicily, in the not at all sleepy eighth century B.C. To found the city of the Phaeacians, Nausithoos did four things: he marked out the city precinct, he built temples for the gods, he constructed houses, and he divided the land among the citizens.[30] The founding of Phaeacia provides a blueprint for a Greek colony such as that discovered, after twenty-five years of intelligent research, by the archaeologists led by Georges Vallet on the site of Megara Hyblaea.[31] A city-founder worked out an overall plan, as a geometer, designating spaces that would allow the city to function: an *agora*, or public square, but also a space for the gods, the pantheon that the colonists from Megara had brought with them. These gods were "mental constructs" even more than they were statues or images lying in the ships' holds. They were gods who existed in people's minds, mental representations of invisible powers that made it possible to organize the world, to think it out in a differentiated fashion, classifying its various aspects just as the model of a city constructs a human space with a center, a boundary, various different quarters, and roads on the basis of a particular idea of how to live and act as a community. As they created their cities, implanting dozens of communities in what would one day be known as Magna Graecia,[32] the founders, in the technical sense of the word (*oikistēs*, "men who made somewhere to live," later also known as *kistēs*, "men who cleared the land and were leaders"[33]), thus began to fashion gods to suit their particular political plan.

The inventors of the city proceeded to make citizen-gods out of the Olympians, so to speak, without the Olympians realizing it: these deities were described as poliad; they would rule over the city's particular pantheon and would be closely involved in the social and political aspects of day-to-day life. The Olympians were thus very much in the air, and also in people's heads, whither they found their way via the ears more than via the eyes. It was through listening to epic being sung by the bards and rhapsodes[34] that everyone in Greece knew the Olympians and that, as a result, throughout the Greek-speaking world the forms, or *schēmata*, of Olympus, in the sense of the geometric forms of the world of the gods, were familiar to one and all.[35] That common knowledge centered around two or three essential factors in eighth-century culture, factors that were set out specifically as propositions in the *Odyssey* and the *Iliad*.[36] The first proposition ran as follows: "Each man sacrificed to one of the ever-living gods."[37] The second stated that, on certain occasions, it was necessary to "make ceremonial sacrifices to the everlasting gods"[38]–to all the gods, without forgetting a single one, as the lord of Calydon, Meleager's father, most unfortunately did, thereby provoking the anger of Artemis.[39] The third proposition, also set out by Homer, was that each of the gods had been allotted particular works (*erga*),[40] a particular field of action–marriage for Aphrodite, warfare for Ares, for example–and these fields of action coincided with the respective privileges and honors that had been shared out among the various Immortals. The gods were thus differentiated from one another within a group that included them all, later known as a pantheon, an organized team of contrasting powers with complementary abilities.

Forms, Skills, and Abilities

The theory of these "forms," which constituted a framework for the company of the gods, was restated three centuries later by contemporaries of Herodotus, but this time from the point of view of human beings. The human beings in question were, it is true, those considered to be the closest to the gods, that is to say, the inhabitants of Egypt, several thousand years older than the Greeks but linked to them by pre-Greeks known as Pelasgians.[41] Gradually, through the knowledge of the Egyptians, the first Greeks learned to distinguish the real names (the *eponymies*) of the gods within the hazy mass of "the divine"–the nebulous "god" to whom these primitive people offered sacrifices and addressed blind prayers; they learned how the honors (*timai*) and skills (*technai*) were divided up among the divine powers; and, finally, they learned how to draw or signify (*semainein*) the visible forms of the gods, their *eidea*.[42] The power of each god was completed by his/her figurative representation, name, and particular skill. With or without the patronage of the Egyptians, these first men on earth, in Argolis or Attica, who had eaten with the gods before the latter withdrew from the company of men, invented, instituted, and inaugurated the gods as individuals. Phoroneus, so active in starting but not completing a thousand different enterprises, once he had discovered the fire of the ashtree, set about sacrificing to the sovereign power of the territory, giving her the name Hera and making arms for her, for she was also skilled in the arts of war.[43] And Cecrops, the first human being but one whose body still ended in the tail of a snake, while putting the finishing touches to his plan for monogony, also produced a name while making a sacrifice. The name he formulated was Zeus on High, Zeus Hypatos, and on his altar he offered up cakes made from cereals grown on Attic soil[44]: a sacrifice without bloodshed, involving no living animal, a pure sacrifice for the Sky-god.

There then appeared the first statues of the gods, painted images or sculpted forms, chiseled from the wood of the first fruit trees, the pear, the olive, and the walnut: a whole generation of early statues, tiny, portable idols, easy to hide. Each of the gods was given individual traits and a name, his or her real name, which incorporated all his/her epithets indicating his/her function, attributes, and place of origin. These names that became associated with the individual gods through the stories of their high deeds–those told by the mythological tradition–were then, in their turn, defined by specific forms, a physical appearance, gestures, objects, and attitudes that accompanied their human appearance. And in their hymns and theogonies and their songs celebrating the generation of the gods, the bards and poets listed the particular "skills" and praised the special knowledge and powers of each of the deities of Olympus.

These were the "forms" of Olympus, the *schēmata* of the world of the gods that every Greek learned and knew from the poems of Homer and Hesiod, but also from all the now forgotten poets who competed against one another in competitions, in open recitals in the Pan-Hellenic sanctuaries, when the Hellenes converged from every part of Greece upon Delos, Delphi, or Olympia to enjoy the games that comprised both athletic exploits and poetic performances. At the same time as men constructed the fine places where they could meet one another outside their own respective cities, they set the divine powers to work in their public squares and outside their front doors, distributing them among various forms of activity, the various domains of their social life, and the network that the city wove to link nature with culture. Without noticing it, the Olympians were already caught in the net of the thousand and one services through which they were naturalized in the cities of human beings and turned into active citizens. They were caught even before they became so enraptured by the poliad position and by the idea of being the chief deity in some local, even parochial, pantheon in which, it seemed to them, each of them would at last enjoy visible dominion over these mortals with all their illusory ideas who, in such an ungainly fashion, crept over the surface of the earth.

Generally speaking, the Olympians do not suffer from an inadequate ego. They have too high an opinion of themselves. After all, they need only take a look at the eaters of bread who are so "like leaves . . . for a time they flourish in a blaze of glory . . . and then again fade lifeless."⁴⁵ That is how Apollo, the god known as Phoebus, the Trojans' protector, disparagingly describes them on the day when he explains to his uncle Poseidon how senseless it would be for the Olympians to come to blows over such weakly creatures. Yet the powerful god of the sea has just reminded him of their shared servitude during one whole year, or possibly even a "great year" (that is to say, eight whole years), under Laomedon, the father of Priam, in this very town of Troy, when they built its great ramparts and pastured the oxen, and all without payment, eventually to be ejected violently like miserable day laborers mercilessly dragooned for obligatory public drudgery. They had certainly experienced exile on that occasion. On Zeus's orders, they had been deprived of part of their divine power. But it was apparently a less important part than the ambrosia and nectar forbidden to another of the gods, who had perjured himself when undergoing trial by the water of the Styx and had then had to spend an entire great year "spiritless and voiceless,"⁴⁶ radically devitalized, the mere shadow of a god, lying between sleep and death: a god without *aiōn*, deprived of his vital force. As the uncle and the nephew both very well knew, men and gods shared a common mother, Earth (Gaia), even if they had formed two distinct species ever since the day when they were separated.⁴⁷ However Olympian they claimed to be, the gods were still an integral part of the world. They were dependent upon the cosmos. So they were also involved in the political order, the human cosmos constructed by mortals as they set up communities of citizens which, however, remained deeply respectful of the poliad power who had been recognized way back in the past by a distant ancestor.

So now the gods were, if not citizens, at least city-gods, the gods of a particular place, the official protectors of a particular segment of social space, a particular handful of citizens, along with their wives, children, possessions, and slaves. They were diverted from their Ouranian calling, from the attraction felt by the most Olympian of them that was exerted by the distant, luminous sky, the sky that would one day be filled by the "Prime Unmoved Mover," as Aristotle was to call him. For the city-founders had decided that in each city there would be two departments in the State administration, two sides to community affairs: on the one hand, the affairs of the gods, on the other, the affairs of men.[48] Both would be decided by the same assemblies and, together, would constitute what was called the public domain, which was also the sphere in which things were made public. In other words, the legislators would take the gods' affairs into consideration each time they had to write laws, and every time that an assembly of citizens placed "the affairs of the gods" on the agenda, it would decide, by majority vote, on the sacrifices, the festivals, the calendar, and the regulations affecting sanctuaries. It would make the lifestyle of the Olympians as agreeable as possible, for now they were citizens and played an extremely active role at every level of society.

10   A Polytheistic Garden

The first feature to strike one about the gods living in the cities of Greece is how very numerous they were. The Greek term for "many gods" is *polytheos*, from which we have derived polytheism in the course of a long, frenetic history (idolatry, Philo of Alexandria, the chorus of the Church Fathers, pagans everywhere, warfare over several centuries, etc.) veering between monotheism and polytheism.[1] But at the time when Aeschylus wrote the *Suppliant Maidens*, which won him the prize at the Great Dionysia of 463,[2] the landscape of a city teemed with gods. The gods were, quite literally, everywhere, even in the kitchen, next to Heraclitus's stove.[3] The divine powers constituted visible little companies, gathered around the public square or apparently engaged in fervent assemblies somewhere in the territory, perhaps in a precinct behind the mortals' *agora*, or on a hill slightly apart from yet still quite close to the city.[4]

One day a band of women, foreigners with sun-tanned skin, arrived. They were the Danaids, making their way to Argos, the city to which they had been encouraged to flee by their father Danaus, who remembered his family links with the land of Argos and had not forgotten Io, the priestess and lover, a cow maddened by desire and by her hatred of Hera the Sovereign, her own sovereign. Now the daughters of Danaus had come, fleeing sexual harassment and violence and the desire of fifty males, the sons of Aegyptus, their own first cousins. When they reached the outskirts of the city, they discovered a wooded hill inhabited by many gods. Some they recognized immediately: Zeus, Helius the Sun God, Apollo; others were identifiable from various signs: the one with the trident was Poseidon, the one with the wand Hermes; and they noticed that there were others, too. There they stood, around their "common altars,"[5] the local gods, a whole grove of divine powers. When the daughters of Danaus needed to exert pressure on the master of Argos, they were to draw attention to themselves by hanging by their belts[6] from the tall effigies of the territory's divine protectors.[7] This was a "polytheist sanctuary, a sanctuary full of gods."[8] How many? How were they arranged? In what order? In twos? In threes? . . . But this is not the moment to embark on a theological inventory.

Here is another scene: a little city in Achaea. When Pausanias passed through it in the second century A.D.., he came upon the public square, just a simple *agora*, and in it a bearded, quadrangular Hermes standing by the altar of Hestia, the Public Hearth. Hestia's altar represented a center, a fixed point, an enclosed place, while the Hermes in the *agora* stood for open spaces that could be crossed in many directions: Hermes and Hestia formed a strong couple, working together as a partnership.[9] Close by there was a spring, consecrated to Hermes: all fishing forbidden, for the fish belonged to the god. A Hermes with fish, a fishy Hermes was certainly unusual. But Pausanias did not linger, for an even more interesting discovery awaited ahead: alongside the Hermes of the public square and the fish-filled spring lay a field strewn with stones: thirty pillars as quadrangular as the bearded Hermes, but not one of them engraved or carved with a human face or body. Yet the citizens of Pharae "adore[d] [them] calling each by the name of some god."[10] It was certainly an unusual assembly. To forestall the amazement of the readers of his *Description of Greece* at the time of Hadrian, Pausanias returns to the time of origins. Long ago, he explains, all the Greeks used to erect blocks of white stone rather than the statues that later became familiar. Nevertheless, this was still a strange pantheon, formed as it was of rough-hewn blocks, each of which was endowed with a form by being given a name—names that the citizens of Pharai would call out, thereby animating the mute, shapeless *stelae* as they passed among them.

Here is another example of a "polytheist sanctuary, filled with gods," but deliberately non-iconic, unrepresentational gods, set alongside others with the appearance of young human beings. In the mid-classical period, set next to statues representing Apollo as a perfect ephebe with an ever-young body, would be an Apollo unabashedly represented by a small conical stone, placed in front of a house on the public thoroughfare. This was the Apollo of carefully cut paths, the Apollo of streets, known as Aguieūs (from *aguia*, meaning "route, open road"[11]).

There were all kinds of gods—rural ones, urban ones, gods of high-above, earthly ones, subterranean ones, heavenly Ouranian ones, gods of the *agora*, of the nuptial bedchamber, of the larder, of the terraces. There were gods with dazzling bodies and flashing limbs, and gods of stone with opaque names who resembled the *kolossoi*, the substitutes for the unburied dead, or the heavy *stelae* rammed into the ground in Cyrene, beneath the Libyan sun.[12] There were individualized gods and there were deeply anonymous powers such as demons, avengers "on the earth's surface," and others, beneath the earth's skin. Greece was certainly a society with a wealth of gods, both divine powers and demonic forces, and in that respect it bears comparison with archaic societies such as India, the world of the Hittites, or the civilizations of black Africa, in Mali, Senegal, or Dahomey, all rich in "god-things," fetishes, power-laden objects, and invisible forces that are frequently possessed of immense power but that can only be identified by force or when taken by surprise.

There are many different ways of imagining multiple powers, of organizing them, making them circulate, dominating them even when one is feeling dominated by them. One variety of god cultivated in Mali consists of god-things, which are neither genies nor altars but are composed of a wide range of different materials, substances, and ingredients: the claw of a lion, a scrap of cotton, a tuft of hyena fur, or plant substances. Each, as an individual material, represents a condensed diversity and is regularly sprinkled with the blood of its victims. Each is a thing given an individuality partly by the manipulations to which it, along with other objects, is subjected, and also by scraps of lore and fragments of concrete, local history.[13] Elsewhere, practices of possession organize the scene in which ancestral or divine powers acquire a form, in a particular place, at a particular moment, in the body of a possessed person or, literally, on his/her head. Orisha and *vodun* constitute a world of pure forms, of possessive powers that only become perceptible when they seize hold of a human being. A trance is started by an act of ancestral violence. The deified ancestors demand human mounts, men or women, to ride, and also to use as their sacrificial altars. When overpowered by an Orisha, the possessed person becomes its altar, its live altar. He wears the "clothing of blood" from the slaughtered animal on him, coagulated on his body. Such a possessive power can gradually be appeased, attracted despite its violence by songs and sayings, until finally its name is torn from the mouth of the one possessed. Out of the invisible, a name, a form embodied in the spasms of a bloodied body, is organized through this mode of communication.[14]

A quite different way of managing the divine powers is adopted in polities that are centralized around royalty and that have a form of writing in which they can classify the gods. For example, in the second millennium B.C., Hattusa (now Bogazkoy) became "the place of the assembly of the gods." The latter were thus lodged in the capital of the Hittite kingdom. Following a period of disturbances during which the most important sanctuaries were destroyed, a reformer, King Tudhalia IV, proceeded to reorganize the pantheon from scratch. The central authorities decided to redraw the map of the sanctuaries and to restructure the society of the gods. The king appointed administrators for the new pantheon of gods: their task would be to install the new idols in temples constructed of durable materials. Anthropomorphic statues made of iron with a coating of precious metals replaced the old standing stones and clumsily carved *stelae*. Figurative representations from then on provided the foundation for the Hittite concept of gods: the completeness of the new forms coincided with the essence of divinity.[15] Furthermore, the gods were reviewed, registered, listed on the tablets of the administrators and the royal clergy. Ever since Sumer, the Mesapotamians had recorded their gods on tablets of unfired clay. Their scribes, who were scholars and diviners, carefully classified the divine population. In a list dating from the second millennium and preserved in the Louvre Museum, 473 deities are recorded and divided into large families centered on fifteen couples.[16] Thanks to their possession of writing, the scholars were able to produce a theological exegesis of the gods in the process of enumerating all their names. The most remarkable list notes all the names of Marduk. It is the last list in the epic poem of the Enuma Elish, the Babylonian account of the creation (about 1300 b.c.).[17] The names and the properties of the names are explained on the basis of a bilingual reading of the sumerograms and their Accadian equivalents. The list starts off with one name and proceeds until enough Sumerian words have been accumulated to open up a theological space that acts as a pantheon created within a single god, in this case the great god Marduk. A whole group of deities is incorporated within a single material name.

As is generally known in the Western world, the Greek city-gods are not things, matter given a particular identity by being manipulated in a particular way and presented with warm blood to nourish the material part of the god. Nor are they born from a centralizing mind intent upon imposing upon all the provinces of a unified polity one single way of naming and representing the powers of the invisible and forming them into a hierarchy. The whole of the Greek world, from one end to the other, does however manifest, as it were, a particular style of polytheism that has its own distinctive characteristics. First, there is the principle of distinction. Whereas other cultures set the highest value on a permanent circulation and interchange between plants, animals, and the gods, or between the Ancestors, human beings, and the deities, the Greeks conceive of the world of the gods as being autonomous. Heroes who become gods are exceptions, and the men of the cities do not call themselves the sons of gods; they have no ambition to become just like the gods, except perhaps through the very selective process of leading a philosophical life. The second distinctive feature is that the Greek gods are all strongly individualized, great actors set on stage by an ambitious mythology well served by its creators, the bards, singers, and poets, and by its theologians, such as Hesiod of Ascra (late eighth century b.c.), who reflect upon the names, configurations, and stories of the gods, and upon a whole collection of questions that it is possible to formulate through the quarrels that develop between the various divine powers or the organization of the world from one generation of gods to the next. It is thus a highly constructed mythology, on a Pan-Hellenic scale, organized around sanctuaries, such as

Olympia, Delphi, and Delos, whose games, competitions, and festivals help to spread far and wide all the discourse about the divine world, with its great gods, each with a particular domain of authority and each with particular skills. The third characteristic of this type of polytheism is its wealth of established partnerships, organized collaborations involving two or more powers, relationships of explicit opposition or complementarity between deities, and hierarchical configurations that can be worked out from the arrangement of altars within the various sanctuaries or from the rules followed in rituals. As new calendars engraved in stone are deciphered, and sacred laws and religious rules are discovered by archaeologists and published and analyzed by epigraphists, the Greek pantheon appears increasingly rich in groupings of deities, in explicit hierarchies, and in configurations based on symmetry, antagonisms, or affinities.

Hunting for Structures

Over the past few years we have, it is true, become more attentive to the manifestations of polytheism as found in Greece, in Rome, in the Caucasian world, and in India, with its Vedas and its Hinduism. In this domain the work of one man, Georges Dumézil (1898–1986), has been crucial. In the 1940s, at the same time that Claude Lévi-Strauss committed anthropology to an analysis of the intellectual operations of the "savage thought" at work in "the mythological," Georges Dumézil was suggesting that, in societies where there were dozens or even hundreds of gods, any definition of a particular god needed to be differential and classificatory. A god could not be defined in static terms, but had to be identified by the whole collection of positions that he or she occupied at one time or another in the complete series of his or her manifestations.

At the beginning of his career and in his enthusiasm for Sir James George Frazer's *Golden Bough*, Dumézil the comparativist was inclined to think that, in the history of civilizations, it is themes that endure, while the gods have their day, then disappear. The gods were ephemeral, he thought, whereas the cavalcade of the dead and the centaurs had continued to resound in festivals held around the turn of the year ever since the ancient times of the Indo-Europeans and right down to the folklore of contemporary European societies. Progressively, however, as he moved on from words to concepts, Dumézil the young Indo-Europeanist came to realize the importance of the gods, the hierarchies of powers, the conceptual structures at work in the classifications of deities, and the long-term relevance of these "ideological fields" inhabited by the gods.

In a whole series of civilizations, in particular those that rely on highly individualized gods, the divine powers are not evanescent forms but for centuries and centuries continue to classify and organize the world. That certainly seems to be the case of Greece, with its pantheons and their geometric configurations that have been rethought constantly ever since the education of the young Achilles and right down to the Renaissance of the towns of Italy, with a series of sages, philosophers, and other natives prone to reflective thought all taking over one from another.

The best way to apprehend polytheism in the Greek world is to follow the method adopted by Pausanias when he described an open field dotted with pillar-gods right next to a very rectangular, bearded Hermes, accompanied by a little Hestia, in the public square of Pharae. In the islands, on the mainland, in southern Italy, wherever cities sprang up, the eye can spot the elementary structures of active pantheons—that is, the eye of the historical anthropologist, as often as not peering over the shoulder of Pausanias or some other Greek observer. For what you find are often both factual data and also "homemade" models. These are perfectly respectable. Indeed, they are positively indispensable to anyone seeking to understand and reconstruct models of the entire system of divine powers and their relations with one another. In the first place, there are what Dumézil liked to call the "structural facts" (*le fait de la structure*) when he wanted to pacify the "door-keepers of History," the boors who at that time bedeviled the art of making history (and, it must be said, still do, particularly in the decrepit and aging departments for the study of ancient societies). By the "structural facts" Dumézil meant the carefully arranged elements, the little structures of gods to be found on altars or used in some sacrificial rituals (you simply have to be careful not to trample them underfoot as you pass, to pay attention to them, and learn how to collect them carefully together).

For example, there are altars that are consecrated to more than

one god, for instance, to two, as at Claros, in Asia Minor, in a great
sanctuary famous for its oracles. Here, the two deities sharing an altar are Dionysus and Apollo, the two powers who live together at the
center or the top of the Greek world, in Delphi.[18] Altars sometimes
are consecrated to two, sometimes to twenty, or even to twenty-four
deities. A great crowd of gods is accommodated on the altar of Amphiaraos, twelve stades distant from Oropos, between Tanagra and
Attica. It is an altar for an entire pantheon, in the midst of which the
diviner Amphiaraos, honored as a god since ancient times, is enthroned.[19] The surface of the altar is divided into five sections. One
is for Heracles, Zeus, and Apollo the Healer, known as Paiōn. The
second is occupied by the Heroes and their wives. The third brings
two couples together: Hestia and Hermes, and Amphiaraos and his
son Amphilochus, also a famous diviner. The fourth is reserved for
Aphrodite, Panacaea, Jason, Hygia, and Athena Paiōnia. Finally, the
fifth is taken up by the Nymphs, Pan, and the rivers Acheloös and
Cephisus. It is a complex construction, but assuredly not a confused
company: the groups are well defined; recurrent triads and couples
mark out separate units for interpretation, all clustered around the
waters of Amphiaraos the diviner and healer, an underground
stream from which Amphiaraos is supposed to have emerged after
being swallowed up with his chariot by a hole in the earth that
opened up in its path.[20]

But whether they add up to twenty-four powers or to twenty, depending on the number of Heroes with their wives, this group would
not have represented the entire company of gods despite the Greeks'
view. When Dionysus, during a country celebration, decided he
wanted to stand for the whole company of the gods, he had twelve
altars set up to himself. When, in the Arcadian night, Hermes prepared to sacrifice Apollo's cattle in a bid to gain recognition as a full
Olympian, he cut up the victims in twelve portions,[21] since the gods
number twelve in all, or at least they do when they are imagined as a
complete group. Ever since the seventh century, in Delos, Olympia,
Athens, and Cos they seem to have been known as the Twelve
[gods].[22] On the single altar erected on the *agora* of Athens by Pisistratus the Younger, the tyrant's grandson, there were twelve gods.[23]
Usually, however, the Twelve were divided either into six couples or
into four groups of three.

In Delos, the Dōdekatheon, the primitive sanctuary detectable beyond the Letōon, the area consecrated to Leto, seems to be an enclosed space (*temenos*) with four altars, each one devoted to three gods.[24] The first group comprised Zeus, Hera, and Athena: the sovereign of the gods, his legitimate wife, and the daughter born from her father. The second group was made up of Demeter, Core, and Zeus Eubouleus: the mistress of cereal foods; her daughter, who became the wife of the god of the dead; and a Zeus with Good Advice, who operated in the underworld. The third probably consisted of Leto, Apollo, and Artemis, for the children of Leto were born here, in Delos. The fourth group is unidentifiable.

In Olympia, Heracles' position is that of a founder, a founder of altars and the founder of the Olympic Games. Alongside the tomb of Pelops, Zeus's son founded and consecrated six altars for the Twelve.[25] The precinct in which he gathered them together may have been similar to the one that, according to Pindar, he "measured out"[26] for the sanctuary of the Zeus known as "of Olympia," an echo of Zeus the Olympian. The inauguration of the games and the sanctuaries took place in the presence of the Fates (the Morai) and Time, the god Chronos, "the sole declarer of the very truth."[27] Six couples were installed here by Heracles, acting as a theologian inspired by the circumstances. The river Alpheus, who was inclined to flow backward to his source, was included in this Twelve, sharing an altar with Artemis, whom he longed to enfold in his watery, oceanic arms.[28] The other couples represented complementarities that were reaffirmed elsewhere all over Greece: Hermes and Apollo; the Charites (or Graces) and Dionysus; Zeus Olympios and Poseidon; Cronos and Rhea, honored here by their grandson; and finally the feminine pair, Hera and Athena, powers who operated in alliance. In Olympia, Cos, and other places too numerous to name,[29] one and the same god could thus occupy three different positions, all of which were essential for the purposes of any classificatory definition of him or her. Hermes could be positioned alongside Aphrodite and in the company of Ares, thus forming the triangle referred to by Apollo in the entertainment sung by Demodocus about the love affair between Ares and Aphrodite, in which Hephaestus figures as a magnificent cuckold.[30] In Cos, Hermes was coupled with Dionysus, who on several occasions acted as his accomplice. And in

Olympia, he was reunited with his elder brother Apollo, in spite of whom, but also with whom, he won recognition for his privileges as an Olympian.[31] In similar fashion, Apollo was associated, now with Artemis, now with Leto-Artemis, now with Hermes, now with Poseidon, his respected uncle and companion in exile and his collaborator in his great plans for new foundations.[32]

Sometimes it even happened that the Twelve were simply statues with no permanent altar, precinct, or sanctuary—statues that were carried in procession on the day of the festival of Zeus the Savior of the city (Sōsipolis), as at Magnesia-on-the-Meander.[33] In Megara, their effigies were housed in the sanctuary of Artemis the Savior (Sōteira).[34] The Twelve were honored in various ways, sometimes with altars, sometimes with sanctuary-precincts, sometimes with temples in which they were housed. And sanctuaries sometimes incorporated not only several altars but also several temples. A temple, more spacious than an altar, sometimes accommodated three gods, as on the road leading from Aulis to Delphi, where three gods of the Phocidians—Zeus, Hera, and Athena—were installed in the place reserved for the general assemblies of the people of Phocis.[35] Meanwhile, in Lesbos, the land of Alcaeus,[36] a more perverse trinity was composed of an enthroned Zeus along with a Hera Genethla, the Generator of all things, and a Dionysus who declared himself to be the son of Thyōne, the Olympian name for his mortal mother.[37] This was a doubly conflictual trinity, what with the strained relations between, on the one hand, the sovereign spouses, and on the other, the stepmother and the son of Zeus, who insisted on being called "the son of his mother."[38] No secret was made of those antagonisms. This was an overtly venomous Holy Family.

Configurations of Gods, Hierarchies of Power

Some associations were less emotional and more intellectual. In Argos, the temple of Apollo also extended a welcome to Hermes and Aphrodite.[39] Apollo was there as the city's poliad sovereign god, but also as the wolf-god Lykeios, echoing the victory of Danaus, the father of the Danaids, who had come there as an exile, like a wolf, and had fallen upon and seized the city. Argos still remembered Apollo of the Wolves, who intervened as a terrible god, avid for vengeance. But what were Aphrodite and Hermes doing here? The goddess may

have been the Aphrodite of Persuasion, who came to the aid of Hypermestra, the Danaid who, on that murderous night, spared the
life of her cousin, in defiance of her father. And possibly Hermes was
there because he too was a god of amorous words, the one who
would murmur in Aphrodite's ear as a prelude to sexual pleasure
and the eroticism in which they were both respected experts.

Strange genealogies are sometimes expressed in out-of-the-way
places. In the deme of Colonus, the one to which Oedipus came, on
the edge of Athena's domain, there stood a sanctuary/precinct (a
temenos) consecrated to the deity who gave her name to Athens,
which contained an ancient statue of Prometheus and also an altar.
But on the lower part of this altar was a bas-relief sculpture, which
represented another altar, just like that dedicated to Prometheus,
the Titan who invented fire and the arts dependent on fire, but
shared by Hephaestus and Athena. Hephaestus was represented
holding a scepter and in the position of an elder sibling: Hephaestus the Elder, a match for Prometheus in skills and ideas but, like
him, at another level eclipsed by Athena, the Sovereign of the sanctuary, the other Athena, who was hierarchically superior to Athena
the younger sister of her scepter-bearing brother.[40]

Other elementary structures can be deduced from the various
ways of performing sacrifices, whether these are described by an observer interested in ritual, such as existed at least from the fifth century on, or are recorded more succinctly in some set of sanctuary
regulations or in a calendar of sacrifices. Particular gestures, the
contents of a libation, the ways of producing fire using particular
woods, the ways of burning particular parts of the sacrificial victim
while eating other parts or else leaving them untouched. In a sacrifice, on the occasion of an annual festival or some regular ritual, all
such procedures could draw attention to the hierarchical positions
of the deities and the forms of subordination that, in certain circumstances, would be imposed upon some in relation to others; or
else they could underline the double nature of a particular deity, the
ambivalence that was reflected in one of his functions; or even show
how a single divine power could combine two statuses, passing from
one level to another, either in similar but distinct rituals or within
the context of one and the same sacrifice.

In the mid-fifth century B.C., the assembly of the people of Argos produced a long document setting out the protocol of an agreement between the mother-city, Argos, and two of its Cretan colonies, Tylissos and Cnossos.[41] This protocol is much concerned with the relations between Hera, the sovereign of Argos, and the Cretan sanctuaries of Zeus Machaneus and of Ares in association with Aphrodite. If sixty rams are sacrificed to Zeus Machaneus, Hera must receive sixty legs, one from each victim–choice, honorable portions that would fall either to the goddess herself or to her priest.[42] The same inscription mentions that every time a ewe was sacrificed to the Artemis Orthia of Argos, it was understood that Apollo should be offered a ram,[43] presumably in his sister's sanctuary. Sacrificing to one god on the altar of another could indicate their respective places in a hierarchy, possibly a hierarchy observed in one particular place, or on one particular day. In Magnesia-on-the-Meander, Apollo the Pythian was offered a sacrifice on the altar of Artemis on the day of the ritual addressed jointly to Zeus Sōsipolis, the Zeus who was the Savior of the city, to Artemis Leukophryene, and to the Pythian,[44] while Apollo, the founder of the city of the Magnesians, along with Dionysus, dominated a thickly packed pantheon.[45] Zeus was very used to sacrifices made to him on the altars of others, so much so that on such occasions he would be called the Zeus of Hera (Zeus Heraios) or the Zeus of Demeter (Zeus Damatrios).[46]

Zeus was also double in a ritual addressed specifically to him, in which he was not only Zeus the Benevolent but also Zeus Meilichios, the honey-god.[47] Here, he had two faces: he was a power from above but also a deity of the underworld. The calendar of Erchia, in Attica, describes a ritual in two stages, separated by the consumption of the roasted viscera (the *splanchna*). Before eating these, cooked on spits, no wine could be drunk, as befitted a chthonic god whose name, Melichios, indicated his preference for honey, or hydromel.[48] But wine was allowed as soon as the sacrifice entered the second stage, when the meat was divided up, under the sign of the Benevolent Zeus, the Olympian. Two aspects of the same divine power were recognized, the chthonic and the Olympian, in a ritual where the Olympian dominated, with both the gods and mortals receiving their respective shares, as the meat of the victim was consumed. Only the wine marked the difference between the two faces of Zeus, the one absent, the other present.

In the case of Aphrodite of Sicyon, a different technique was adopted.[49] Here, access to the sanctuary was limited to two women. One was married but, so long as she served the sanctuary, could have no dealings with any man. She was the "Neocore," and was in charge of the sanctuary. The other was a virgin, a *parthenos*, who was priestess for one year. She brought the water for bathing, and so was known as the *loutrophoros*. The Aphrodite of Sicyon could only be looked upon from afar, from the sanctuary's threshold, which was not to be crossed. The two women performed the ceremonial rites, which fell into two phases and operated on three levels. The haunches of the sacrificial victims were burned in the Olympian manner, producing aromatic smoke for Aphrodite on high. What remained, that is to say, most of the animal, was entirely devoured by the flames on a fire of juniper wood. This was a holocaust in the chthonic manner. But the division between the Olympian and the chthonic modes of sacrifice was modulated by one detail. A plant known as *paiderōs* ("passionate desire for a body") grew only on this spot, around the statue and the altar. The priestess would pick one leaf and place it on the roasting thighs, the aroma of which would be breathed in by Aphrodite. The *paiderōs* leaf was not itself aromatic, but it was two-toned, pale on one side, dark on the other, like the leaves of the white poplar, the tree that grew in the underworld.[50] Both aspects of Aphrodite came together at the Olympian level, in the hands of the ancient Aphrodite, the Black Goddess crowned with a wreath, who held a poppy in one hand and an apple in the other.

Also in Sicyon, a similar but slightly different sacrificial ritual was performed for Heracles.[51] It was inspired by his double origin and his two statuses. The people of Sicyon were accustomed to address to him the kind of cult reserved for heroes. But one of Heracles' sons, named Phaestus, who became king of Sicyon, refused to follow this custom, arguing that Heracles was a god and so should be offered sacrifices in accordance with the ritual for the gods. As a result, in the days of Pausanias still, when the citizens of Sicyon sacrificed lambs for Heracles, they began by burning the thighs on the altar, in the Olympian manner. The rest of the meat was treated in one of two ways. Half was consumed by meat-eaters, once they had set aside the portion for the gods; the other half was consecrated in accordance with the heroic ritual, that is to say, was not touched by the mortals and was totally destroyed. This ritual thus comprised two phases, but the second, which reflected the two natures of Heracles and in which meat was eaten, gave the Olympian aspect priority over the heroic. The duality of Heracles was even reflected in the two names given to the festival, which lasted for two days: one term was the Heracleia; the other, the actual name of which has not come down to us, must have commemorated either the story of Phaestus or the divine name for Heracles.[52] The Olympian who married Youth, Hebe, and became immortal, retained signs of his double status in the ritual devoted to him but had the divine aspect outweigh the heroic, in keeping with the whole orientation of his exploits and a life devoted to winning recognition for his status as the son of Zeus. It is a hierarchical model that seems to be in competition with the dualist model approved by Herodotus of Halicarnassus. Herodotus refers to his "inquiries" as follows: "The result of these researches is a plain proof that the worship of Heracles is very ancient; and I think that the wisest course is taken by those Greeks who maintain a double cult of this deity, with two temples, in one of which they worship him as Olympian and divine, and in the other pay him such honor as is due to a demi-god, or hero."[53] A spatial division was thus made in the social and religious topography of the city of Thasos, which Herodotus knew well (and which is the subject of an excellent study by J. Pouilloux, summarized here). On the *agora*, Heracles the Olympian received offerings as befitted a god; meanwhile, near the gates, the hero Heracles, the defender of the city and a master of warfare, presided over sacrifices of victims slaughtered and totally consumed in the flames.[54]

In the Greece of the early days of beginnings, cities were rising from the ground and gods were springing up on all sides. Cities appeared by the dozens, by the hundreds. Most were tiny, with fewer than a thousand citizens and a territory consisting of a small valley or a strip of coastal plain. Some were linked with others in phratries, groups of brother-towns, or *demes*, small territorial units. But all of them were full of gods. Each city had its own strategies for coping with the invisible and set up its own structures of deities, organizing complex local pantheons that seemed as autonomous as the cities themselves in their desire for self-sufficiency and completeness. But just as the cities, whatever their size, all seem to have presented the same morphological characteristics, the divine powers, whatever their concrete form and whatever their individual traits anchored in the specific details of their locality, all seem to have been structured in the same general way, recognizable from one city to another and operating according to the same principles–abstract principles modified, on the one hand, by the many nuanced variations of these microsocieties of deities, heroes, heroines, and demons and, on the other, by Pan-Hellenic declarations that paid lip-service to the rival powers of the Twelve Gods; the public Hearth and its poliad deity; and also to the Hellēnion, the sanctuary that was for all the Greeks. Hellenism was thus converted into a divine power, except, that is, where–as at the sanctuary of Delphi–the forms of the divine world were crystallized around the fundamental pair, Apollo and Dionysus.

This was a polytheism with a framework sufficiently pliable to accommodate the needs of small, rival, independent communities and, at the same time, strong enough to constitute a world of forms that recognized its own particular rules along with values that were shared by the whole of the Greek world.

11 Dealings with the Gods

Once upon a time, seemingly before the advent of the citizen-gods, the company of gods were in the habit of leaving Olympus at regular intervals. They would take a break from the current business and day-to-day concerns of their assemblies, and off they would go to the world's end, to the Ocean, to the land of the Ethiopians, heading sometimes westward, sometimes eastward. They would spend an extended, twelve-day weekend banqueting with the irreproachable men who were known as the "Burnt Faces" (Aithiopes, Ethiopians) by reason of their proximity to the sun when it rose and set.[1] There, they would enjoy a banquet of the Golden Age type, with perfect hecatombs and the gods and the Ethiopians seated alongside one another at the same tables, for the Burnt Faces and the Olympians were still eating together.[2] Then, relaxed and no doubt with rather deeper suntans, the gods of Olympus would return to their activities amid the rest of the human race, who were, without doubt, less irreproachable.

But now things had certainly changed. There were quarrels in the public square, injustice was honored, and the age of iron was already under way. The disappearance of the gods was announced by Hesiod, the theologian from Ascra, and this time, he said, their retreat was definitive. Tomorrow, the only two deities left on earth would leave it for good: "Then Aidōs and Nemesis [Reverence and Righteous Indignation], with their sweet forms wrapped in white robes, will go from the wide-pathed earth and forsake mankind to join the deathless company of the gods."[3] But could men really be definitively separated from the gods at the very time when, in dozens of new cities, altars and sanctuaries were sending the smoke of burnt offerings up to the divine powers, inviting them to enjoy the aromas from the lambs and the oxen sacrificed almost daily and to share them with the political communities then in full expansion? Who among the Greeks of these fledgling cities could possibly believe Hesiod when, aiming his words against the "kings who passed twisted sentences," he warned that, on this earth that nurtures us, thirty thousand or even countless Immortals "keep watch on judgments and deeds of wrong as they roam (*phoitān*), clothed in mist, all over the earth."[4] The Greek cities were not haunted by fear of the gods. Neither the citizens of Megara nor those of Syracuse felt themselves to be dominated by supernatural powers who spied on their actions, listening to their every word, keeping them under constant police surveillance. To judge by the way that men took care of the gods and were keen to devote cults to them and have dealings with them, the citizen-gods were neither remote powers nor oppressive deities.

For the Greeks, "believing in the gods" simply meant recognizing their presence in the city, their importance in the lives of human beings living in societies, in particular when the social group organized itself into a political community (*theous nomizēin*).[5] In our language as we use it today, the word "believe," when applied to gods, is so heavily charged that this will, I hope, justify our digressing to consider the strangeness of cultures that have made "believe" and belief mean precisely what they themselves, sovereignly, have decided it should mean. In Vedic India, for instance, Belief is a goddess by the name of *Sráddhā*.[6] In the Vedas, Belief rules over the celebration of rites. She is particularly fond of those who thoroughly explore the mysteries of sacrifice.

Those who are madly obsessed with sacrifice are very dear to Belief, who allows them—whether they be Brahmins or gods with a passion for sacrifices—to be recognized as capable of making sacrifice work, to be credited with competence in this domain, and to be "believed" as experts in ritual sacrifice. Belief is thus "immanent in the

Veda inasmuch as the Veda teaches what is to be done"; she is the one who makes possible the relations that are established by sacrifice; she is its moving force, upheld by the words of the Veda, the spoken pronouncements that accompany the rite of sacrifice. However, there is nothing in Belief, as represented by the Vedas, that alludes to any knowledge of the invisible, any religious "believing" such as that fashioned by the Christian culture. The twelfth-century Christian theologians distinguished between three degrees of belief: believing that God exists (*credere Deum*),[7] the very lowest degree for a Christian life; believing what God *says* (*credere Deo*), while pursuing one's own life; and believing *in* God with love (*credere in Deo*), as true Christians should. Then, from the thirteenth century on, a distinction was drawn between implicit and explicit faith, the clergy now requiring laymen to make their faith explicit in a *credo*–a formula carefully composed and written down, but to be read out loud, professed, along with attendant dogmas on the Trinity, the Incarnation, the Passion, and the Resurrection, etc. This was a faith founded upon an obligatory *credo* for all, and was at the heart of a religion that took the form of a Church.[8]

Those are two different models, the one Vedic, the other Catholic, but they are equally alien from the point of view of a society that set out to manage the affairs of the gods and the affairs of human beings within one and the same political space, and that regarded patterns of behavior regulated by tradition as all part of a single whole, whether they concerned the divine powers or social relations. "Belief," in this instance, Greek belief, incorporated everything that was due to the gods: sacrifices, prayers, hymns, dances, purifications, that is to say, all the "rites"–the recognized practices, which were in conformity with what it was seemly to say and to do.[9] This constituted a code of good conduct, which had to do with order, rules, an organized world, a *nomos*, an order thanks to which, for example, humankind, unlike wild beasts, did not devour one another and did offer up to the gods sacrifices that were carefully prescribed.[10] But "belief in the gods" also meant that one lived with them, had dealings with them, sought out their company. Socializing with the gods, cultivating them (*therapeūein*), in both senses of the expression–both devoting a cult to them and maintaining amicable relations with them–frequenting their altars, getting along

(*phoitān*) with the divine powers: all were commonsensical ways of
saying that one believed in the gods, that one dealt with them so-
cially, or, to be more precise, "politically" –that is to say, in the way
that was expected in a city.[11] If two cities happened mutually to recognize each other's rights of citizenship, they would arrange for
their respective citizens to sacrifice on the same altars as their own
natives, and to frequent (*phoitān*) the same public cults as the home-
citizens and in the same conditions.[12] "Living the life of a citizen"
meant showing oneself in the temples and at the festivals, as well as
taking part in the deliberative assemblies and playing one's part in
the law courts.[13]

"Believing in the Gods": A Social Practice

Honoring the gods according to custom and devoting a cult to them
was an eminently practical kind of "belief" in which the gods were
surrounded by gestures and rituals, a whole system of civic ceremonial as much as "piety," a system of values that imposed respect for
ancestors, the dead, and suppliants, as much as for the divine powers who were the guarantors of the social and religious order. Not to
"believe in the gods," in this sense, was to exclude oneself from the
human community, to sink into madness and abandon oneself to violent excess. The myth of the races uses the mortals of the race of
silver to illustrate the drama of impiety, the tragedy of anyone mad
enough not to believe in the gods. The life of the members of this
race begins with a biological misfortune: they are children born after their time, kept for hundreds of years within their mothers'
skirts, sickly and infantile. And when, eventually, they become ado-
lescents, an overweening lack of moderation overtakes them: "Nor
would they serve the immortals nor sacrifice on the holy altars of
the blessed ones as it is right for men to do wherever they dwell."[14]
There is only one thing to be done with them: bury them, cover
them over with earth, make them disappear.

   According to the laws of the city, impiety was a public crime.
There were, to be sure, benign infractions that were let off with a
fine and that were provided for by the rules that were engraved in
stone and fixed to the sanctuary entrance. But if a citizen entrusted
with a public priesthood or a priest responsible for the mysteries

was convicted of grave negligence, he would be punished for the crime of impiety, particularly if "ancestral" sacrifices or the ceremonies of the mysteries, such as, in Athens, those of Eleusis, were involved. The procedure in such cases was the same as that applied to attempts at revolution: an emergency "message" was announced before the Council.[15] Not to devote a suitable cult to the gods was to strike a blow against the city, against its principles, against its very being. For a minority of individuals such as Anaxagoras, the meteorologists and "physicians" arguing about the movements of the stars and the nature of the gods in the sky, and Socrates, who was accused of not honoring the city-gods, "believing in the gods" came to mean "believing in the existence of the gods."[16] An atheist was no longer a poor wretch "abandoned by the gods," such as Oedipus in his extreme solitude,[17] for nowadays he had been taught by the sophists that the gods were an artifact, just as politics was a *techne*, an art, and, by helping to construct a body of discourse on the gods, culture, and language, those same sophists had provided Plato with the chance to sketch out an initial draft of proofs of the existence of the gods. However, in the Greek cities, even in the late-Hellenistic period, no candidate for a magistracy or for citizenship was ever required to confess his belief in the existence of the gods. The cities continued to trust to the evidence of the gods and the rhythms of a liturgy of sacrifices and festivals in which beliefs were never separated from practices, and in which the members of the social group believed in the city-gods because they offered up sacrifices to them, frequented their altars, and recognized their presence behind the whole of social and religious life. So there was no knowledge of the invisible, organized into a creed, and nobody had to be converted to the city-gods, or needed to convert anybody else to them. The fact that one was a citizen gave one access to the altars and, reciprocally, it was the regular practice of sacrificing that sustained the daily exercise of one's citizenship.

The people of the cities of the Greek world were meat-eaters: meat, along with cereals, was of the first importance in their diet and was made the more precious by its association with altars and sacrifices.[18] Of course, everyone would, at some time–indeed, daily, if their income was modest–eat their bread with fish, squid, sepia, or other seafood, as well as olives and onions. Yet, for this people so familiar with the sea, on the altars no saltwater creature could substitute for the products of the earth, or–to be more precise–for the hot-blooded animals whose privilege it was to put men in contact with the gods. Even Poseidon, who had received as his special domain the great expanse of the seas, took delight in hecatombs of lambs and oxen, and the only fish ever to find its way onto his altars, and even then only in exceptional circumstances, was one that dared to bleed, the tunny-fish, whose blood looked like that of the domesticated animals slaughtered before being cooked in the sacred space of a sanctuary.[19] In the eyes of other peoples–such as the Egyptians mentioned by Herodotus, who found meat repugnant[20]–the combination of three instruments summed up the Greeks' way of eating, which was also, in general, their way of sacrificing. The instruments were the knife, the spit, and the cauldron: a knife to make the victim's blood spurt on to the altar and to cut up the limbs, dividing the various pieces; a spit to roast the viscera over an open flame, viscera that would then be eaten by the sacrificer and those seated in the closest circle; and, finally, a large pot for cooking the rest of the meat, boiling or simmering it before distributing it to those seated in the wider circles at the sacrificial feast. It was important that the sacrifice should never look like a murder: the already domesticated victim would indicate its acquiescence, then the knife hidden under the grains of wheat in the basket would strike swiftly. In the company of the gods, only a gentle violence could justify men eating animals that were so close to the mortal "eaters of bread."

In the entire Greek tradition, eating meant first dividing and distributing. Sacrificial, solemn eating was called a *dais* (a feast or banquet), with the emphasis laid on the sharing of food (*daiein*: to divide, share out).[21] Sharing and equal distribution: banquets in which all the shares were equal were "feasts for the gods," in which the altars where the gods were always offered libations and the aromas of sizzling fat were surrounded by tables "where each man had his share." Admittedly, the shares were equal in the sense that the distribution tended to be made between equals, between peers, rather than between all the city's inhabitants. In these "banquets of equal shares" (*dais eisē*), the equality had more to do with the sharing than with the actual portions distributed. In the aristocratic society of Homer's epic, the equality is more geometrical than arithmeti-

e most prized pieces, the thighs and the filets, were first set
⌐r the gods or for the most important figures present as guests
or officiating at the sacrifice.[22]

The sacrifice was the basis of the relations maintained between
men and the gods, and it fulfilled a number of functions. It helped
the Greeks to think about "others" and also about themselves, as
can be seen from Herodotus's inquiries, which concentrate on the
peculiarity of the Scythians or the strangeness of the Egyptians,
epitomized by the Scythians' custom of cooking the ox wrapped in
its skin and the Egyptians' disgust at the slaughtering knife used by
the Greeks. Sacrifice also helped to classify the gods, to differentiate them from one another, or at least to establish certain differential signs: the double aspects of a single deity, the hierarchical relation between two deities in certain, particular circumstances; the
outstanding nature of one particular deity. One reservation needs
to be made here, however: in Greece, not only did a sacrifice not represent the occasion *par excellence* for speculating about the gods
but, furthermore, it was not even really the occasion that most
clearly revealed the distinctive system according to which the gods
in the pantheon were arranged. The practice of sacrifice said more
about the proximity or distance between men and the gods in general than about the differential features of the gods themselves. But,
within the space of the city, sacrifice also fulfilled another, more direct function: it spelled out the political rights of each individual,
revealed the structures of the social body, and in some cases even
pronounced on the nature of the relations that obtained between
two or several cities.

Political Rights: Meat and Sacrifices

In a Greek *polis*, the nature of butchery was dictated partly by di-
alectic and even more by weights and measures. For there were two
ways of cutting up a sacrificial animal. One was based on the joints.[23]
In the *Phaedrus*, Socrates praises this method, "that of dividing
things again by classes, where the natural joints are, and not trying
to break any part."[24] A good dialectician proceeds in just the same
way, if he knows the art of dividing things up. Clearly, this was very
helpful when it was a matter of offering a god, a priest, or a distin-

guished guest a haunch or a filet from the victim. The other method, more rough and ready, required less skill: what remained of the meat was simply divided into portions of the same size.[25] The portions were equal in weight, and the pieces of meat cut into portions were checked on a balance just as they came to hand, regardless of quality.[26] Thanks to the part played by the butcher, the sacrifice activated a powerful egalitarian machine. It was to continue to function for centuries in public sacrifices, always obeying the rule of equal shares; and democracy then complemented the rigor of the weighing scales by the practice of drawing lots, which so convincingly reaffirmed the absolute equality of the citizen-banqueters.[27] It was during the great sacrifices attended by the entire citizen community that the equal rights of all citizens were remembered. During the competitions held in honor of Hera, in Argos, a sacrifice of "one hundred oxen" was offered up, and the meat was then divided equally between all the citizens.[28] All those with citizens' rights received a portion of meat of identical weight if not size. In Delos, during its period of Independence, all the citizens, that is to say, probably about one thousand, two hundred people, were invited to the banquet of the Poseidoneia, the festival in honor of Poseidon. Each of them received a portion of meat or, if they were unable to get to the banquet to claim their due, would be allotted the equivalent in coins.[29] These were thus sacrifices that would have made it possible to take a yearly census of the active citizens, had the city deemed this advisable. They certainly sometimes help modern historians to make an approximate calculation of the size of some of these political communities.

In the Minor Panathenaea held in honor of the goddess Athena, although a considerable quantity of meat would be indiscriminately divided between the citizens of Athens, the first shares were distributed to the magistrates, seated in order of importance: the *prytaneis* were allowed five shares each, the nine archons three, the goddess's treasurers one, the *hieropoi* in charge of the administration also one, the *strategoi* and taxiarchs (military leaders) three.[30] There were two concentric circles of participants, the first of which reveals the hierarchy of magistracies observed within the space of distribution at sacrifices. Elsewhere, at Haliarte in Boeotia, for example, it is the procession in which the sacrificial victims were led to the altar

that presents us with the spectacle of an entire city, led by its most
important magistrates, taking to the sanctuary of Apollo Ptoios an
ox, one of whose haunches and whose grilled parts were to be offered to the archon, the principal magistrate; to the three pole-
marchs, the ministers for War; and to the guardians of the Boeotian
Law and Rights, that is to say, all the political authorities who had
to "be present" at the sacrifice offered up by the city of Haliarte.[31]
The banquet that followed the sacrifice, or rather that of the outer
circle of participants, was sometimes subject to rules that laid down
how it was to be organized: the citizens were to eat in tribes, or in
"family groups," "neighborhood associations," or in "families."[32]

These sacrifices, which were plenary but spaced out in time, were
balanced by daily sacrifices celebrated by the representatives of the
city around the altar upon which the Public Fire burned, the altar
of Hestia, the Common Hearth.[33] Forming a college, the citizens
acting as archons or *prytaneis*, or as the administrators of the Council, daily took turns to offer up libations, salt, and victims sacrificed
to Hestia and then taken in charge by the public treasury. Sharing a
table set up in the banqueting hall in or alongside the Prytaneum,
the magistrates in office would observe the rule of equal shares of
food. At Tenos, in the Cyclades, the Prytaneum would receive, in the
company of the archon, between twelve and twenty "companions,"
guests elsewhere sometimes known as "parasites," in the sense of
"those who eat with . . . ,"[34] such as the official parasite-guests to
be found round the tables in the sanctuaries of Athena, Heracles,
Hera, or Apollo more or less anywhere in the Greek world. The practice of commensality was part of the political policy of a city: in
Athens, Solon ruled that all citizens should, in turn, take part in the
public banquets. To act as a "parasite" was, precisely, to demonstrate one's attachment to the community and "the affairs of all"
(*koina*).[35] In Naucratis, three times a year at least, all the male citizens would eat together in the Prytaneum, clad in dazzlingly white
Prytanic garments. We know that the menu was abundant but not
what it consisted of. Everything had to be consumed on the spot, in
the precinct consecrated to Hestia, by fellow citizens eating at the
communal table.[36] The entire political body would share and consume the same food, thereby affirming its cohesion, its unity around
the idea of a city that took the form of a Public Hearth (or Home).

Just as the political bonds between citizens were formed around the altar and the dining table, the legal relations between cities could be expressed within the space reserved for sacrifices, in terms of the numbers of victims offered up to the gods and destined then to be eaten. In western Locris, two small cities, Myania and Hypnia, concluded an agreement and had the clauses of their pact of *sympolitia* engraved in stone in about 190 B.C. Their respective contributions of soldiers to defend the territory, of judges to decide legal problems between the two communities, of ambassadors to foreign places, and of magistrates for the new, merged community were fixed "proportionally, according to the contributions made toward sacrifices"—in other words, according to the number of victims provided by each partner for their common sacrificial ceremonies.[37]

Also in Locris, two other cities quarreled over their membership in the Amphictionia (the association of those who lived in the neighborhood of a sanctuary), in particular over the allotment of one vote, that of the Epicnemidian Locrians, in the assembly of the Amphictionia members. One of the cities claimed that its rightful share of representation was one-third since, it declared in the arbitration document made public in Delphi, it had "always contributed to the supply of beasts for sacrifice and all the offerings that have in the past concerned the Amphictions."[38]

Whatever its role in the public sphere, in a city the practice of sacrifice constituted a means of having dealings with the gods, dealings that were structured more by the differences between them than by the distance that separated them that is so strongly stressed in Hesiod's theology. In his account of Prometheus's crime and its consequences for the first division of a sacrificial victim between the gods and the mortals, the author of the *Theogony* describes the misery of the human race, devoured by hunger and condemned to nourish itself on the flesh of dead animals, which, in its turn, committed it to experience old age, decline, and death. The gods, in contrast, despite apparently having been duped by Prometheus, received as their lot the animal's imperishable bones, smeared with fat and consumed in a fire that changed them into fragrant smoke, immaterial aromas, as befitted divine powers who lived on the peaks of Olympus.[39] Hesiod's vision is extremely somber: the Golden Age was over, and henceforth the distance between men and the gods would be insurmountable. But the city did not agree with the pessimism of the theologian from Ascra. It was more inclined to believe that mortals and the gods, different though they were, were all born from the same mother and were all part of the same world, even if, at a certain point in their history, the two races had parted company and each developed in its own, different ways.

The Presence of the Gods

A number of features of the sacrificial ritual seem to indicate that the gods actually take part in the ceremony, watching the slaughtering of the victims and then, in a way, participating in the celebration and banquet of the human beings in the city.[40] In the first place, there is the procedure of calling to them, the invocation addressed to the deity whose altar it is, to the god of the sanctuary, the divine power who inhabits the temple. He/she is invited to come, to step forward, to show himself/herself, to appear in the temple, by the altar, where the sacrifice is to take place.[41] Several of the hymns of Callimachus are composed as "advent" songs, celebrating the god's arrival, his *epidēmia*–that is to say, his coming to the spot, or his "epiphany," on the occasion of a festival or sacrifice in his honor. In Cyrene, the laurel of Apollo trembled, the whole temple began to shake, and the keys of the sanctuary turned in their locks when the feet of Phoebus kicked at the doors: "Not unto everyone doth Apollo appear, but unto *him that is good*. Whoso hath seen Apollo, he is great."[42] In Olympia, the city of the Eleans, the college of the Sixteen Priestesses summoned Dionysus on the day of his festival known as the Springing Forth when, mysteriously, the wine would begin to bubble in the vats behind the closed doors of the house of the god. They would invite him to come to the pure temple of the Eleans, "leaping on his bull's hoof." Each year they would sing the same refrains, which were noted down by an observer interested in rituals and were then preserved by Plutarch.[43] Just as Apollo revealed himself and was present in his temple in Cyrene, the Eleans claimed that Dionysus manifested himself during the festival of the Springing Forth and Leaping, mingling (*epiphoitān*[44]) with the Elean faithful. He was present and he communicated.

A second pointer is provided by the Greek theorists of festivals, in particular by Plato, in the *Laws*: "The gods, in pity for the human race thus born to misery, have ordained the feasts of thanksgiving with gods as periods of respite from their troubles; and they have granted them as companions in their feasts the Muses and Apollo the Master of music, and Dionysus, so that these deities maintain the correct rituals and the right way of behaving during these feasts celebrated in the company of the gods."[45] Later on, Plutarch too testified to the firm belief that the gods were present at festivals and banquets,[46] and that men entered into their company,[47] thanks to the offerings, the prayers, and the whole apparatus of sacrifice. It was within the space where sacrifice took place that men and the gods were in "mutual communication,"[48] sharing their enjoyment and pleasure. The gods were present at the festival banquets that the Greeks called *thaleia*, after the name of Thallo, one of the Seasons, or else one of the Graces known as the Charites.[49] These were "feasts for the gods" and were so much regarded as such that eventually, courtesy of Sophocles, "Festival Banquet" (Dais Thaleia) came to be consecrated as "the most ancient of the deities."[50]

The sacrificial laws and the sanctuary rules confirmed that the gods were present alongside their fragrant altars, concretely present at the table set up next to the fire, the fire that consumed the share reserved for the gods, while the other portions were set down on the table, the ones that the inscriptions refer to as "the sacred portions," "the morsels for the god," or quite simply as "the shares for the table." Frequently, priests or their helpers would "set the table up," "adorn the table," "serve at the table." The portion for the gods would lie close to that of the priest, who was likewise well served with choice morsels, to which "the god's morsel" would be added, passed from its table to another, or possibly the god's portion actually was the priest's portion all along.[51] As in a festival known as a Theoxeneion or Theodaiseion, in which the gods received hospitality and were made welcome in the cities where, it was said, they resided in person, or as when they themselves were offering the hospitality, as Apollo did at Delphi, the table was accessible to the gods of Olympus, to the Heroes, and to all the citizens who had been invited to the festival.[52]

Such sacrifices may have been exceptional but they manifested, in exemplary fashion, the combined presence of men and gods at the altars. To the Phaeacians, being together with the gods seemed quite natural, for they were on such familiar terms with them that if any of them, walking alone, chanced to meet an Immortal, the deity would not bother to hide but would greet him in a perfectly friendly way, "for they have always shown themselves to us without disguise when we have offered them our sumptuous sacrifices, and at our banquets they sit at our side."[53] They would sit at the same table, even on the same bench. And although, while telling this, the king of the Phaeacians may seem to have been boasting of the conviviality between the human race and that of the gods, he was certainly not harking back to a Golden Age or to times long gone. In the epic tradition, it was normal for the deity receiving hecatombs and exceptionally prestigious sacrifices to be present. He/she would respond to the prayers and smoke rising from the altar and would "stand before"[54] the animal victims. Athena did so close to the palace of Nestor at the sacrifice of a yearling heifer whose horns were gilded before it was delivered up to the ax and knife in honor of the daughter of Zeus. And at the beginning of the *Iliad*, everyone is expecting Apollo to come, as usual, to "attend" the sacrifice of lambs and goats, the smoke from which always gives him such great pleasure. Gods stand *facing* you, full on, as can be seen from the vase paintings depicting sacrificial processions wending their way toward altars where a divine power awaits, facing toward the sacrificers.[55] Poseidon, likewise, at the banquets of the distant Ethiopians, "stood facing" the bulls and lambs destined for the hecatomb, a god at a festival, looking forward to the pleasure of a perfect sacrifice.[56] Right down to the third century A.D. at least, the cities of Greece and Asia Minor continued to associate manifestations of the gods, taking the form of dazzling epiphanies, with the meals, altars, and festival liturgies that they continued to treat themselves to, for the delight of themselves, the gods, and all those who lived the lives of citizens.

12 The Altars and Territories That Were Home to the Divine Powers

At the very end of the fourth century B.C., Colophon, in Asia, positioned between Smyrna and Ephesus, recovered its liberty, thanked Alexander and above all Antigonus for it, and decided to extend its boundaries to incorporate the "old town" which, it seems, had fallen into ruins and been abandoned many years earlier.[1] The ancient city of Colophon was the home of Xenophon the philosopher and Mimnermus the poet and had been built "with the permission of the gods" by their ancestors, who had "founded" its temples and "consecrated" its altars. A committee of ten was to organize the town planning and, in consultation with the chosen architect, decide upon the layout of the streets and allotments, and designate the sites for the *agora*, the workshops, and all the necessary public areas. First, however, the assembly decided to make a tour of the altars that had been set up by the ancestors and there perform all the traditional sacrifices. Led by the priest of Apollo, the other priests, the priestesses, and the *prytanis* (the chief magistrate), surrounded by the Council and accompanied by the Ten in charge of the project, went to the ancient *agora* to offer up sacrifices "on the altars that the ancestors had left for their descendants for praying to Zeus the Savior, firmly seated Poseidon, Apollo of Claros, the Mother known as Antaia 'she who appears facing you,' Athena poliad, and all the other gods and goddesses, as well as the heroes, those who own the city and the territory." In this way, the ancestral city was refounded, and its land, which had reverted to the common domain, was put up for sale rather than being distributed, as would be the custom in a newly founded city. But first the ancient gods were reawakened, roused by prayers and sacrifices, and reestablished in their temples and on their altars and in all the places that were theirs in the old days. The city and territory of ancient Colophon were restored to the heroes, the local powers, and the forces of the land, now recalled into action after a long fallow period. Just when Antigonus, the master of Asia, was proclaiming the liberty of the Greek towns, in Colophon the gods, goddesses, and heroes were recovering their altars, sanctuaries, and temples. They did so in the simplest possible manner: as a result of the new sacrifices that were made to the old gods and heroes (who were, in all likelihood, the very same as those of the new Colophon).

A different procedure was followed when it came to refounding Messene, under the direction of Epaminondas, following the battle of Leuctra, in 371 B.C.[2] This had brought defeat to Sparta, which had so harshly reduced Messenia to slavery in a series of wars that had ended with the destruction of the last of all its fortresses. Victory now fell to Thebes, which immediately called for the return of the survivors, all the Messenians who had emigrated to the four corners of the earth. In a dream, a priest of Demeter announced to Epaminondas that the gods were no longer angry; the resentment of the Dioscuri, who had been offended by two young Messenians, had now been appeased. Another dream led to the discovery of the site of the new Messene: on Mount Ithome, on the spot where, one night before the inevitable end, the last king of the Messenians had buried the talisman that would ensure the rebirth of his people.[3] This was a bronze urn containing fine sheets of tin, rolled up like papyrus leaves, upon which were written the Mysteries of the Great Goddesses. The site was approved by the Messenians, and Epaminondas proceeded to convene the diviners, for it was necessary to ascertain that the gods, for their part, "wished to live there." The diviners made sacrifices; and the omens were favorable, so the foundation could begin. Experts were summoned, "people clever at plotting out streets and communication routes, and at erecting sanctuaries and houses, and surrounding a town with walls." The architects and town-planners were assisted by teams of builders and craftsmen.

But before they could start work, Epaminondas and his co-founders of Messene addressed themselves to the gods, the gods who, when consulted, had accepted the new territory chosen for the Messenians. Together, the Thebans, Argives, and Messenians went to offer victims to the gods. Epaminondas and his followers sacrificed to Dionysus and Apollo Ismenios in the Theban manner, as befitted the two major deities of Thebes. The Argives did likewise for the sovereign gods of Argos, Hera the Argive and Zeus the Nemean. The Messenians addressed themselves to Zeus of Ithome and the Dioscuri. Their priests also made the required sacrifices to the Great Goddesses, whose Mysteries were so closely associated with the survival and rebirth of the Messenian people, not forgetting the initiator of those Mysteries in Messenia, whose name was Kaukon. The great gods of the Messenians thus returned, accompanied by the major deities of the Argives and the Thebans, who were so actively involved in the foundation of the new city. Together, raising their voices in unison, the Messenians, Thebans, and Argives then called upon the heroes, begging them to return and "live with them": first Messene, the daughter of Triopas, the toponym-heroine and power of the Messenian land; then Eurytus, Aphareus and his children, the early ancestors of the Messenian people, and the sons of Heracles, Cresphonte and Aipytus, who were associated with the very first occupation of Messenia. The longest, loudest, and most unanimous appeal was that made to the hero of the most recent Messenian resistance, Aristomenes.

A whole day was taken up by prayers and sacrifices. As Pausanias points out, for the previous three centuries the last of the Messenians had been living in exile, far from the Peloponese. Now the gods too seemed to be returning from exile. In the ancient town of Colophon, they had simply had their altars abandoned and replaced by others in the new town. But in Messenia the citizens had disappeared; the territory had been emptied of those who used to feed the gods and burn the victims whose throats had been cut in honor of the local heroes.[4] Colophon, like Messenia, was in Greek territory, where, ever since the second half of the eighth century, local heroes, the little "gods of the soil," had been the object of cults, usually close to a tomb that we would call "Mycenaean" but which, for the Messenians, simply represented the visible mark of a man who lived long ago, in the heroic age, and who was commemorated by the bards in the songs of one epic or another.[5] That is why, in Messene, in Colophon, anywhere that had been Greek for a long, long time, these heroes "who owned the city and the territory" were so important. They were local heroes, powers of that little place, who good-naturedly bore its name, toponym-heroes who rubbed shoulders with others whose genealogies were not much more impressive but might, in the most prestigious cases, be traced back as far as Heracles. The reason why the returning Messenians called so intensely for them as the sun went down was that the heroes who had "lived among them" in the past (the verb also means "to marry," "to live together"[6]) constituted the community's point of anchorage, or rooting, in its own land. When Epaminondas saw to it that the gods of the Messenians were asked if they wished to *dwell*[7] on the site of the new Messene, it was no rhetorical question: the gods were their own masters; they could perfectly well have rejected the selected spot, except that they were already the "local" (*enchōrioi*) gods, the powers who had owned the territory forever, or at least for as long as men could remember.

The situation was different if, instead of refounding an ancient city that had died or fallen into ruins, the founder undertook the task of planning a new city totally from scratch,[8] particularly if it was to take shape in a foreign land, on the coast of southern Italy or Sicily where, since the eighth century, the Greeks had been founding cities very much in the manner of Nausithoos and the Phaeacians. In such cases, the procedure seems to have been quite different. The founder of a colony was not concerned to know whether the gods, the ones he had brought with him, were or were not willing to live on the plain or hilltop where he had decided to set up altars and sanctuaries. Nor, on disembarking, was he about to solicit any "local gods."[9] The Delphic oracle had given full powers to the founder: when indicating his approval, Apollo spoke in the name of all the gods, first and foremost those of the metropolis of which the founder was a native. As for the distant land for which the Greek ships set sail, it would, in principle, be a land without inhabitants, empty, deserted since the beginning of time.[10] So what "local gods" could there be there to solicit? The sanctuaries that the founder was about to set up, the altars that he would be building, and the temples that he would be constructing would be reserved for the gods of the city, the powers who from that time on would become "the gods who own the land and the city."

From Altar to City

Altars, sanctuaries, temples: these were structures that clearly indicated the establishment of a new foundation, a newly organized space. The altar came first, for it would be the deity's favorite place. Whenever he/she paid a visit, this is where the aromas of sacrifices would be found.[11] For every divine power, the altar was the special place to receive offerings of wine and of fat, and for banquets of equal shares.[12] The altar would stand in the area reserved for the gods, the space "cut out" for them, the *temenos* as the Greeks called it (from the verb *temnein*, "to cut out"[13]). The most ancient built-up altars, in Samos, in the sanctuary of Hera, were contemporary with the altars described in the *Iliad* and the *Odyssey*.[14] By the eighth century B.C., a Greek altar was already distinguishable by a number of features. In the first place, it was built-up, a definite construction, however modest, made from the interlaced horns of sacrificial victims, uncut stones placed one on top of another, or else the careful creation of someone expert at "building up in even, superposed rows."[15] An altar invited ritual gestures. People would approach it, set down offerings or pieces of sacrificial victims upon its table, and would process solemnly around it at every sacrifice.[16] Thirdly—and we know this from the epic discourse—some gods were more keen on altars than others. Apollo was a case in point: the major sacrificial rituals in the *Iliad* take place around an altar consecrated to the god of the bow, the god who, "like the night," steps forward at the beginning of book I.[17]

In the overall plan of a sanctuary, a holy place consecrated to the gods, from the point of view of the cult, the altar was the most important feature, for it was the altar that made it possible to communicate with the divine powers. It was there that the fire was lit, that the blood of the sacrificed animals dripped down, that the gods' share was consumed by the flames, and that the mortals' portion, the viscera, threaded on to spits, was grilled before being eaten by the sacrificer and his assistants in the ritual. The altar played an inaugural role: it inaugurated the establishment of a sanctuary and was the first stone to be laid in a new city. Its installation signaled the beginning of a process of territorialization: fashioning a space, building it. When Apollo, after approving the site at Delphi, began to think about builders for his sanctuary, he changed himself into a dolphin and leaped onto a ship manned by Cretans, who then became his priests, the technicians of his "works" (denoted by the old word *orgia*, from the *ergon* family), the works around his altars. As soon as he had driven the ship on to the seashore, he set about teaching its occupants their ritual tasks. Where the land met the sea, Apollo had them build an altar. They lit a fire, made a sacrifice of white flour and then, grouped around the altar, the Cretans began to pray, invoking the Delphinian Apollo, who was both the god of Delphi and also the dolphin-god (*delphinos*). The altar thus erected on the edge of the Apollonian domain was to remain, as a memorial that the god himself dubbed "Delphinian."[18] Similarly, the first colonists of Sicily, led by Thoucles, their founder, set up an altar on the seashore of Naxos, in honor of the god of Delphi, Apollo the founder. For centuries, the *theoroi* (the observer-ambassadors sent by all the Greek cities implanted in Sicily to represent them in Delphi, in the sanctuary of Apollo[19]) would come to this Apollonian altar, to sacrifice before setting sail.

After Delphi, it was the turn of Rhodes, where an altar was built, a sacrifice was made, and a city appeared. It represented a double foundation, one effected by Tlepolemus, who is mentioned in the *Iliad*, the other by the Sun-god, whose story is told in one of Pindar's *Olympians*. Tlepolemus was violent and hasty. One day, in Tiryns, he killed the bastard brother of Alcmene and was forced to go away, pointed in the direction of the island of the Sun by the oracle. There, Tlepolemus became a Founder, an *archegetēs*, with an annual cult and sacrifices like those offered "to a god." However, his foundation renewed another, more ancient one that was as old as the Sun itself. Sun had been absent on the day when the earth and its cities were distributed between Zeus and the Immortals, and "nobody had designated his share." There was already talk of drawing lots all over again, when suddenly an island surfaced from the depths of the sea;

Sun spotted it, and it was allotted to him. On their father's advice, the children of Sun climbed up to the Acropolis. They wanted to be the first to found an altar and offer a sacrifice in honor of Athena, who had sprung forth from the head of Zeus, a sacrifice "without fire," in order to lay the foundations of a sanctuary and of Rhodes itself, with its three cities, Lindos, Ialysos and Camiros.[20] The building of the altar represented an initial clearing of the land: the wilderness was "put under cultivation"; a portion of space was marked out and surrounded by a line. It enclosed a precinct, an enclosure that contained an altar, around which the sacrificer, once he was in action, walked in a circle, purifying it with lustral water and a basketful of grain. An altar was thus but a step from a city, and that was a step that Apollo would always take when he felt like doing so, striding through the sanctuaries that it pleased him to build. This was Apollo the architect, the master of foundations: "It was by following in the tracks of Phoebus, Apollo, that men learned to measure out cities with a cord,"[21] to draw plans and mark out the perimeter on the ground, as they built altars, temples, and houses for people to live in.

It was necessary not only to surround the town with a wall, divide up the land between the colonist-citizens, and build houses for them, but also to construct temples for the gods.[22] When Nausithoos founded the city of the Phaeacians, he was careful to set aside allotments of land for the divine powers.[23] The gods, like the citizens, each received a portion of land for their altars, to which they would be attracted by frequent sacrifices and at which they would thus be present, and they also received land for the sanctuary that marked out their domain and for the temple that "allowed them to live there"[24] in the form of idols or statues. A sanctuary was both an allotment and a deserved honor.[25] A *temenos* was a particular piece of land, cut out and given, as a privilege, in the *Iliad*, either to a warrior chief, such as Meleager or Bellerophon, or to a god. Thus Zeus, on the summit of Ida, could enjoy the aromas rising from his altar and his "sanctuary" (*temenos*[26]) or seek out the river Spercheios at the spot where it gushed forth from this very precinct comprising "a sanctuary with an altar."[27] An altar was a place where offerings were made to the gods, in the form of aromatic smoke rising up from burnt meat. From the time of Homer on, the Greek word used to denote a sanctuary was *hieron* ("consecrated place"): a sanctuary was where the ceremonies of the cult (*hieron*) took place, in particular the act of sacrificing victims (also called *hiera*) to the gods. Close to the altar, usually opposite it, in this same enclosure reserved for the god, his dwelling place would stand. This was known as the *nāos*, the house in which men "got the deity to live" by consecrating his image or statue and placing it there. In the Homeric epic, the gods already have temples, some of them built of stone,[28] with doors and locks, in which stands a statue, such as the statue of Athena visited by the Old Women who climb up to the Acropolis to lay a richly embroidered veil "upon the knees"[29] of the goddess.

This was a new way of organizing space, which made its appearance in the geometric period, in the early eighth century B.C.[30] It marked a break with the Mycenaean model. Most of the gods were already listed on the tablets that were the administrative documents of the palaces of the Mycenaean age, but the offerings, which were also recorded, would be deposited in domestic chapels, in ordinary houses, or in the palace, which sheltered the holders of sovereign power: not only the king but also the idols of the deities. Between about 800 and 750, a number of large cult sites made their appearance, separate from the dwellings of human beings, yet accessible to large numbers of people, not all of them necessarily inhabitants of that territory.[31] Olympia, Delos, and Delphi were, all three, sites where offerings for the gods, such as great bronze tripods and statues, would accumulate. The earliest were left at Olympia; in Delphi they appeared around 800. The first constructions in stone appeared in about 730, but sometimes wood was used, as in Eretria, for Apollo the Laurel-bearer (Daphnephoros). Many of the offerings were brought from far away: Etruria, Italy, or the west coast of the Adriatic.

In Delphi, Delos, and Olympia, the great Pan-Hellenic sanctuaries began in this way, accumulating precious objects, sumptuous metalware, and the first statues in which the forms of the gods were crossed with those of human beings, the two becoming easily interchangeable.[32] The *temenos*-sanctuary constituted a domain of the gods that was quite distinct from the kingdom of mortals, and its boundaries would be marked either by boundary stones or by a low wall running all around it (*peribolē*), or else by receptacles filled with lustral water and positioned at the entrances to the consecrated ground. The new sanctuaries served to assemble not only individuals but also different cities and peoples. When festivals and games were held there, the great sanctuaries, by virtue of their extraterritorial status, became places where all these people could come together. Several localities or "peoples" occupying the same region would form an association or federation around a shared sanctuary. Such a grouping was known as an "amphictionia," an association of "those who live round about" (*amphi*, around; *ktiones*, from the verb *ktizein*, "to found, to dwell")–neighbors who all recognized a particular deity and his/her domain, established beyond the borders of the territories of each of the peoples represented.[33] Close to Mykale, in Asia Minor, the sanctuary of Poseidon Helikonios was the seat of the Ionian confederation, and here the Panionia, "the festival of all the Ionians" was held, open to all those who practiced the same cults. At Calauria it was likewise Poseidon who gathered together the maritime cities of the Saronic Gulf. Near Thermopylae, the sanctuary of Demeter Pylaia periodically assembled some of the peoples of northern Greece. In all these places, the federation members became table companions, eating and drinking together. The wine for the libations would be mixed in a crater owned in common.[34]

The Pan-Hellenic sanctuaries of Olympia, Delphi, and Delos were thronged by the people of many cities, all with the same language and the same gods, who recognized one another as "Hellenes."[35] They were keen to meet at these *panegyria* and to compete, challenging one another in the games.[36] As used by Homer, *agōn* means both assembly and competition, a gathering and a contest, and in the *Homeric Hymn* the two activities become one in the eyes of Apollo, the god of Delos, who is in the position of a *theoros*, a spectator absorbed in watching: "In Delos do you most delight your heart; for there the long-robed Ionians gather (*ageirein*, related to *agora* and to *agōn*) in the wide ways (*aguia*, wide road, evoking the Apollo known as *aguieūs*) in your honor with their children and their shy wives; mindful, they delight you with boxing and dancing and song, so often as they hold their gathering [competitions, *agōn*]."[37] Seeing them "assembled" in this fashion, "a man would say they were deathless and unaging."[38] Absorbed in the pleasure of the assemblies and contests, these human beings resemble divine powers, and thus reflect his own image back to the Olympian who is contemplating them from on high, in the assembly of the gods, those divine sovereign spectators, the ever-young Immortals.

The Uniqueness of Greek Temples

Dwellings for the gods came in many forms, but three models seem to have dominated, two of which rate as real "temples."[39] The kind of construction called a "treasury" does not really count. It was kept locked and bolted: inside were the precious objects, including statues, that were deposited there; outside were the cult, the public, and the sacrificers. By virtue of its contents, the treasury building itself counted as an offering. The god did not ever reside in the treasury: there was no altar in it for sacrifices, no statue specially positioned facing the faithful. The proper temples, those inhabited by the gods, were of two types: the one, with its indoor altars and cult statues, contained all the various elements of a religious picture or image; the other, with its external altars, opened outward, so that the figure of the god could be seen, visible to all and sundry.

The sanctuary "of Erechtheus" in Athens and that of Apollo in Delphi were "image-temples." The Erechtheion was a mass of niches, clustered altars for a number of gods, ancient kings and venerable heroes, and, scored in the ground, marks of famous epiphanies, the scars left by a whole history of autochthony. It sheltered, indeed concealed–lest it should be stolen–an old statue of Athena carved from olive wood. This was said to have fallen from the sky; perhaps it did. In Delphi, the temple was built on the site of the oracle, over the Earth's prophetic mouth. The great hall, called the Megaron, contained the hearth of the Pythian Apollo, the ever-burning fire of Hestia, and the altar of Poseidon. And at one end, a secret part, the *adyton*, a forbidden place, contained the Earth's navel, the sacred laurel tree, the tomb of Dionysus, and the prophetic mouth.[40] All these were signs representing the Apollonian pantheon, guarded by priests known as the Pure Ones (Hosioi). This temple was closed upon the oracle that inhabited it. However, this did not prevent the sanctuary of Pythian Apollo from also offering outdoor altars and, for those attending its Pan-Hellenic festival,

large open spaces where the games could be watched and where po-
litical decisions and sacred regulations could be announced. The second model of a temple was designed with publicity particularly in mind. The cult-statue would be on view in the principal
hall, and the temple would be constructed in such a way as to draw
attention to the figure of the god, so much so indeed that, progressively, architects dispensed with the internal, axial colonnade and
replaced it by two parallel rows of columns that gave direct access,
visually at least, to the statue, which in many cases would be of monumental proportions.[41] Two conceptions of the representation of
the gods were thus in play.[42] One is exemplified by the idol in the
Erechtheion: a wooden statue, uncouth, with a primitive air and
something strange, even disturbing about it. Such "xylographs" of
gods that had fallen from the sky, surfaced from the sea, or were
sculpted by some unknown, mysterious craftsman, were objects to
be kept hidden or only exhibited on carefully judged occasions, for
they could madden or kill whoever gazed upon them at the wrong
time. Between the seventh and the sixth centuries there appeared,
in contrast to such idols, great statues of stone, marble, or bronze.
Such a deity would be set up in the middle of the temple, in the guise
of a nude adolescent or a young woman with youthful breasts, statues that glorified the perfect form of the human body. In a religious
representation such as this, the god inhabited a human form in the
prime of life, and the statue exhibited in the middle of the open temple "exteriorized the presence of the god."[43]

It sometimes happened that a sanctuary took root on the exact
spot where a deity had revealed himself/herself by means of a statue
that had appeared miraculously from nowhere. An idol of Artemis
of Ephesus came to light in the marshes surrounding the mouth of
the River Caystre and a temple was repeatedly rebuilt on the same
spot,[44] just as the temple of Delphi was always rebuilt over the
Earth's mouth. Any vigilant historian following in the steps of Pausanias as he pursued his virtually exhaustive pilgrimage to all the
cult sites in Greece might here and there come across sanctuaries
that are half-open on only one day in the year. However, it is the
model of the temple set in a space envisaged as empty and designed
to make public both the gods and the affairs of the city that is pecu-

liarly typical of the Greek world, as compared to the civilizations of
the ancient Near East or Hinduism.

In the Mesopotamian tradition, it was the king who designed and
constructed the temple, but on the basis of a plan established by the
great god Enki, or Marduk. Just as the gods of Mesopotamia invented the Town before creating Man, they began by founding a
Temple,[45] or, to be more precise, by drawing and writing. In the second millennium, in the evidence testifying to the foundation of temples, engraved stones took over from the ancient nails that had once
riveted the dwellings of the gods to the earth. Temples fallen from
the skies now acquired a whole collection of written signs, tablets
which, along with the Assyrian dynasties, became the palimpsest of
sanctuaries constantly newly built but always copies of other more
ancient ones that stretched right back as far as the borders of the divine world.

The same relationship between the gods, the king, and the temple characterized ancient Egypt, but here its cosmogonic impact was
greater: the first Temple emerged from the waters of Chaos. It constituted the first hump of earth, formed at the very beginning, a primordial hillock over which a divine being, the Falcon, came to
hover. Every temple subsequently consecrated by the Pharaoh was
to reproduce the creation of the world, thanks to the skills of Seshat,
the goddess of writing and the measuring line. The construction of a
temple proceeded in accordance with the written instructions of the
architect-god, the architect who had become a god, Imhotep. The
Egyptian gods were always themselves the master-builders of the
sanctuaries inhabited by their divine statues.[46]

In Hindu India, finally, which set great store by the sacrificial area
but, in contrast to Vedic India, limited it to one particular spot, the
siting of a temple was decided by the epiphany of a divine power, by
the emergence there of a goddess or a god in a directly material
form. The space was rigorously laid out, with its cardinal points, and
with symbolic meanings ascribed to various spots, and representations of the same gods always positioned in the same places. The
space was centered on the Holy of Holies reserved for the Brahmins,
the highest caste, a group that expanded or retracted depending on
whether it integrated or rejected the more or less numerous clusters

of inhabitants of the dominated territory.[47] The great temple of Siva, in southern India, somehow spawned around its complex of buildings a whole collection of new localities, towns that were not quite palaces, not quite villages, and that all considered themselves to be kingdoms, which is hardly surprising given the importance ascribed to the royal function and its great social authority.[48]

In contrast, in the model of the city evolved by the eighth-century Greeks, the temple was part of the domain assigned to the gods by the architect-founder, the *temenos* did not drop from heaven, and, although the Olympians might be housed in dwellings "all of bronze," like that of Hephaestus,[49] none of them claimed to have designed the first temple or to have laid down a canon of rules for it. A Greek temple did not conform to any cosmogonic model. It conveyed no cosmic symbolism. It was not obliged to face either West or East. The terrain, the design, and the constraints of the landscape or the town plan dictated how it should lie on the ground. No priests or diviners were empowered to cut out the space for it or to order its erection. Nor did a Greek *temenos* at all resemble a Roman "temple," a *templum*, which was a space for consulting the gods.

Rome employed augurers, priests expert at questioning the gods and skilled in the art of "carving out" directions in the sky and observing and classifying all the signs sent by Jupiter. As a place of augury, on the ground a "temple" was a quadrangular terrain previously "liberated" from all hostile or impure powers. The temples of Rome assigned to the gods in this way were fixed, immovable establishments.[50] But when Nausithoos, having divided the land into allotments, set about giving the gods somewhere to live, he consulted no one but himself, for he was the founder and had received his legitimacy from Delphi. All operations of founding new cities thus rested upon oracular authority, but each "leader" of a colony was left free to assign the most adequate space possible both to the city and to its gods.[51]

A Greek temple was not a microcosm, but was a part of the city. It belonged to the spiritual and social order of the city, that is to say, to the *cosmos* in the political sense that the Ionian philosophers gave to the term. As such, the great sanctuaries of the principal cities were designed to be used as public spaces, in the same way as the *agora* (the public square) or the *prytaneum* (the center of decision in which the *prytaneis*, the magistrates who took it in turns to administer the affairs of the community, met).[52] The most ancient laws, those of Crete, were engraved on the walls of the temple of Pythian Apollo, at Gortyn. At Dreros, the first political texts were put on show in the sanctuaries of Delphinian Apollo, or Apollo the Dolphin. The great temples were veritable lapidary museums. They were so crammed with *stelae* covered by writing that in the Hellenistic period the monumental altars were, in their turn, also covered in inscriptions, as were even the stairs leading up to the sacrificial table. From the geometric period right down to the end of antiquity, the Greek sanctuary remained a space that was accessible to all the members of the community.

Questions of Territory

However, as well as having these official residences, the gods of those temples might also maintain close links with the city's territory: in deepest Greece in particular, that is to say, in mainland Greece, the Greece of the old metropolises and also of more recent ones, even in the islands, that were more inclined to state explicitly that only those who were natives of the territory had the right to sacrifice to certain earth powers such as Zeus "of the Earth" and an equally "chthonic" Demeter, both of whom were to be found in Mykonos.[53] In some places the local gods were very fussy about the "typical" local or regional way of sacrificing or making offerings and expected herbs from a particular sanctuary, cereals grown on the land surrounding their own temple, or "local" cakes, the taste and appearance of which were unique. There were particular regional ways of cooking sacrifice meat, as Thucydides (about 455–400 B.C.) has the Athenians explain: "Under Hellenic law whoever was in control of a piece of country, whether large or small, invariably also took possession of the temples in that country, with the duty to maintain, as far as possible, the usual religious ceremonies."[54] It is true that among themselves Greeks recognized one another from their way of sacrificing, which distinguished them from non-Greeks, or Barbarians. But at the same time, they were very attentive to the religious peculiarities that overlay the basic forms of their dietary behavior.

Secrecy seems to have characterized certain territories, which were entrusted to divine or heroic powers whose locations, which were kept carefully hidden, would frequently be visited, under cover of night, by high-ranking city magistrates.[55] If an enemy discovered the way to them and sacrificed to them first, there was immediately a danger that the power of those protectors might be subverted. It is said, for instance, that Solon grabbed Salamis in this fashion, sending a boat there by night, to sacrifice victims to the "local founding heroes."[56] The Athenians, who were experts in autochthony, were apt to go somewhat over the top in this respect. When they were one day urged by the oracle to give their neighbors in Epidauros two olive trunks, to embody powers of fertility and fecundity that were much in demand, they went so far as to specify that the recipients of the idols should repay them by making annual sacrifices to show that these goddesses of Epidaurus still in reality belonged to the land of their own territory, the only soil to grow the olive tree with evergreen leaves that Athena had introduced. Nor was that the end of the matter. When the people of Aegina one day seized these statues that brought such fecundity, the Athenians insisted upon the same sacrificial recognition so imperiously that the Aeginetans–who were appalled by the intrusiveness of these proprietorial Athenians who were determined that the idols made out of wood from their territory should remain forever Athenian–decided in an emergency assembly that they would never again import anything from Attica, not even so much as a clay cup.[57] They would boycott all Athenian exports and drink their wine from goblets made in Aegina,[58] not from the Attic pottery that at that time monopolized the export market. This altercation between Aegina and Athens over two powers represented by olive-tree trunks underlines how very ridiculous the Athenians, with their "earthy bottoms," could be when they indulged so fatuously in those proclamations of autochthony that were so alien to the manners of other Greeks who, ever since the eighth century, had been perfecting the art of creating cities in new lands. The two territorial deities, known as Damia and Auxesia, involved in this particular episode seem to have been devoid of any trace of Pan-Hellenic spirit, as was only to be expected of powers that were so obviously parochial.

In the Greece of the early beginnings, the newest, most modern gods were those to be found in many of the cities. These were the gods who gathered unoppressively in the large public spaces of the great Pan-Hellenic sites and who owed no allegiance to aboriginal practices or to materials peculiar to any locality, but were powerful enough to embark upon a life with its own rules, without however renouncing their particular territorial duties and their particular concrete modes of being present on certain occasions.

13 The Affairs of the Gods and the Affairs of Men

There was nothing accessory or superfluous about the gods. They were part of the essentials of everyday life. Whoever led the life of a citizen had to visit their altars and sanctuaries almost every day. Just as in mythical tradition it fell to the first mortals on a territory to decide which of the Olympians to appoint as their poliad deity, so in real life every member of the city took part in the assemblies that, in sovereign fashion, decided all questions relating to the gods–the city-gods, those divine powers who were an integral part of the very definition of the city. Communal life, the aim of which was "the good life," according to the Aristotelian definition of the city, required that every citizen should be mindful of the gods and attentively concerned with their affairs, all of which were strictly part of the affairs of the whole community.

A Greek was born Greek but had to become a citizen progressively, step by step, by taking part in city affairs at three cumulative levels.[1] First he had to be recognized by a *phratry*, then he had to be registered in a *deme*, finally he had to play an active part in the *city*: he acquired first brotherhood, next territorial roots, finally a political space.

The phratry was an association based on family links, marriage alliances, and a neighborhood.[2] The members of a phratry called themselves "brothers," classificatory brothers, not blood brothers (*adelphoi*). A phratry included rich and poor, aristocrats and people of humble birth; it was not hierarchical. It functioned as a structure to which you had to be admitted. You gained admittance as a result of being introduced by your family. In principle, you were first introduced at birth. A Greek child would be recognized by his father, integrated into the home, at the hearth of the house, and would be given a name. He was given his first identity by the household and family gods: Apollo Patroōs[3] and Zeus Herkeios, the two powers whose altars he would one day have to "show" publicly, if he ever became archon, one of the foremost city magistrates. Zeus of the Enclosure and Apollo of the Ancestors represented the household, both as a separate precinct and as a group with blood connections that went back over three generations. But these gods of the family circle, who would perhaps one day be called upon to testify in favor of their devotee being granted citizenship, were also, already, powers in the phratry.[4] When the time came, the would-be phratry member would be presented before them.

At sixteen, the age of legal puberty and, in the scale of Athenian age-groups, two years before becoming a civic adult, the future "brother" was presented to an assembly of Brothers.[5] The phratries celebrated convivial sacrifices, had their own altars, met in assemblies, voted, had decrees engraved in stone, and kept a register of members, whom they provided with an official identity. They had their own public places, where the names of the candidates for membership, painted on wooden tablets, would be exhibited, to be perused by all the phratry members congregating there. The official introduction of a new "brother" was marked by a sacrifice known as a *koureion*, named after the word for a victim immolated after being shorn. All sheep and goats destined for sacrifice would be shorn, but so too would young boys once they became pubescent. The sacrifice took place on the third day of the Apatouria festival, the festival of "those with the same father."[6] It was a communal festival shared by all the phratries, under the patronage of a select group of Olympians: Apollo, Poseidon, Zeus, and Athena.[7]

The second stage involved the deme.[8] This was a territorial unit, part village, part mini-city. Before the reforms of Cleisthenes in 508 B.C., the demes were all ranked as cities. Each had its own assembly and magistrates, led by a demarch, the deme leader. In contrast to the phratries, which had no calendar of their own and no autonomous sanctuaries, the demes boasted packed pantheons, drew up their own calendars, and organized sacrifices and festivals unknown elsewhere. For example, at Thorikos, a deme in Attica, the calendar, engraved in stone and now an exhibit in the J. Paul Getty Museum, mentioned three specifically territorial festival days: the day known as green (Chloia), when the first buds appeared; the day known as the beginning of the ploughing season (Prerosia); and the day known as that of the first ear of wheat (Antheia), the harvest of Demeter.[9] The demes held three kinds of festivals: those which were peculiar to their respective demes; those in which all the demes participated, in the city; and those that the demes shared with "the city" but celebrated on their own home ground.[10] Once you were a member of a deme, you were a citizen. To be inscribed in the deme, on the register and the list kept up to date by a scribe, was to count as an active member of the city. Primarily, however, it meant taking part in everything that was shared by those mini-citizens, the deme members; it was "to sacrifice in common" and to meet together at gatherings[11]; "to hold festivals that are a common delight"[12] and "sacrifices, with all their common business" (*koina*).[13] Just like the great city, the *polis* proper, the deme associated the cult of the gods with the welfare of the community, the affairs of all its members. It aped, or prefigured, the city's discourse about itself, its values, and the hierarchy of those values.

In the mid-sixth century b.c., "masters of public writing" made their appearance in the cities of Greece.[14] These were figures of importance in that setting out the city laws in writing, in a monumental form, made them public, organized the political domain, founded a polity based on "isometric" law–that is to say, one that valued equality before the law. The public scribes were expert in the use of "red," or "Phoenician," letters, as they were called, and played an essential role in the definition and formulation of the "common good" (*xunon*) and the city-state (*koinon*). The written laws encouraged political practices, actively affected social relations, and one by one fashioned the public life of the city. At first, the public scribes used to be elected by a show of hands: "Formerly this clerk was elected by a show of hands, and the most distinguished and trustworthy men used to be elected."[15] There are three archaic statues on the Acropolis of Athens that show them at their work: with writing tablets on their knees, sitting up very straight, and wearing stiffly pleated cloaks. By a lucky chance, the contract drawn up for one of them affords us a glimpse of both their privileges and the new way of defining the public domain in the city.

The name of the man in question was Spensithios, and his contract was discovered on a mountain in Crete. He was a "demiurge," that is to say, a first-class citizen, expert in red or Phoenician letters, who was employed, at a large salary, by a little city as yet undiscovered.[16] This master of writing was appointed for life, treated as the equal of the *cosme* (the top magistrate), and engaged as a scribe "for the city, in the public affairs of both the gods and men." His job was thus to record in writing anything to do with public or communal affairs (*damosia*). But the contract of the scribe Spensithios returns no less than three times to the division of the public domain into two spheres: that of the gods and that of men. The affairs of the gods are dealt with first, then those of men. The field of politics, that is to say, city affairs, is divided into two departments. And the contract of Spensithios, who was neither simply an archivist nor simply the city's chronicler of events, stipulates that "every time matters of the gods or those of men are concerned, the scribe should also be *present and participating*, whenever the *cosme* is there" (italics added). Through writing, assuredly engraved in stone, Spensithios was made a political actor or even protagonist, because he conferred a new publicity and efficacy upon what the city considered to be essential. His contract specifically made him an actor, for it was part of his job to "make the public sacrifices for all the gods for which there was no designated priest, and to be in charge of their sacred domains." So he was responsible for ritual and for sacrifices and was thereby invested with an equal dignity, an equal share of honor (*timē*) as the magistrates, whose authority came from the common Hearth, from Hestia—as Aristotle, in the *Constitution of the Athenians*, reminds us.[17] These were magistrates with the rank of archons, kings, or *prytaneis*, magistrates responsible for performing the "communal sacrifices," those which in Athens were sometimes called "ancestral" and were, on that account, fixed in writing, inscribed "on tablets and *stelae*" by the Athenian legislator Solon who, long before his Cretan colleague, was also a scribe and "master of public writing."

Spensithios's contract confirms the importance of the affairs of the gods, alongside those of men, in the city's definition of itself and political, or city, matters. His job was to perform and also to record the sacrifices. And the city-gods were all closely associated with the most political of all of them, the communal Hearth, Hestia, who had started out as an Olympian deity but had come to symbolize the very concept of a city and who, of all the divine powers, had thus become a citizen in the fullest sense.[18]

It was at the third level, in the city, that the concept of "the affairs of the gods and the affairs of men" really came into its own. It was a formula that was retained by the cities of Crete right down to the Hellenistic period. In the third century B.C. the citizens of Itanos were still swearing that they would be "citizens equal and the same in everything that concerned the gods and men"[19]; and a decree passed by the assembly of the Itanians specified that whoever refused to swear the oath would be punished by being "excluded from the affairs of the gods and the affairs of men."[20] The domain of the gods and the sphere of men encompassed everything in which one participated once one received citizenship, once one became a fully integrated citizen.[21] Some cities would refer to "the sacrifices and communal affairs,"[22] or, in a more humdrum manner, to "the sacred things and the civil things" (*hiera kai hosia*),[23] as in the oath of the ephebes of Athens, who swore to defend the city, its territory, "the boundaries of the motherland, the Wheat, the Barley, the Vines, the Olives, and the Figs."[24]

Gods at the Heart of Politics

Whatever the exact words, the formula always included two terms: the gods, and men, always mentioned in that order; that hierarchy clearly never changed. An examination of the processes by which a new citizen became part of a political community into which he had not been born shows that he was required to take part in the public sacrifices, to have access to the altars and sanctuaries of the city-gods, and also to the assemblies and to the magistracies. In the case of a foreigner who received the rights of citizenship, real ones rather than the nominal rights that were often granted to city benefactors,[25] he ceased to be regarded as a passing stranger who always needed the intercession of a qualified citizen if he wished to approach an altar. He probably also ceased to be considered as one of the city's resident foreigners,[26] known as metics or *perioikoi*, who were excluded from the civic community even if, from time to time, the city would invite them to some banquet in which the entire community took part, or would tolerate their presence in minor cults of the local heroes or at the festival of Hephaestus, the god who welcomed craftsmen and all those who plied a trade, in contrast to free citizens, who led a life of leisure.[27] The future citizen would thus be admitted to a phratry, and inscribed in a tribe, which secured him a legal share in sacrifices and a legitimate place at a banquet of equals.[28] He might possibly be asked to appear before an assembly of "brothers" or of the "tribe" in order to explain the motives for his inscription and to try to win the acceptance of the members of his city in miniature.[29] Once accepted, he could take part in everything in which active citizens could participate, first and foremost in communal sacrifices.

That initial right might be backed up by another which, although it would not be granted to him automatically, explicitly demonstrates how important the affairs of the gods were to the city. This further right, which was granted quite selectively and parsimoniously, allowed the citizen to take part in the deliberations of the assembly authorized to discuss the affairs of the gods. To be more precise, it gave him the right *also* to sit in the first part of the assembly, the part that was devoted to "sacred things" (*hiera*), accession to which was limited to citizens with full rights, those who enjoyed "all the rights." This was a privilege seldom granted, as the story of Tisamenus and the Spartans shows. Tisamenus was a famous diviner who, the oracle predicted, would be victorious in five battles directed by him. Sparta was immediately keen to engage him. Tisamenus asked that his contract should include a clause that gave him complete citizenship "with full rights." The Spartans reacted with indignation, and Tisamenus went elsewhere.[30]

"Full rights" were exactly what the Athenians, in quite exceptional circumstances, granted to the Plataeans, their allies to the death, or rather to such Plataeans as survived the town's horrendous siege by the Spartans: "It is decreed that the Plataeans shall be Athenians from this day, and shall have full rights as citizens, and that they shall share in all the privileges in which the Athenians share, *both civil and religious.*"[31] Even in their case, there were two restrictions: first, a Plataean did not have access to the priesthoods and mysteries that were passed on hereditarily; second, he could not become one of the nine archons. By virtue of this decree, the Plataeans were distributed among the demes and tribes and were admitted to the assembly that handled the affairs of the gods. Another way of expressing full citizenship was the formula "participating in the cults and the magistracies," which was used in the regulations applied to the small fortress-town of Pidasa when it was absorbed by Miletus. But here only those who had sworn the oath and who appeared on the list drawn up by the commissioners sent from Miletus qualified. Only they could take part, without any explicit restrictions, in "everything in which the other Milesians participated."[32] It was far more common to share the city altars and sacrifices than to be granted access to the management of the affairs of the gods. In 198 B.C. the Roman consul T. Qu. Flaminius, campaigning against the Macedonians, besieged Elatea, in Phocis. The town fell, and the Elateans found refuge in Arcadia, among the citizens of Stymphalus, who had been their "kinsmen" from ancient times.[33] They were lodged in the latter's houses, welcomed to family hearths and sacrifices, and allotted plots of land from the public domain. Several years passed, and eventually the Elateans returned to their own country where they immediately passed a decree honoring the city and citizens of Stymphalus: as well as being granted the right of asylum, the citizens of Stymphalus were to "take part in the public sacrifices of the Elateans, and the affairs of the Elateans were to be examined immediately after the assembly for 'sacred things.'"[34] It is not clear whether this meant that the Elateans offered the citizens of Stymphalus the right to oversee their most symbolic affairs, nor do we know whether they themselves had ever crossed the threshold of such a closed assembly in Stymphalus.

Many cities drew a temporal distinction between the affairs of the gods and the affairs of men by using the formula "first, after the sacred things" to indicate the "political" affairs that most urgently needed to be discussed.[35] But they also did so in honorific decrees that granted the rights of citizenship to carefully chosen foreigners: "They will be admitted to the council and the assembly *immediately after* the affairs of the gods."[36] The gods' business came first and was handled by citizens of the highest rank, precisely those for whom the most important priesthoods and magistracies were reserved. In Delphi, the first-class citizens were called "demiurges," or "public officials."[37] It was they who acted for the city. In Marseilles, they were known as *timouchoi*. They were well-born people "who had enjoyed citizens' rights for three generations."[38] In Perge, in Pamphilia, the highest priesthood, that of Artemis of Perge, could only go to a "female citizen" who lived in the town and was descended from ancestors who had been inhabitants for three generations on both her father's side and her mother's.[39]

In the political space of the city that included the affairs of the gods and the affairs of men, the "sacred things" were the province of the innermost circle, a reflection of that formed, in the old days of blood sacrifice, by the small group of those who together consumed the animal's viscera, roasted on a spit. They had constituted a select band of table companions, surrounding the sacrificer, who had the right to the victim's vital organs, the parts of the living creature that were composed of condensed blood. These men were the first to eat and what they tasted were the most intensely vital parts of the animal, after the blood, that is, which had to spurt onto the altar for the divine powers.[40] At the level of the city, which was always attentive to the ancestral sacrifices, the tight circle of foremost citizens closed around what was the foremost and highest concern of the city: namely, the gods and their affairs. This was the first, innermost circle in the public domain, positioned right at the heart of what the fifth-century Greeks called "politics" or "political (affairs)," the affairs of the city. This is made clear by, among others, an account by Lysias the orator, a rich shield-producer who composed over two hundred written speeches and thereby left his mark on Athenian democracy without ever being granted citizens' rights.[41] Andocides had been involved in the scandal of the mutilated Hermes statues. When he was denounced, he denounced others. Because he "repented," he escaped being sentenced to death but, by virtue of a decree specially targeted at "repentant" men of his ilk, he suffered *atimiē* –that is to say, he was deprived of his citizens' rights, and the *agora* and the sanctuaries were declared out of bounds for him. Andocides went abroad, where he led the life of a wandering exile. When democracy was restored, he returned and the amnesty restored his rights to him. But his enemies denounced him, seeking his arrest. They complained that he was stained by his impiety yet was still disposed to take part in city affairs (*politika*): "He attends meetings of the Council, and gives advice in debates on sacrifices, processions, prayers, and oracles."[42] That was exactly what would be on the agenda of the assembly for sacred things, the *hiera* that lay right at the heart of "politics."[43]

A long decree engraved in stone around the mid-fifth century was discovered in Argos at the beginning of the twentieth century. It consisted of the decisions of "an assembly watching over the affairs of the god,"[44] affairs that stemmed from a pact between the Argives and two cities in Crete, Cnossos and Tylissos. Most of the decree's articles were devoted to fixing the communal sacrifices, the concomitant offerings in parallel sanctuaries, the hierarchies of victims and distributed parts, and the organization of the respective calendars. The rest of the decree's decisions fixed the etiquette of warfare, legal relations with other cities, and the frontiers between Tylissos and Cnossos, but all these matters, as a whole, were handled by an assembly which, as the reader was reminded at the bottom of the *stele*, watched over the "sacred things" that affected the entire domain of public affairs.

Gods Dominated by Men?

We should not leap to the conclusion that a Greek city was quite simply dominated by the gods. The practice of assemblies that included affairs of the gods on their agendas suggests, rather, that in a way the divine powers were subject to the decisions made by the community of men. Spensithios's task of keeping a written note for the

city of everything that concerned the gods and everything that concerned men is directly in line with the work of the legislators, particularly that of the one who is the best known to us both for his political actions and for his detailed laws, Solon of Athens,[45] who was
so proud of having written the city's laws, applicable to rich and
poor alike, at the dawn of the sixth century. When Solon decided to
make public the fundamental city rules, that is to say, to set them
before the eyes of all and sundry, he wrote, or ordered that there be
written, on bronze and on wood, prescriptions for sacrifices, cal-
endary data, details of the cost of the sacrificial victims, the powers
to whom they were to be offered, and the actors and beneficiaries in
the sacrificial ceremonies. A large section of the "laws of Solon"
falls outside what we should call the "political" domain, in the strict
sense of that expression.[46] His legislation covered both the *hiera*
("sacred things") and the *hosia* ("civil affairs").[47] It was a double
register that was manifestly still operative in the fifth century when,
in 410, the Athenians entrusted to Nichomachus, who was presiding over a law commission, the task of revising Solon's code and having it engraved on a large section of wall in the Basileius-Stoa: a
written code engraved in stone, to which the Athenians could refer,
just as they had to Solon's work.[48]

Draco, the seventh-century legislator, had probably also made
public, alongside his famous laws on homicide (which Solon was to
retain), lists of sacrifices, "sacred laws," and festival calendars.[49]
And when Plato wrote the *Laws*, he advised officially instituting all
practices to do with cults: interpreters and guardians of the laws
would be responsible for composing them and writing them down,
but the city would first consult the Apollonian oracle in Delphi to
find out which sacrifices the city would profit by offering up and to
which gods they should be offered.[50]

The affairs of the gods—all of them, without exception—were thus
handled by commissions and discussed in assemblies, and truly were
the responsibility of the citizens. In 485–484 B.C., the Athenian people, or Demos, decided to protect the sanctuaries on the Acropolis,
in particular the Hecatompedon, to which it was forbidden to bring
cooking pots and fire.[51] If a synoecism or merger of villages took
place, or if several cities fused to form a single one, as happened in

Mykonos in the third century B.C., an assembly would meet to take decisions, elaborate a common calendar, reorganize the local pantheons, and institute new sacrifices, showing respect for tradition of course, but also making changes to "rectify" it.[52] It would be interesting to know more about this work, the difficulties encountered, the advice taken from experts, what was at stake politically, the balance of local interests, the inevitable clashes, the compromises—all that the word "rectify" covered. For that was the word the city would use: the new calendar of sacrifices was expected to be an improvement on the old. The gods would be told of the changes. Sometimes the assembly of citizens would let it be known, when it drew up articles on the festivals and sacrifices, that the rules could only be modified if at least one hundred *demotes* ("deme citizens") were present.[53]

The gods were certainly not at the mercy of the majority. And civil wars did not necessarily lead to the destruction of the statues of the gods of the defeated faction. For all important changes, sanction from Delphi was essential, and the oracle's sense of tradition was as strong as that of those consulting the Pythia. But in the domain of "city affairs" (*politika*), in particular, the action of men was autonomous. It was decisive, whereas in the domain of "the fruits of the earth," sowing and planting, it was the divine powers who set the rhythm of labor, made things burgeon and grow, and who either generously proffered or refused to proffer food for all those who devoted a cult to the Seasons, to Demeter, to the Charites or Graces, and to Dionysus. As Xenophon remarks in his *Oeconomicus*: to cultivate the earth is to devote a cult to Earth, and to the gods who protect the seeds and the fruits.[54] The verb *therapeuin* means both to cultivate and to practice a cult.

In the assembly, on the *agora*, in the council, and in the exercise of magistracies, many gods were conspicuous, among them some of the foremost Olympians: Zeus, Athena, Artemis, and also Hermes, Aphrodite, and Apollo.[55] The gods were even present at political decisions, although not to the same extent as in the domain of warfare and that of agriculture, where men seemed positively dependent upon the divine powers.[56] But it was certainly men, mortals, who were the inventors of the city. It was they who organized the political domain, thought out and designed the space within which things were made public, progressively affirming their authority with institutions, rationalized practices, and a concerted effort of conceptualization coupled with abstraction. For example, the first of Cronos's children, Hestia, became the communal Hearth, the symbol of the city, a political ideal,[57] "legality itself,"[58] attracting into her orbit other equally abstract figures who together imposed a political symbolism the like of which had never been introduced by other polytheistic gods.

The city's political symbols, like the rest of the divine powers, were an integral part of the world, but over and above this, they bore the mark of the kind of thinking that went on in cities. They were remodeled right through, precisely adjusted to fit the abstract ideas produced by the various theorists of "human affairs" and of all the experiments made in the government of men by men. In short, living the life of a citizen could mean not merely devoting an almost daily cult to the gods recognized by the city, but also belonging to the small, bold–even rash–company of men who decided on the right place for symbolism from the vantage point of the space opened up by the strict, unflinching division between human affairs on the one hand and the affairs of the gods on the other.

The gods of a Greek city were not activists, unlike Homer's gods, so many of whom suffered for men, going through appalling torments in order to please the wretched mortals. But nor were they the indifferent figures imagined by Epicurus, distant gods, isolated in their beatitude and absorbed in self-contemplation, knowing nothing of human affairs and troubles. As citizens, in some cases as poliad deities, the gods were associated with the entire gamut of practices, ceremonies, and institutions that made up the social fabric of the life of a citizen. They reigned over all the acts of human beings engaged in living "politically" in both new cities and more ancient ones. They reigned; but, as has quite rightly been pointed out, they did not govern.[59]

Let us next consider two examples that will show us how the divine powers intervened in two specific domains, without, however, controlling them altogether: on the one hand, the domain of the identity and education of citizens; on the other, that of what we should call sexuality. In the first case, we shall be seeing how feminine powers were at work both in the foundation of cities and also in the female urge to reproduce without the intervention of any man. In the second, we shall inquire into the role played by Dionysus, starting with his effigy in the form of a phallus.

We shall be trying to fathom a company of gods of which every individual in Greek antiquity had a perfectly clear idea,[60] which the familiar statues of the gods helped him or her to imagine in a concrete form but the complexity of which, intuitively sensed from the customary practices of the citizen body, was far beyond the descriptive powers of any anthropologizing Homer.

14 The Power of Women: Hera, Athena, and Their Followers

In the search for a city and a territory that would acknowledge his sovereignty, Poseidon cuts a sorry figure. He was always ruled out of court, even though, by virtue of certain aspects of his divine personality, he seemed more qualified than many of his rivals to exercise an effective dominion over these expanses of land.[1] In the daily prayers repeatedly addressed to his altars, he was, after all, the god who maintained a firm, possessive grip on the earth, the god who was securely and unshakeably established on a firm foundation.[2] Sometimes he was even addressed as the Lord-Husband of Earth in her pre-lunar form of a black Demeter, as black as the Arcadia in which her mares ran wild. Perhaps, in truth, it was his immediately recognized nature as a god who was somehow generically a foundation and support that thwarted his career as a sovereign god who reigned over a city from on high. But although Poseidon was always, or almost always, a loser in this domain, as often as not he certainly did not lose everything. It even seems to have been in his opponents' interests to grant him certain rights without which they themselves would not have been able to enjoy their coveted cities.

In two places, Argolis and Attica, Poseidon came up against powerful goddesses and was defeated by women: first by the Athenian women, who held a majority under Cecrops's brief reign, and then, still in Athens, by Praxithea, who did not hesitate to sacrifice her own daughter in order to ensure the triumph of Athena and her victory over Poseidon, who was then forced to respect the cult of Erechtheus, housed in the foundations of the Acropolis.[3] He was likewise defeated in the land of Argos, again by women, who in this case had come in from outside in order to institute the reign of Hera.[4] Here, Poseidon had to knuckle under in a different way, subjugated this time by desire, persuasion, and a mutually agreed marriage. Won over by the beauty of Amymone, one of the fifty Danaids, the god of fecund springs lifted the blockage of the waters of the rivers of Argolis to which, in his anger, he had subjected the first inhabitants of the Argive territory when they had taken Hera's side and rejected his own claims. An extreme drought had followed his action: all the waters had withdrawn to the frontiers of the city territory. These, as it happened, abutted onto the shore where Poseidon, the god of springs, ordinarily made fountains of sweet water spurt forth from the very depths of the sea, into whose waves harnessed horses were brutally hurled, in an attempt to appease him.

When the Danaids arrived, returning to the land of their forefathers, they landed near Lerna and immediately searched for water, for without it they could not sacrifice to the local gods. While exploring the woods surrounding Argos, one of Danaus's daughters, armed with a javelin, came across a doe, took aim at it, missed her mark, and awakened a sleeping satyr who, in his turn, provoked the intervention of Poseidon. A chain of reactions was started. The god of underground waters forswore violence: for Amymone, he invented a form of contract that linked spouses in mutual respect. In this way, Poseidon gained access to the domain of Hera, his rival, and ruled over not only the land of Argos but also the deity who claimed to be "equal in rights" to Zeus, the king of the gods, whom she legitimately treated as the companion of her bed rather than as an overlord or a domestic despot. Thanks to Poseidon, Amymone came to preside over marriage ceremonies and over the lustral and fecund waters of the territory, alongside Hera, who, in Samos, was known as "the birth and root of all things,"[5] Hera, who, when she wished to, so closely resembled Earth, her accomplice, who, bypassing the male entirely, brought about the birth of offspring, children, some of them monstrous but others as perfect as Youth or Hebe, Hera's daughter, who was born one evening from a crisp, juicy lettuce.[6]

Meanwhile, in parallel to Amymone, another of Danaus's daughters defied her father and stood up for the right of a daughter to choose her own husband and love, instead of fulfilling her duty to kill, to shed blood when ordered to do so by her father. Hypermestra was the only daughter of Danaus who refused to shed blood on the night of the wedding between themselves and the sons of Aegyptus, their own cousins. She then became the first priestess of Hera of Argos and, at the same time, the first queen of the territory of Argos. In the hemicycle of the kings of Argos consecrated in 369 B.C. by the Argives, the statue of Hypermestra precedes that of Lynceus and follows immediately after Danaus. The country's kings were descended from Hypermestra and Lynceus. The royal power was thus originally feminine, as befitted a territory placed under the protection of the Hēraion, the sanctuary in which Hera was enthroned, scepter in hand, with at her feet a conjugal bed ornamented by her Charites, the deities of exchange. Opposite her hung the shield of the armed poliad goddess, Hera the warrior, who doubled up with Hera the sovereign. Ever since that time, Poseidon, bearing no resentment, had supplied the nocturnal waters of Lerna for the beautiful water-carrier—or seeker—and the spring of Amymone, destined for the use of newlywed wives, flowed regularly, winter and summer alike. The subterranean power of Poseidon, released by the hand of a Danaid, became the foundation of the power of women, mediated through the royalty of Hera in the land of Argos.

Athena the Misogynist

In the Argive tradition, the women intervened after the judgment of the water-gods. In contrast, an account of the Attic tradition, paraphrased by the author of the *City of God*, tells of the decisive action taken by the race of women when the entire city, rather than the first autochthonous being, was called upon to decide between the two candidates for the position of poliad deity.[7] The women sat alongside the men, at the invitation of the first king of Attica, the snake-tailed Cecrops, who represented the most ancient autochthony. This was a strange mediator indeed, the first-born Cecrops, half-snake, half-man, and the inventor of monogamy. In place of confused unions like those of animals, he had instituted the couple: one man and one woman. Every child would now know both his father and his mother.[8] The women possessed political rights, went to assemblies, and voted in them. And when Cecrops's progressive city met to decide whether Athena or Poseidon should be their poliad deity, the males and the females clashed, married couples split apart, and the whole party of women approved Athena's candidacy while the men rallied to Poseidon. Cecrops, who was a great organizer, had already discovered the principle of the majority vote, and the feminine party, marked by asymmetry, had one more vote than the masculine party. So Athena won, and Poseidon was defeated. The first female "Athenians" chose a feminine deity, one of themselves really, to fill the first symbolic magistracy in the city. No doubt they were unaware that Athena had already declared herself a "motherless virgin," born from her father "alone." Did they think that, as a *parthenos*, a virgin, she would be devoted entirely to things feminine, entirely wrapped up in pure femininity? They can hardly have imagined that, clad in bronze from top to toe and bursting with warrior violence, the Athena who had sprung forth from the head of Zeus would soon be declaring to the whole city, in another assembly, that she was "altogether on the male side," marriage apart, and wished to remain forever untouched by the femininity that experiences desire, that makes love, then conceives and produces children.[9] The female "Athenians" seem to have got themselves the wrong Athena.

For the Athenian deity of fire and ice was not the only Athena. In the territory of Olympia, at Elis, there was another. She was called the "Mother," and in very interesting circumstances.[10] There had been a war, the city was destroyed, and its warriors in the flower of youth had been decimated. The female citizens of Elis wanted to save their city and have it reborn. They turned to Athena and begged her to enable them to bear sons the moment they had made love with their husbands. Athena complied without protest and without the slightest show of virginal horror. Out of gratitude, a sanctuary was built for her, in which she bore the name "Mother," Athena Mētēr. So far, so good: this was a patriotic Athena, who had made it possible for them to make love and then, without delay, produce children, in order to save the country. But the strangest thing, according to this same account, was that the spot where these female citizens were united with their husbands was then dubbed Pleasure (Badu, in dialect), so great had been the enjoyment of both the men and the women. So this was an Athena made sensitive to erotic pleasure, an Athena more sensual than Hera, who had been so offended when Tiresias, having undergone metamorphosis and become a woman, and who therefore knew what he/she was talking about, told her that the sexual pleasure of women was immensely superior (nine times as great, according to his/her reckoning[11]).

However that may be, once consecrated as poliad deity, the most virgin Virgin of Attica was not going to lift a finger to come to the defense of women's rights. Poseidon, meanwhile, was so irritated that he got Athena to rescind and abolish those rights on her territory. In the *City of God* (413–426 A.D.), Augustine, who is apt to paraphrase Varro (the first-century A.D. Roman antiquarian), is none too clear on the matter: Neptune (the Latin name for Poseidon) was angry and to *appease* him, the women were punished three times over. They lost their right to vote, their children were no longer to bear their mother's names, and they themselves would no longer be called female "Athenians." The days of Cecrops were over; from now on the women were under the regime of the Virgin who was "altogether on the side of the males." There were, of course, other ways to calm the fury of Poseidon, as we have seen from Hera's methods in Argolis. But Athena was a misogynist; she said so herself and she showed it in her actions. The only exception that she made was for her priestesses, strong women totally devoted to her personally: Praxithea, for example, in a version of feminine autochthony produced by Euripides in late fifth-century Athens.

Was Euripides against women or on their side?[12] This is perhaps the moment, now that interest has been reawakened in the subject, to pause for a moment to consider the question of mythological sex.[13] It is a question that has recently been much debated, and in a polemical spirit intent, both in France and elsewhere, upon repudiating the injustice done over thousands of years to the feminine condition. *The Flounder*,[14] Hesiod, the city, and Aristotle, to mention only the principal witnesses, are all in the dock.[15] Consider the affair of Pandora, Hesiod's dream (and possibly that of Greek men generally) of a world without women, or the even more telling and more subtle ploy of the version of the story of Athena, the little

Erichthonius and his mother Gaia that was purveyed by perfidious males, which clearly sets out to deny the little that remained to women in this masculine world, stripping them of their maternity and instead attributing it to the Earth "to be on the safe side."[16] Some may wonder whether that was really such a good idea, and whether it was wise to draw attention to the thwarting of masculine desire, the discomfiture of Hephaestus, a child rendered fatherless, and the triumphant complicity of women left to themselves: Earth, Athena, and her three accomplices–Aglauros, Herse, and Pandrosos. And when, from Zeus's head, split by the two-edged sword of Hephaestus-the-Midwife (performing a cesarean, as an exploit of a demiurge), the Virgin with a bronze body leaps forth, uttering a terrible cry, does it really make sense to hasten to blame this masculine deity for usurping the process of birth, for revealing the female womb to be unnecessary, and for, yet again, inflicting a "huge rejection upon . . . the maternity of women"?[17] Those, word for word, were the reproaches heaped upon Zeus *by Hera* precisely when she saw that he was pregnant, right up to his head, with bright-eyed Athena: "Would I not have borne you a child, I who was at least called your wife among the undying gods?" she asks him. The rest of the *Homeric Hymn to Apollo* recounts at length how Hera, so active in her battle against her husband, resorts to a series of sophisticated procedures in order to produce her own offspring without any intervention from Zeus, who is thus totally marginalized.[18] But is this really the insult to the paternity of citizens, symbolized here by Hera's husband, that it has promptly been claimed to be? Interpretations of mythology that claim that it "reflects" the class struggle have never been very convincing, and those that key into the war between the sexes seem no more decisive.

All things considered, a more profitable method for the analysis of myths is first to read all their different versions, comparing stories that echo one another in Argos and in Athens, or even on different levels within Athens itself: for example, Athenian autochthony in the feminine as compared to autochthony in the political masculine: the story of Praxithea and Aglauros as compared to that of Erechtheus on the same Acropolis (as we shall be doing presently).

Seen from a distance, autochthony seems an obsession of the

Athenians who, indulging in the delights of narcissism, produced, in the form of funeral orations, an immense volume of repetitive discourse on the autochthonous, perfect Athenian "born from the very soil of the country, always identical in his virtues, exploits, words, and actions."[19] It was in the fifth century B.C., when the city of Athens was at the peak of its sea power and its predominance over all the tribute-paying allied cities, that its ego was at its most inflated. Alarm bells ought to have been ringing.

Upon closer examination, the diversity of Athenian autochthony becomes apparent, as has skillfully been shown by Nicole Loraux.[20] There are many versions of it, many points at which it is anchored, and successive examples of it: Cecrops, then Erechtheus the Most Chthonic One, he of the *Iliad*, raised by Athena, who installed him long ago in her triple sanctuary–Erechtheus, rightly called the Most Chthonic One since the ploughed Earth (*chtōn*, in Greek), so full of life, conceived him, then "bore" him in her dark womb.[21] Cecrops, the snake-tailed king who introduced monogamy, introduced the idea of autochthony even before Athena, an autochthony that afforded a fine role to the female species confronted by the male. Then there is the considerable distance that separates Erechtheus and Erichthonios. Linguistically, the former appears to be an abbreviated version of the latter, but their roles are quite different. Erichthonios is the newborn babe in the scenario in which Hephaestus, pursuing his sister, with whom he is in love, prematurely ejaculates his semen in a passageway on the Acropolis. And when Hephaestus has disappeared down another alley, Athena, who was hiding from him, hurriedly turns back to gather up her brother's sperm in a twist of wool. She then places this in a basket and entrusts it to Earth, who, as ever, does the rest, just as she does for Hera, at her request. Erichthonios is thus a little autochthonous male surrounded by women, what with the shadowy Earth, his wet nurse, and his three female cousins, sisters bigger than him who have to look after him but without seeing or knowing all the fateful secrets. Erechtheus, in contrast, is a mature, adult king who inaugurates the triumphal processions of Athena and her princely festivals, the Great and the Minor Panathenaea. Upon close examination it is also possible to see that there are differences between, on the one hand, the Agora, with its abstract, founder-heroes, the ten

Eponymous heroes who include in their ranks Cecrops and Erechtheus, and, on the other, the Acropolis, which is the place of royal births and childhoods. And there are also differences between these two and the Ceramicus, with its rows of tombs and monumental burial places that exalt the idea of dying for the city, where the motherland is hymned as it is presented with its harvest of the dead, all of them identical Athenians who are to be reborn, eternally the same.[22]

As it wends it way up from the Ceramicus, through the Agora, toward the Acropolis, Autochthony is declined in the political, masculine case. Only males, leaping to her defense, die for the Mother-Country. Fortunately, however, Euripides surprised everyone by setting on the tragic stage a feminine version of Athenian autochthony: an autochthony for women, based on the strength of women, which re-explored the whole mythology of the origins of Athens. Inevitably, all this was spurned by those who pronounced the national funeral orations and those who spoke for the undertakers' profession.

Praxithea, an Anti-Clytemnestra

Around 430 B.C. according to some, 420 according to others, the Athenians set about constructing a new Erechtheion on the site of the old one built by the Pisistratids, which had itself been the third sanctuary consecrated to Erechtheus. There is a line in Euripides' tragedy entitled *Erechtheus*[23] that alludes to a stone edifice erected in honor of Erechtheus-Poseidon, upon Athena's decision, once the town had been saved from danger.[24] The play begins with a confrontation between Athena and Poseidon. The two deities are quarreling over the Acropolis and their respective rights over Attica. The quarrel had begun under Cecrops, flared up again under Erechtheus, and seems an essential part of the claim to autochthony.[25] In this version of the story, Poseidon has a territorial base at his disposal, namely Eleusis. The city of Eleusis was at war with Athens and was threatening the existence of the autochthonous city. The Eleusinians revealed themselves in their true colors when they appealed to foreigners for help. They turned to the Thracians, positive barbarians, led by Eumolpus, the Fair Singer, who was a son of Poseidon. Faced with "others," "otherness," in the wild form of Poseidon and Eleusis, Erechtheus and Athena reaffirm the Athenian identity and its intact autochthony. This time the battle is to be decisive, so Erechthteus goes to Delphi to discover how to be victorious: by sacrificing one of his daughters, the oracle tells him. Erechtheus returns to Athens, tells his wife Praxithea of the condition imposed by the Delphic oracle, and then, with her complete agreement, leads his daughter to the altar and slaughters her, to save the city. Her blood flows. But Praxithea and Erechtheus have three daughters in all; the other two commit suicide by the sword.[26] Now the outcome of the battle is assured. Erechtheus kills Eumolpus, thwarting Eleusis and the Thracian mercenaries. At this point, Poseidon intervenes. Furious at the death of his son, with a blow of his trident he splits the rock of the Acropolis, causing Erechtheus to be swallowed up in the ground, and threatens to destroy the city by an earthquake. Athena protests, telling Poseidon to return to the sea and be satisfied with the death of Erechtheus. She then announces to Praxithea, the sole family survivor, that her daughters, who have become goddesses, will forever be devoted a cult in the city, and that her husband, Erechtheus, who has also been deified, will now become the August Poseidon, in a sanctuary in the middle of the city. As for Praxithea herself, Athena makes her the priestess of her poliad cult. "I want you to be the first to carry offerings to my altars, in the name of the city," she declares.[27] Eleusis was defeated by the Athenians, but the rival city retained the right to celebrate the Mysteries founded by Eumolpus.

In that tragedy about autochthony, the heroic role really fell to Praxithea rather than to Erechtheus.[28] The name of this queen of Athens was almost functional, its meaning derived from the words of Athena that consecrated her status as an official priestess; she acted for the goddess. "Praxithea" was constructed in the same way as *praxidikai*, the word denoting the executors of Justice, who represented one aspect of the Erinyes-Eumenides.[29] "I want you to be called my priestess (*hierea*) and to be the first to carry offerings to my altars, in the name of the city." She was responsible for the public sacrifices offered up, in the name of the city, to the poliad goddess who lived on the Acropolis. The autochthony of this city was proclaimed by the priestess acting for Athena. When it came to action, it was Praxithea who expressed the Athenian identity. Erechtheus was no longer a protagonist; fate had swept him away and he was now entombed inside the Acropolis. Praxithea declared the autochthony of Athens even before she was left to embody it on her own: "As for us, we are autochthonous,"[30] by birth, by nature. "We" meant the city, a city unlike any other. In other cities the people came from somewhere else, they were alien, foreign. Athenians, in contrast, had always lived on the same land. They knew nothing of any founding. "Other cities were formed from a variety of elements, as are coins collected up at the throw of the dice, founded upon a hodgepodge of many origins."[31] Athens alone was a "natural" city; all the rest resulted from chance, a series of foreign occupations, mixtures and meetings between metics of every kind and "paper" citizens (although "papyrus" citizens would be a more apposite expression for Aristophanes' public, who would be more inclined to draw a contrast between "straw" and "grain"[32]). All around Athens were cities of straw, then, populated by immigrants, citizens "in name only," without consistency, who were not, could not possibly be true shoots grown from the soil of the city. Between 430 and 420 B.C., Athens was teeming with resident non-citizens, working there. It was rich in metics, who brought to it their intelligence, their creativity, and their knowledge, as well as their financial wealth. And it was they whom the queen of Athens was addressing with her megalomaniac discourse: "Whoever leaves a town to come and live in another is like a piece of wood added to a framework: he is citizen in name, but not in fact (in his actions)."[33]

That was the kind of praise that Praxithea produced for autochthony, speaking as herself. She was in no way a spokeswoman for Erechtheus. As queen, she spoke in the name of Athens, with the "we were born autochthonous" of male Athenians, and also—in fact—of female Athenians, "all the Athenian women" who were declared by a decree of about 450 B.C. to have an equal right to act as priestesses of the Athena of Victory, Athena Nike.[34] Praxithea knew what she was talking about, for she was directly descended from the Athenian territory, being the daughter of the Cephissus, a local river[35]: she was the daughter of a father whose waters irrigated the Athenian earth. There could be no doubt that Praxithea was autochthonous.

She had to be if she was to do what Athena and the city expected of her: sacrifice her own daughter, abetted by Erechtheus, shed the blood demanded by the oracle, in order to save Athens. Praxithea was certainly not unworthy of her autochthonous birth. When Erechtheus had left the oracle to bring home its terrible message, he had been convinced that Praxithea would revolt, wrest the child away from him, try to impede the salvation of the Town. On his way back, he had thought of a compromise solution: he would adopt a daughter, and she would be the victim required by the oracle. Praxithea would lose nothing. But Erechtheus underestimated the strength of Cephissus's daughter, the strength of an autochthonous Athenian woman. Praxithea had just denounced the idea of borrowed citizenship, false citizens, not part of the finely milled barley that was the quintessence of the earth. How could an adopted child be a substitute for an authentic one? The fruits of nature were stronger than the products of legal measures.[36] At the very suggestion that another life could be worth as much as the blood of her daughter, Praxithea flew into a rage, let fly: she would show Erechtheus and everyone, all the assembled citizens, how an autochthonous woman behaved, how an autochthonous mother could shed the blood of her own flesh, in order to offer it to the Earth that was thirsty for it.

Unlike Clytemnestra, Praxithea herself volunteered: "I shall give my own child to be slaughtered."[37] She sang in praise of dying for one's country: "My daughter alone shall win the crown by dying for the city."[38] She would save "the altars of the gods and our motherland."[39] It was a motherland behind which, as the autochthonous queen showed, lay the Earth, Gaia: "This girl (*korē*) who is mine purely by nature, by birth, I shall give as a sacrifice to the earth."[40] Here, Praxithea occupies the place assigned to Erechtheus in another work very close to this one, also by Euripides. In the *Ion*, Creusa pays homage to Erechtheus, saying, "He had the courage to kill his daughters, slaughtering them for the earth."[41] And that "I" of Praxithea's makes us forget the "we, the autochthonous ones"; it is an "I" that makes Erechtheus disappear, just as though war and death had already closed in on him, bearing him away to the sanctuary and underground caverns of the Acropolis. Praxithea is most certainly the protagonist,[42] and she already stands alone in her autochthony, declaring, "Without my consent, nobody can abolish the ancient laws of our ancestors."[43] As queen, one who knows how to give Gaia her due, she solemnly takes Athena's side and, for the sake of salvation for the citizens and for victory, offers up "the fruit of her womb,"[44] her womb that is also the womb of Gaia, no longer shunned as it was by Athena, who preferred to play at nursemaid and was determined to know nothing of the matrix. Praxithea and Gaia stand shoulder to shoulder.

Foundress and Motherland

In one version, by Demaratus, the slaughtered girl is even given the name Chthonia, Daughter of the Earth, and her blood gushes onto the altar of Persephone, flows into the entrails of Earth, and fills the mouth of the one who is so often called Core, the Girl.[45] Everything that takes place is between women. The Attic earth is marked by the blood of women. Athena institutionalizes this situation: the three sisters, buried together, are to be the official protectresses of the territory, goddesses who will be the object of a cult similar to that of the Eumenides: before any military engagement, blood sacrifices to them will ensure victory for the city.[46] Whatever their names may have been, whether a feminine equivalent to Erichthonios, Prōtogeneia or First-Born, or Pandora[47] (but in this context in the guise of a suntanned young girl), the daughters of Praxithea were granted a fine death. The first, sacrificed daughter, who was dressed by her mother in her finest clothes, as if to head a festival procession or *theoria*,[48] was set apart in her solitary glory, whereas, as Praxithea remarked, "The sons of the city who fall in battle share a tomb and the common glory with many others."[49] This is an allusion to the national funeral ceremony in the Ceramicus cemetery that was open to the democracy of the dead who fell for the city, those for whom Athens and its orators would pronounce the Epitaph in praise of Autochthony. Once the other two sisters had killed themselves, as befitted brave autochthonous girls, they joined their sister and all three were given "a name to be famous throughout Greek lands: mortals will call them the Hyacinthid goddesses."[50] They were thus granted not only a fine death and the glory of warriors who died to save the motherland, but also an annual cult: "Every year, so that they are not forgotten as time passes, the citizens must pay homage to them with sacrifices and blood victims."[51] The cult involved the entire city, with choirs of young girls and possibly armed dances performed by young men.[52]

Nor was that all. As warrior powers entrusted with the defense of the territory, the daughters of Praxithea were "to have an inviolable precinct": "Any enemy that tries to sacrifice to them in secret must be prevented from doing so: for it would mean victory for them and disaster for this land."[53] A technical description of this ritual exists: it consisted of a sacrifice before engaging in battle, similar to the sacrifices that the Spartans would make to Artemis, except that in her case they were performed actually upon the battlefield, in the sight of the enemy. Athena was very precise: "It is to the Hyacinthides that victims must first be sacrificed, before setting out to fight the enemy, but without touching the vine, without pouring libations on the fire, and offering only the fruit collected by the industrious bee, mixed with fresh water drawn from the river."[54] Chthonia and her sisters thus became powers of the earth, deities as chthonic as the Eumenides, who also held wine in horror and refused all libations other than those of honey mixed with water.[55] The Hyacinthides were not substitutes for the powerful Eumenides, but they backed them up in the domain of warfare, as guardians of the city who lived underground but were constantly vigilant in defense of the frontiers and in the thwarting of foreign conquest. Positioned sometimes on the Acropolis, sometimes on the frontiers,[56] the daughters of Praxithea watched over the city territory, the territory that the ephebes swore to protect when they presented themselves in the sanctuary of Aglauros, that other autochthonous girl of the time of Cecrops, who had played the roles of both Praxithea and her daughters who killed themselves in order to save Athens.

Earth had drunk the blood of those autochthonous girls, but still demanded another victim, Erechtheus, the Most Chthonic One, whose body, enclosed in the Acropolis rock, helped to strengthen the foundations of both the city and its very autochthony. At the very point when the power of Poseidon was unleashed against the king of Athens, that autochthony seemed trapped and immobilized in the service of Athena, his rival, who had again won the day. Poseidon, the god of earthquakes, "made the ground of the city shake,"[57] and his trident, plunged into the Acropolis, opened up a tomb for Erechtheus, who was swallowed up by the earth. The Most Chthonic One in this way returned to the depths whence he was born when he became Erechtheus. Athena, no doubt aided by Zeus, put a stop to the violence of the god of the seas and pinned Poseidon down with his victim, telling Praxithea, "As for your husband, I command that he be built a sanctuary in the middle of the town, with a surrounding stone wall." And this sanctuary was to contain both Erechtheus and Poseidon: "Erechtheus will take the name of his murderer: that is how the citizens will invoke him when they sacrifice hecatombs of oxen to him."[58] Poseidon-Erechtheus or Erechtheus-Poseidon?[59] The former appears in cult inscriptions, as also does the more common Poseidon *and* Erechtheus. The latter does not appear anywhere but would be in conformity with the intention of subjecting the murderer to his victim[60]: Erechtheus was deified as Poseidon, in this instance the god of firm foundations, Poseidon the god of foundations forever reliable, a Poseidon now integrated into autochthony.[61]

After the death of Erechtheus and the disappearance of the three sisters, that autochthony was entirely taken over by the priestess of Athena, Praxithea, who had opposed Poseidon so energetically: "And on the rocks of the Acropolis, in the place of the olive tree and the golden Gorgon, never shall we see the trident crowned by Eumolpus and his Thracian warriors, nor Pallas stripped of all her honors."[62] Not only was Praxithea certainly the executor of the works of Athena, but the victorious Athena even dubbed her "foundress": "You are the one who knew how to re-establish the foundations of the city."[63] Athenian autochthony, in Euripides' version of it, needed to be founded, rooted, deeply anchored—by the very blood of the autochthonous ones returned to the Earth, and also by the stabilizing power of an alien god who had seemed to threaten the autochthonous quality of Athena. What the autochthonous Earth demanded of her citizens was that they should die for her. Praxithea, by sacrificing her daughter, born from the earth as she herself was fathered by Cephissus, had set the example. So homage was paid to the Athenian women, and to the strength of the women of Athens,

who were proud to be autochthonous, were indeed the very
foundresses of autochthony.

A Woman in Charge of Ephebes

Just as Praxithea embodied[64] Athenian autochthony when she addressed the citizens with the twofold authority of the queen who had
sacrificed her own daughter on the altars consecrated to Earth and
also of the priestess of Athena Poliad, who represented the whole
city in the public sacrifices, there was another Athenian heroine,
who was both a mother and a daughter, who affirmed the autochthonous qualities of Athens through blood and warfare, but in
her case by officially acting as the one who supervised the initiation
of young men of an age to bear arms and become major citizens. Her
name was either Aglauros or Agraulos,[65] and she was the daughter
of Cecrops, or one of his daughters, or possibly the mother of the
Cecropids (the children of Cecrops). Translating those two names
with the aid of expert etymologists, for Aglauros we obtain something like "Clear Water," and for Agraulos "Daughter of the
Fields," preferably uncultivated fields, or even, according to one ancient philologist (known as the Quiet One, Hesychios), "She who
sleeps at night in the fields on the edge of the woods."[66] This name is
preferable to Clear Water, which is, to be sure, very suitable for an
autochthonous girl, but distracts us from what is essential here: her
dark, violent side. So we shall leave her the name Aglauros, which
is the one used in the oath in which the ephebes swore solemnly to
die for her,[67] but at the same time we should remember the passion
of Agraulos who threw herself from the top of the Acropolis in order to save her city.

The version of the story produced by Philochorus, an attidogra-
pher or historian of Athens from its origins to the then present day
of the third century B.C., runs as follows: The country was at war,
with Eumolpus attacking Erechtheus[68]—as in the story of Praxithea.[69] Also, in similar fashion, the oracle declared that the outcome would be dire unless somebody sacrificed himself/herself for
the city. In the tradition of Thebes, which was similarly under threat
under the reign of Creon, it was Menecaeus, the son of the king,

who cast himself from the high walls of Thebes, for Tiresias had predicted victory for the Thebans if Menecaeus was sacrificed to Ares.[70] Aglauros/Agraulos, for her part, made her own decision to die. She climbed onto the ramparts, cast herself into the void, and crashed to earth at the foot of the wall. At the spot where Agraulos/Aglauros killed herself, where her blood was shed, the Athenians built her a sanctuary, at the foot of the ramparts surrounding the Acropolis.[71] It was there that the ephebes came to swear their oath before setting out to war.[72] Aglauros/Agraulos was thus likewise a priestess of Athena,[73] a heroine who combined both the role assumed by Chthonia and that of her mother Praxithea in Euripides' tragedy. She was like a Praxithea, consecrated as the priestess of Athena, but one who killed herself instead of helping Erechtheus to have her daughter slaughtered. Here, there is no mention of Earth, nor of Persephone and her altar, nor even of Ares, who is a constant presence in the space of Agraulos/Aglauros. There are just the city walls and the sanctuary erected at the gate, and the blood required to strengthen the ramparts, the blood of an autochthonous woman[74] to "re-establish the foundations of the city," as Euripides' Athena puts it–or, more directly, to found Athens, to root it in its autochthony, anchoring it in blood beneath the Earth's skin.

Aglauros/Agraulos, the autochthonous foundress, embodied not only the warrior values, those of Ares and the ephebes, but also the feminine values, those of women in society and of the powers of fecundity possessed by the earth, the Seasons, the fruits and the branches of trees. Aglauros and Ares formed a couple.[75] They were the first deities to whom the priestess of Aglauros offered the "sacrifices of the entry" in the month before Boēdromion (September–October), when the ephebes began their military service.[76] Aglauros was wedded to Ares,[77] and had long been a warrior, even "before the Trojan War." That, at least, is what is declared in a sanctuary in Salamis, a Cypriot city founded in the eleventh century B.C., which is the date of the ramparts that have now been excavated. In Salamis, "the most Greek of the Cypriot cities," according to Isocrates (436–338 B.C.),[78] Agraulos presided, along with Athena, over an ephebic and bloody ceremony.[79] A man chased by ephebes entered the sanctuary. With the ephebes in hot pursuit, he dashed around the altar three times. The priest of Agraulos then speared him through the throat[80]: a warrior's death in honor of Agraulos. The body, placed on a pyre that was already prepared for it, was entirely consumed by the flames. Later on, Agraulos was replaced by Diomedes, but he was the Diomedes of Ares, a homologue of the heroine who, in her sanctuary, now positioned to the east of the Acropolis, close to the Prytaneum, had assembled together all the powers of war, both the ancient ones, Enyō and Enyalios,[81] and also Ares, who formed a pair with Athena Areia[82]: an Athena of Ares, just as there was an Ares of Agraulos, the Agraulos of the ephebes, youths on the way to becoming adults, citizens in arms, but also the Agraulos of women. This was the Agraulos by whom married women customarily swore[83] when they gathered together on their own at the festival of the Thesmophoria, from which males were excluded and during which the women fleetingly constituted a city, themselves offering up blood sacrifices, and in which, according to imaginary representations, they seem to have acquired a mastery over weapons, certainly over the weapons used in sacrifice, but also over the weapons of warfare, which they could at last wield as they wished.[84]

Agraulos is thus on the side of active women, for she is the mother, or the sister, of Pandrosos, who likewise is closely associated with Athena and also with ritual sacrifice.[85] Pandrosos, another daughter of Cecrops, was the first to weave with wool, making clothes for men to wear[86] and thereby moving them along the path toward civilized life, in the same way as the bee-women, the *melissai*, who surrounded Demeter Thesmophoros, bringing, along with their honey, clothing woven for the purpose of covering up nudity and establishing new relations between the sexes.[87] Just as Agraulos, by virtue of having offered up her life for the land of Attica, represented a model of behavior for every ephebe, Pandrosos, and with her the Kourotrophos, she who made the young grow, were feminine powers who invented the first civilized space on an equal footing with better-known masculine initiators such as Erechtheus and the snake-tailed Cecrops.

In her eminently political sanctuary, Aglauros marshaled around her two groups of divine powers. One was directed toward war, the other toward fecundity and the glory of the Athenian territory. Aglauros's personal brilliance was fostered by her violence against all agressors. When the priestess of Aglauros performed the sacrifices on the occasion of "assuming her functions,"[88] she began by sacrificing to the armed couple formed by Aglauros and Ares. Then she turned her attention to Sun (Hēlios), the Seasons (Hōrai), Apollo, and the other gods, "according to ancestral custom." Sun and the Seasons presided over the fecund time of the earth, when it brought forth its fairest fruits. The Athenians sacrificed to them jointly in May and in October, offering up boiled rather than roasted meat, one liturgist tells us, so that the fruits of the earth (like the Seasons, known as Hōrai) should ripen, helped along by moderate heat and regular rains.[89] Apollo, next on the list, was by no means out of place, for he reigned over not only the city assemblies but also its gates and the defense of the territory. A similar division between gods of warfare and deities of the fecund earth accounts for the selection of the powers invoked by the ephebes when they came to the precinct of Aglauros to swear an oath to fight to defend the territory of the city, those who lived there, and their gods.[90] In this oath, Aglauros was given pride of place, before even Hestia, the Common Hearth and the goddess of the Prytaneum, the center of the *polis*, where the ephebes entered upon their military service. Next, after Aglauros and Hestia, came the compact squad of the powers of warfare: the archaic couple Enyō and Enyalios, with the female deity leading her male companion; then Ares leading the Athena of Ares, Athena Areia. Ares was a familiar figure in Athens, and his sanctuary in the Agora of the city sheltered a statue of the female warrior Enyō (later known in Rome as Bellona), who stood there alongside Athena and Aphrodite.[91] Behind the Athena of Ares came Zeus, leading the Seasons, whose names were Thallō ("the Season of the branches"), Auxō ("the Season of growth"), and Hēgemonē ("the Season that leads"). Zeus was given no specific attribute but may have been the Olympian, the Zeus of the sky and of water from the sky. Then came the Chthonic One, a god of the soil and the nourishing earth, and, finally, the Poleius, the god of the political city, balancing Hestia and Athena Polias.

Hēgemonē, "the Leader," brought up the rear of the file of Seasons but was positioned directly in front of Heracles, who was followed by "the Boundaries of the Motherland," along with Wheat, Barley, Vines, Olive Trees, and Fig Trees. Heracles was thus present partly in his capacity as the protector of the *ephebeia* but also playing the role that he shared with Apollo, warding off danger and defending the territory, his integrity symbolized by the Boundary markers, and also drawing attention to the riches brought by the fruit-laden Seasons, the fields, and the orchards.

A Tour of the Sanctuaries

From her tomb, in her sanctuary, Aglauros watched over the military novitiate imposed upon the youths who were soon to embark upon the life of citizens. The ceremony for the ephebes began in the Prytaneum and ended on the Acropolis.[92] It started with sacrifices under the sign of Hestia, the Communal Hearth, and the deities close to her; and it ended with sacrifices to three feminine deities: Athena, who lived on the Acropolis, Athena Polias; the Kourotrophos, that is to say, the Nurse of the Young, who was very close to the nursing Earth; and Pandrosos the weaver, the daughter of Cecrops who opened up the space of civilized life for the ephebes,[93] just as the Poliad Athena assured them of the exercise of citizenship, both potentially and in action. In all probability the ephebes would move on from the Prytaneum to swear their oath in the sanctuary of Aglauros, just a couple of steps away from Hestia.[94] There they received their arms. Then came the third stage: led by the *kosmētēs*, the officer elected to head the present batch of youths, the ephebes made a "tour of the sanctuaries."[95] We do not know in what order, following what route, or whether they just visited the urban and suburban sanctuaries or went further afield to take in those in the countryside or even out on the frontiers. The Spartans had a similar ceremony but reserved it for the man of the greatest merit who had reached the age of sixty and was a newly elected senator to the Council of Elders, the Gerousia. Crowned with a wreath and in a procession, the new senator would go from sanctuary to sanctuary, accompanied by a throng of young men who would shower him with compliments and praise, and escorted by a

large band of women singing the praises of his virtues and past behavior.[96] But in the Athenian city it was the young men, on their own
and wearing no crowns, who, no doubt at an athletic pace, made a
first tour of reconnaissance, so that they could recognize the gods,
both those of the city and those of the territory as a whole.[97] There is
at least one mention of the epehebes offering sacrifices "to the gods
of Attica," while they are "at the frontiers," those same frontiers
and "Boundaries of the motherland" invoked in their oath.[98]

Throughout their military service–during which they were
known as *peripoloi*, "those who go around"[99]–Agraulos's young
men moved from festivals to competitions, from sacrifices to processions, week after week throughout the year taking part in the festivals held in honor of the gods, in the order decreed by the calendar.[100] From mid-September on they would constantly be doing the
rounds of the pantheon: the Artemis of Marathon, the Virgin of the
boundaries, for whom they ran grueling races in full armor, which
tested them to the very limit; then the Young Girl and the Angry
Mother, Core and Demeter. There would be "sacred objects" for
them to transport from Eleusis to Athens, to the Eleusinion, and
then back to where they had come from, always clad in full armor,
but crowned with fresh myrtle and provided with portions of meat,
to keep their strength up. There would be the festival of the Mother
of the gods, known as the Galaxia (for she was a milk-drinker), in the
course of which they would offer her a vial from the libation cup.
Then there would be more races, this time for Theseus, the
Oschophoria, with vine branches laden with bunches of grapes to
carry as they ran. The first to reach the winning post would quaff a
coveted mixture of oil, wine, honey, cheese, and milled barley. Then
came a march that carried them on from Dionysus to the Athena of
the stony hills, the Skiras; and, of course, the Epitaphia for the war-
dead, a funeral service and a march-past in impeccable order and
full dress uniform: disciplined, with perfect kit, and led by their
commanding officer (the Kosmētēs), with a censor or Sophronistes
bringing up the rear of each of the ten tribes, carrying a long sup-
ple switch with which to inculcate *sophrosynē*, self-control, into his
young charges, who had to bear themselves erect, as befitted citizens. One of Aglauros's young men's favorite exercises was per-

formed when a handful of them laid hold of an ox, bull or cow, never mind which, then lifted it on high and carried it on their shoulders, still alive–or almost–and presented it to be sacrificed, all of them still in good order, in uniform, albeit splashed with blood by the time the animal fell still.[101] When the sacrifice was completed, there would be congratulations from their officer and from the censor. An inscription in stone would testify to their trainers' satisfaction with a truly fine sacrifice.

Dionysus too had to receive his due: there were nocturnal processions with his statue, an old idol, to be carried from the altar known as the Eschara to the Theater; the Dionysia held in Piraeus; the urban festivals known as the Lenaea and the Great Dionysia; and processions, one of which solemnly featured an enormous phallus representing Dionysus, leading into the tragedy and comedy contests.

And still they continued to keep up with the calendar: Artemis on the seashore, Marathon, then Salamis, with regattas and sacrifices; then Ajax and the Zeus who made enemies turn on their heels, Zeus Tropaios (from the verb *trepein*, "to turn"). For Ajax, represented by an armed statue laid out on a bed, there were races, "long races," and mock naval battles. For Athena and for Zeus, whether Zeus the Savior or some other, there were many festivals. Sometimes, on an occasion of a more than usual "political" ritual, one particularly essential to the city, the young ephebes seemed to be already integrated, endowed with the status that awaited them on their return from military service. One was the festival of the Venerable Ones, the Semnai theai or Eumenides–the ancient deities of the hill of Ares, the seat of the Areopagus, the city's nocturnal council. According to their cult, the Eumenides were drinkers of milk, which would be left out for them in jars; and they fed on succulent wheat-cakes prepared by the best of the class of ephebes with their very own hands: local cakes prepared by local children. At this family "tea-party," the Old Ladies of the Hill wanted only free men and women around them, all of irreproachable reputation. Not a slave was to be seen,[102] let alone a foreigner. Ancient Athens opened its doors to its own children. The sons of Aglauros were permitted to climb up to the Acropolis and offer up their parting sacrifices to the feminine triad that awaited them there: Athena Polias, the Kourotrophos, and Pandrosos, the excellent weaver. They were received with open arms, for now they were back home, worthy autochthonous Athenians, duly instructed as to the great configurations of the company of the gods and the principal ways of integrating the divine powers into the city's social space and, equally, as to the eminently active role that was reserved, in Athena's kingdom, for the goddesses, the heroines, and–quite simply–Women.

15   A Phallus for Dionysus

In polytheist Greece the gods constituted a society; they were carefully organized, with their respective fields of activity, each with privileges that the rest respected, and with particular knowledge and powers that were limited by those of their neighbors or associates. A division of labor, as it were, operated within the pantheon: each of the gods had been allotted his/her tasks in a particular sphere of action. In some cases these were very general: the labors of warfare for Ares, marriage for Aphrodite.[1] But in such a complicated pantheon a single deity could not be altogether confused with a single domain of intervention. Aphrodite reigned over not only marriage but also sexual pleasure, the *aphrodisia*, the act of "making love" (*aphrodisiadzein*[2]), intertwined bodies, living creatures–animals and humans alike–impelled to intermingle their limbs and their bodies.[3] Then there was also the armed Aphrodite, the Ouranian power, a black deity associated with the Erinyes, the forces of vengeance, and with the powers of Fate, the Moerae; not to mention the Aphrodite with a beard, who combined the two sexes and was very much out of place in the marriage scene, an institutionalized space within which Aphrodite was, besides, carefully surrounded by eight or nine other deities, mobilized to share the domain of conjugality, under the supervision of Hera and Hera's Zeus, who officiated together, clad in ceremonial costumes.[4]

One way of defining the presence of the gods within the domain of social life would be to select an institution, such as marriage, and assess how much of it was allotted to each of the gods involved in the marriage ceremony, from the very first of its rituals down to the very last. Each divine power could in this way be analyzed in relation to his/her specific mode of action, which would then, in its turn, be tested out within the whole collection of fields of human action deployed by Greek society. The absence of expected gods within the framework of a particular institution would in itself be significant: for instance, in marriage ceremonies Dionysus is not present, yet he seems to lurk not far away.

Another approach was successfully adopted by Georges Dumézil.[5] He would take a concrete object and confront a series of powers with it to see how they would react, how they would approach it, how they would see and conceptualize it: a horse, for example, or a chariot, or a horse's bit. Athena and Poseidon were both powers who intervened with horses and chariots, but not in the same fashion. Athena acted through the bit, intervening in the domain of horses and chariots in her own particular way: with the horse, by means of the technical instrument that gave her control over the animal; with the chariot, through the assembly of the pieces of wood from which the vehicle was constructed. Poseidon, in contrast, manifested himself in the disturbing, impetuous, uncontrollable power of the horse itself, a creature that had sprung from the waters or a force born from the very Earth. Both were powers connected with the horse, but Athena was more equestrian, Poseidon closer to the animal itself.[6]

A concrete object or a part of the body, the foot, the head, the heart, or the phallus, could attract a whole group of gods around it. Let us consider the phallus, the male sexual organ, at once a fabricated object and a body-object that operated on an eminently day-to-day basis and was very much the center of a packed configuration of divine powers: in the first place Dionysus, on whose account there was a phallus parade; but also Aphrodite, directly involved with it through her birth: her admirable female body was formed from the seed or sperm that spurted forth from the member of Ouranos swiped off by Cronos at the instigation of Gaia, the All-Powerful One.[7] Alongside Aphrodite, and already closely associated with her in the ritual of marriage, was Hermes, very prone to huge erections when represented as a pillar. And just beyond him, Priapus and the god Pan. Priapus was the tiniest of the gods but was endowed with definitely the largest penis of all.[8] Pan was the billy goat in human form who was always falling upon his victims with his phallus at the ready, a god so violent that he could give erections to the entire male population of a city.[9]

Clearly then, in the Greek pantheon Dionysus did not possess a monopoly over the phallus. Some experts have even claimed that "originally" the phallus had nothing to do with Dionysus.[10] It is true that Dionysus is never represented figuratively with an erection, unlike the satyrs in his train. Nevertheless, Dionysus was the only god manifested by and through the penis, the figurative representation of which occupied a place of central importance in his cult and in the greatest of his festivals. Dionysus, who appeared in the form of a phallus and instituted a phallus procession in which the whole city took part, clearly has things to tell us about the penis, about how, as a god, he himself acted through and on the phallus, about his sexual strategies with regard to obstinately chaste Maenads, about the satyrs whose sexual energy was so exuberant, and also about the pleasure derived from sex in everyday life by both men and women.

First, here are some brief remarks about these "political" phallophoria, the phallus processions that the city organized for all its citizens, including its female members. The phallus was carried aloft in procession in broad daylight and in a highly official manner on the occasion of the Great Dionysia, in March–April,[11] that is to say, after the "Dionysia in the fields" of December, followed by the Lenaea in January–February, and the Anthesteria in February–March. Now it was the turn of a winter Dionysus on the brink of spring, with summer just hoving into sight. The Great Dionysia constituted an urban festival,[12] which attracted huge crowds of people, for it included the dithyrambic competitions, and the performances of tragedies went on for four whole days. In Athens, and in Delos too, the phallophoria occasioned extensive preparations. Allies of the Athenians, colonies such as Brea, in Thrace, were required to send a phallus for Dionysus, to mark the occasion of the Great Dionysia.[13] Just as at the Panathenaea, they were expected to offer up to Athena, the goddess who lived on the Acropolis, an ox and a panoply of arms. The Panathenaea and the Dionysia were festivals of equal importance, and a phallus was as welcome to Dionysus as a set of warrior equipment and the largest of sacrificial victims were to Athena.

The phallus had to be made. Carpenters would set to work with wood, glue, and nails. The accounts of Delos that have come down to us provide a list of all the components and what they cost, from 321 to 169 B.C. This was the phallus of Independence. It took the form of a bird whose head and neck were replaced by a penis. This phallus-bird would be painted and set on a chariot that needed to be balanced by the attachment of lead weights.[14] (In rural Dionysia, the phallus would stand on its own feet and would be smaller.) Once it was freshly painted and carefully mounted, the phallus-bird of Dionysus was ready to appear. On the appointed day it would be paraded before the whole city, flanked in particular by well-born girls acting as *canephoroi*, that is to say, carrying the sacrificial baskets.[15]

The phallus-bird in honor of Dionysus was an autonomous object. It was, of course, a penis, but it was equipped with wings and was not just the sexual member on a statue of a god. The difference was noted by Herodotus. Of course, the Egyptians were familiar with Dionysus; in fact, they were the first to know of him. They celebrated Osiris-Dionysus in a fashion similar to the Greeks, except that instead of parading the phallus, as the Greeks did, the Egyptian women would walk in procession holding little articulated statuettes that they moved with strings, making the virile member wave vigorously about, a penis that was quite as long as the whole of the rest of the statuette.[16] In Greek, a Priapus is what Herodotus would have called the disproportionately long sexual organ mounted on an Osiris-Dionysus. Just such a figure has been found in Lampsacus, although it dates from one century later.

The Epiphany of the Phallus

The invention of the "carrying of the phallus," the *phallophoria*, came in the wake of Dionysus's first appearance, which in Greek was called his *epidēmia* or "arrival in the country." Dionysus was frequently represented as a god who arrived suddenly, surfacing in an eruption, as when he demonstrated how to use wine in the land of Icarius or in the Athenian city of king Amphictyon. To be precise, in both the accounts known to us "parading the phallus" was introduced between Dionysus's epiphany at the side of Icarius (an unfortunate grower of vines who fell victim to pure, undiluted wine) and his arrival at the dining table of Amphictyon, who learned from Dionysus's own lips the rules to be followed when drinking wine and the exact proportions to use when mixing pure wine with water.[17] The first story runs as follows.[18] There was a little city called Eleutherae situated on the borders of Attica. A mediator by the name of Pegasus set out from here for Athens, carrying in his arms a "statue" of his god, for Pegasus was an ambassador and missionary of Dionysus. This was the very Dionysus who, later, each year, on the occasion of the Great Dionysia, was to be returned to a chapel-depot positioned at the side of the Eleutherae road, to be carried from there to the town and the theater by the ephebes engaged upon their military service. On Pegasus's first visit he was rudely received. The Athenians turned away from him, causing Dionysus to become violently enraged, with an anger as black as the shirt made from goatskin that he had been wearing when he first appeared as Melanaigis–a beardless god, wearing a belted black goatskin–to Pegasus's daughters.[19] In his anger, he struck down the impolite Athenians with a disease that afflicted the male sexual organ. There appeared to be no cure for the disease, no treatment to bring relief. The Delphic oracle, consulted in this emergency, made it known that a cure would only be forthcoming if the people of Attica "paraded" the god with all the honors due to his rank. The Athenians immediately set about "constructing" or "fashioning" phalluses, some privately, some publicly, paying homage to the god with objects that commemorated their suffering.

In this story, Dionysus is angered at not being honored by a cult, and chooses the male penis to convey what form his effigy to be honored should take. When he was at last duly recognized, in "homage" to the god the people of Attica set up phalluses in all likelihood imitated from the "effigy" (*agalma*) that Pegasus had brought with him from Eleutherae. Dionysus was thus a doubly strange god, for in the first place the people of Attica had not heard of him before, and secondly, the form that he took was that of a single erect penis with sovereign power. Statues consecrated by cults would often take the form of faithful reproductions of the epiphany that had first introduced them. For instance, when Dionysus appeared to the fishermen of Methymna as a wooden mask surfacing from the waves of the sea, he was indicating that this was the form in which he expected to receive a cult. The god liked to choose his own effigy.[20]

Was there really a statue of Dionysus in the form of a phallus? The inscriptions in Delos testify that there was, for the phallus-bird riveted and stuck together and duly painted for the day of the procession figures in the sanctuary accounts in two forms, now as an "effigy" (*agalma*) *for* Dionysus, now as an effigy (*agalma*) *of* Dionysus.[21] And we have long known that on these same engraved stones the word for "effigy" (*agalma*) alternates with "phallus."[22] The phallus *for* Dionysus, presented by the colonies and the beloved allies, was thus the phallus *of* Dionysus, or indeed was Dionysus himself, the organ of virility.

In the second version of the story,[23] Icarius, a peasant of Athens, receives the first vine cutting and generously tells everyone around about the new drink. The pure wine works wonders, but the drinkers then fall into such a deep stupor that their neighbors, arriving late for the banquet, believe them to be stone-dead. They accuse Icarius of killing them and strike him, mortally wounding him. Once again, Dionysus is enraged. This time the god appears in person, in the disturbing guise of a boy in the full flower of youth. Icarius's peasant neighbors are mad with desire, "desire to make love with him. And he himself even incites them to seduce and violate him." Then, suddenly, Dionysus disappears, making himself invisible. Icarius's neighbors, whose desires the lovely boy had just promised to satisfy, reach the peak of excitement, quite carried away. But once the handsome Dionysus has disappeared, "they remain in that state forever, possessed by an erotic urge that cannot be satisfied, on account of Dionysus's anger." They hurry to Delphi, and the oracle tells them to "make earthenware figurines. These they consecrate, to take their own places, and in this way halt the madness (*mania*) that possesses them." As in the first story, Dionysus is placated when he is offered phalluses, free-standing male sexual organs, not whole male bodies with erections.

Once again Dionysus struck at the male penis, subjecting it to an erotic impulse that nothing could calm. He unleashed a veritable spate of sexual madness in Icarius's neighborhood: the men, who alone were affected by his anger, were possessed by a desire arrested at the highest peak of excitement; they were sexually maddened. According to the Greek doctors, this was a well-known state: *pathologia sexualis*. It was classified under two headings: "priapism" and "satyriasis."[24] Satyriasis was when the sexual act took its course, with infinitely copious ejaculations, accompanied by enjoyment which, however, was so excessive that it led to mortal exhaustion. Priapism, in contrast, was characterized by the penis unstoppably increasing in size, but bringing no enjoyment. It became paralyzed, with no prospect of satisfaction, like a wooden rod: a penis of dry wood that was both painful and impotent.

The reference to satyrs and Priapus is particularly apposite in connection with the sexual madness dispensed by Dionysus, for he was certainly a god frequently surrounded by phalluses in a state of erection, those of his train of satyrs and asses, although he himself is never depicted with an erection or, *a fortiori*, with an excessively large phallus. Dionysus is not to be confused with the satyrs, with their pointed ears, their horse-tails, and their penises that are as long as those of their asses. In vase paintings satyrs are to be seen indulging themselves in every way, masturbating, copulating with animals, harassing women surprised as they sleep, or maenads who, however, defend themselves most successfully. On the sides of cups and drinking flasks, the satyrs are equipped with a whole set of sexual props, phallus-objects: phalluses in the form of switches, javelins, *thyrsoi*–all kinds of manipulated phallus-instruments that seem to be endowed with a life of their own, for they display an eye in the tip, the eye of desire and life, the eye of the animated force of the phallus.[25]

Priapus is not as close to Dionysus as the satyrs are. His distinctive appearance is well known[26]: he is an ugly little god, deformed, anthropomorphic, with no bestial features, a child with the head of an old man, afflicted with a monstrous sexual organ as long as the entire rest of his body and, what is more, not only useless but painful, too. In his short biography, Priapus more than once crosses Dionysus's path, but only to be further differentiated from him. He was born from the womb of Aphrodite, who in some versions of the story had been seduced by her own father, but who may have been making love with Adonis or even with Dionysus. Hera, as always full of hatred for Aphrodite, touched her pregnant body, promising that the child would be a perfect monster. Aphrodite withdrew to Lampsacus, on the shores of the Hellespont, and there gave birth to the little freak, whom she promptly rejected. But the ladies of Lampsacus had other ideas and eyes only for him and his sexual organ. The young Priapus "with his big tool" seemed quite prepared to satisfy their demands and declared himself ready to "engender citizens." The husbands protested, and Priapus was exiled. In tears, the ladies then addressed the gods, beseeching them to come to their aid. At this point a serious illness afflicted the penises of the citizens of Lampsacus. The oracle declared that it would persist until Priapus was recalled to his homeland, where, however, he was to be limited to the functions of a "god of gardens," albeit with his own temples and sacrifices. So Priapus was detailed to keep away thieves and the evil eye generally and to ensure for his vegetable patch the fecundity that he had earlier promised the population. The "great tool" with which he had been endowed by nature, aided by Hera, would never know a commensurate enjoyment or satisfaction. His sexual organ was frozen in the priapism that he had wanted to inflict upon the recalcitrant husbands of his female admirers. Regularly denied erotic fulfillment, impotent and sterile, Priapus found himself confined to the role of a hypochondriacal gardener, committed to tending his plot of vegetables and suffering from a shameful affliction that would forever make him uglier than ever.[27] Priapus would never be a rival for the joyful Phales or Phallus, who held himself "very erect" as he followed behind the girl who led the procession in the rural Dionysia.[28] No phallophoria for little Priapus, then! In fact, the distance between him and Dionysus unrelentingly increased. The sexual malady provoked by Priapus in Lampsacus was condemned to be a pseudo-priapism, whereas the phallic madness unleashed by Dionysus, far from being merely satyriasis for his entourage, hinted at the super-power of this god who could manifest himself through the phallus.

Beyond Eroticism:
The Heart and the Virile Member

As a god given to "arriving" and "making an entrance," Dionysus appeared in many, diverse forms. Never, however, in any of his sudden appearances, did he choose to inspire aphrodisiacal madness, erotic delirium, even though such forms of madness were certainly not unknown in the regions of Greece where Dionysus himself was apt to descend and drive the female population into a mad frenzy. In Argolis, the daughters of Proetus were afflicted with "debauchery": naked and crazy for love, they ran wild in the countryside. But the deity responsible for their madness was Hera, who was angered by the mockery to which the Proetids had subjected her.[29] Also in Argolis, Dionysus, for his part, turned women into Maenads, driving them out into the countryside, yelling the *euoi*, the Dionysiac cry, and running wild in the mountains. The girls of Eleutherae, who burst out laughing at the sight of Dionysus in his little black shirt, were also struck by "madness," but it was in no way erotic. Neither the Bacchae nor the Maenads are represented as experiencing a sexual madness, either in stories or in paintings. The Attic vase paintings depict them as chaste and modest, cultivating "moderation," the wisdom upon which they pride themselves in Euripides' *Bacchae*. Similarly, a Maenad was sober, drunk with Dionysus himself but not with his wine. In that respect, they were no different from the women depicted on Dionysiac vases, pouring out wine, or drawing it from a bowl, demonstrating how to handle the divine beverage, close to a Dionysus-pillar dressed up in a mask and a robe.[30] The Meanads might fall into a trance before an uplifted phallus *of* or *for* Dionysus, but never (not in the documentation so far available, anyway) do they become "Bacchic," possessed by Dionysus through sexuality, either their own or his. Eroticism was not a means of escaping from oneself in Greece, nor was it the medium of Dionysiac possession.

Dionysus in the form of a truncated bust on a pillar established his presence through his gaze, the face that he turned toward the spectators or the Maenads dancing round him.[31] He did not display a sexual organ, his robe did not protrude over a thrusting penis. On the other hand, the quadrangular Hermes-pillar (commonly known as a *hermēs*), the form bestowed upon this god by the Pisistratids in Athens, did, for his part, display an honest phallus, forthrightly erect. But its size was in proportion to the human body, never anything like the endlessly long phallus of the bald Priapus. The latter was, for obvious reasons, never invited to marriage ceremonies, whereas Hermes would invariably be there, anxious to help, having brought Aphrodite along with him in his chariot. He was the god who ushered the bride into her husband's house, leading her over the threshold and into the nuptial chamber. Hermes the messenger would then prompt the young couple with suitable words of love, words of seduction; furthermore, as the inventor of fire produced by rubbing two sticks together, he was also active in promoting sexual union between the woman and man who now lived together, close to the same hearth, within the space that he, Hermes, shared with two other deities, Hestia and Aphrodite.

There are two vases that display figurative representations of the phallus as a cult-object. One is a small *kotylē* (bowl) in Munich,[32] on which a long phallus, with an open eye on its tip, stands erect by a table for offerings, cheerfully overtopping it by two-thirds of its height. The other is a black-figured *lekythos* in the National Museum of Athens.[33] It shows two satyrs performing a dance around a phallus in the process of becoming ever more erect, amid a décor of vines festooned with bunches of grapes. The epiphany of the phallus, the phallus-god, is celebrated by a rhythmic dance executed by two of Dionysus's companions. Two other satyrs are also present, one equipped with a large seven-stringed lyre, the other saluting the erection of the phallus-god with an erection of his own.

As we are warned at train crossings, one train may obscure another from our sight. The same goes for phalluses. The meaning of the phallus *of* or *for* Dionysus should thus be sought first in the local discourse, the ancient Greek semantics of the phallus when it appears in specifically Dionysiac configurations, and particularly in the physiology typically displayed by the "son of Semele," as Dionysus liked to introduce himself. His appearances, or epiphanies, show that he affected the spurting or leaping forth mode.[34] In the land of Elis, Dionysus presided over the gushing forth of pure wine in a festival consecrated to him, in which Sixteen Priestesses invoked him in the guise of a "leaping" bull. The festival was known as the "Seething" (Thuia) because, during it, sealed bowls suddenly filled up with seething, frothing wine. Like a liquid fire, the new wine spurted forth in the jars. But this same god of pure wine also reigned over blood, in particular the boiling, bubbling blood that coursed through the body of a Maenad. Ever since Homer, a Maenad had been a woman "with a palpitating heart," a woman driven out of her mind, far from the town, up in the mountains. A Maenad seized and possessed by Dionysus leaped wildly about, carried away by an inner boiling that originated in the heart, the organ full of blood, the part of a feminine body entirely possessed by agitated, pulsing blood. Maenads were known as Thuiades, literally "Seething Ones."

In the biological tradition to which the physiological model of Dionysism belongs, it is the heart[35] that inaugurates life; it is the first part to be born in any living creature, and it is also the last to die when life withdraws from the body. The Orphic theology, that of the disciples of Orpheus, recounts how Dionysus, as a child-god slaughtered by the Titans, escaped complete destruction thanks to his heart, the only part of his body that was not devoured and from which the god was then reborn, thereby proving that Dionysus recognized himself to be particularly present in the organ of the blood, boiling, pulsating blood. As Aristotle stressed in the *De motu animalium*, the heart has a life of its own: it is a separate living thing, with its own spontaneous movements and an autochthonous vitality.[36] But it is not the only part of the body to be endowed with an autonomous life. The phallus is, likewise. It is another living part that, like the heart, possesses a "vital humor." Its autochthony is clearly manifested by the power of the sperm that spurts forth from it like some kind of animal (Aristotle's description).[37] The phallus signifies "the power of generation," as Iamblichus observed in the fourth century A.D., in his work entitled *On the Mysteries*, in which he produces an interpretation of the custom of setting up phalluses in festivals devoted to Dionysus, in particular the Dionysia of March-April.[38] This is the time when the earth is filling with sap, juices, and humors, the time for celebrating springtime, when the Dionysus-phallus is aroused in the presence of leaping satyrs.

The phallus and the heart both constitute embodiments of the power of Dionysus, just as pure, bubbling wine does. Let the feminists not be dejected, however: Dionysus, who loves them and gives such a fine role to the Maenad (whereas he always tends to bestialize the masculine body), never did favor the male sexual organs over the female. Dionysus cannot be confused with a vulgar phallocrat, for the phallus, which is a manifestation of the "vital power" of nature, does not belong to any male body. It transcends the body, is beyond human sexuality, just as the power of pure wine exceeds the limits of the banquet and the *krater* that is set down amid the drinkers and guests. The day of the phallus is the day when the omnipotence of Dionysus is on show, presenting the entire city with the spectacle of the vital force that irrigates nature–plants, trees, and all living beings, whatever their sex and their individual relationships. The task of organizing those is something that Dionysus leaves to others.[39]

Reference Matter

Notes

Introduction

1. Henri Lefebvre, *Everyday Life in the Modern World*, trans. Sacha Rabinovitch (London, 1971) (following a number of works on the same subject, beginning in 1946). The "a la Hachette" quotation is from pp. 60-61.

2. As Henri Lefebvre notes, after every revolutionary failure, everydayness rushes back (p. 149).

3. Jean Starobinski, "L'Ordre du jour," *Le Temps de la réflexion* 4 (1983): 101-25; see also "Espace du jour, espace du bonheur," in *Studi filosofici*, vol. 1 (Naples, 1978); "Les Journées plurielles de Ronsard," in *Mélanges J.-P. Vernant* (Paris). Many other analyses also exist.

4. See Michel Foucault, "L'Ecriture de soi," in *Corps écrit*, vol. 5: *L'Autoportrait* (Paris, 1983).

5. Through self-examination, covering the past day, but also through setting oneself a specific program each morning; see Iamblichus *Life of Pythagoras* 256.

6. Seneca *Letters to Lucilius* 83.

7. See, in general, S. Accame, "La concezione del tempo nell'età omerica ed arcaica" (1962), reprinted in *Gli albori della critica*[2] (Naples, n.d.).

8. Ibid., 312.

9. *Odyssey* 18.136-37.

10. *Odyssey* 21.85: only the uncouth are constantly concerned with *ephemeria*.

11. *Ephemeral*: depending on the day; marked by daily changes. See H. Fraenkel, "Man's 'Ephemeros': Nature According to Pindar and Others," in *Transactions and Proceedings of the American Philological Association* 77 (1946).

12. See E. Degani, *Aiōn da Omero ad Aristotele* (Padua, 1961).

13. Hesiod frag. 1.6–8 Merkelbach and West.

14. *Iliad* 21.464–66.

15. Pindar *Nemean Odes* 6.1–10.

16. As is declared by the Muses who attend Apollo (*Homeric Hymn to Apollo*, 186 ff.), who are also responsible for the scornful expression used in the *Iliad* 21.462–66.

17. Herodotus 1.131.

18. The following view of Olympian society is presented by Giulia Sissa in *Le Grand Atlas des religions* (Paris, 1988).

Chapter 1

1. Public readings of the Homeric poems seem to have been instituted in Athens in the sixth century by the tyrant Hipparchus, the son of Pisistratus (Ps. Plato, *Hipparchus, Or the Covetous Man*, 228b).

2. *Iliad* 2.13–15.

3. *Iliad* 1.2.

4. *Iliad* 1.8 (italics added).

5. *Iliad* 1.44–45. It should straightaway be pointed out that, in the present work, we shall not be reopening the huge question of the liberty of human beings with respect to the gods, that is to say, Greek ethics more or less guaranteed by the principles of divine justice. In short, we shall not be entering into the debate in which A. W. H. Adkins (see "Homeric Gods and the Values of Homeric Society," *Journal of Hellenic Studies* 92 [1972]: 10 ff.) stands in opposition to Hugh Lloyd-Jones (see *The Justice of Zeus* [Berkeley, 1971]), in which the former refutes what the latter suggests, namely, that Homeric society was governed by moral values. Another perspective that we have also eschewed, one adopted by J. Strauss Clay (in *The Wrath of Athena: Gods and Men in the Odyssey* [Princeton: Princeton University Press, 1983]), is that of an examination of the interventions of particular deities into the lives of particular heroes. An approach with which we do feel an affinity is that of Jasper Griffin (see "The Divine Audience and the Religion in the *Iliad*," *Classical Quarterly* 28 [1978]: 1–22), who sets out to reread the *Iliad* from the point of view of the gods. We are convinced that, as Griffin most pertinently remarks, "Only in the light of the nature and perspective of the gods is human life intelligible . . . ; the conception of life and

death which characterizes the *Iliad* is the poetic heart of the poem and of its greatness" (p. 6).

6. Olympus is not an empty space. It has physical attributes: It is said to be steep (*Iliad* 5.367, 868), with many precipices (*Iliad* 1.499, 754), rising to several peaks of unequal height (*Iliad* 5.753). Sometimes it is snow-covered (*Iliad* 1.420), despite the idea that its climate is invariably mild, which is expressed in the *Odyssey* (6.41–46). Surrounded by walls (*Iliad* 8.435) and with gates that open on to the outside world (*Iliad* 8.11), the space inhabited by the gods should be imagined as a cluster of separate dwellings. Zeus's palace is where the gods gather for assemblies and feasts, and the only function of the personal houses of each of the other gods appears to be to provide them with somewhere to sleep (*Iliad* 8.607). Olympus is served by a whole team of staff: a doctor, Peon (*Iliad* 8.899); a maid of all work, Hebe, who works sometimes as a chambermaid (*Iliad* 8.905), sometimes as a groom (*Iliad* 5.722); a herald, Iris, who is regularly dispatched on missions to human beings; doorkeepers, the Seasons (*Hōrai*), "to whom are entrusted great heaven and Olympos, whether to throw open the thick cloud or shut it to" (*Iliad* 8.393–95).

7. The epicurean aspects of the life of the gods will be the subject of Chapter 5, "Savoring the Sweetness of Life."

8. These are questions that must be asked by any historian interested in material history, as is pointed out by Fernand Braudel in *La Dynamique du capitalisme* (Paris, 1985), 17.

9. [Apollodorus] *Library* 2.4–5.

10. *Iliad* 19.95–133.

11. Hesiod *Theogony* 39–41.

12. On the sometimes beneficial effects of oblivion, see Nicole Loraux, "L'oubli dans la cité," *Le Temps de la réflexion* 1 (1980): 213–41.

13. Aristotle *Metaphysics* 12.1072b.

14. Aristotle *Metaphysics* 1704b.

15. Aristotle *Metaphysics* 1704b.

16. The parallel between Hesiod and Aristotle could be extended. For the author of the *Theogony*, the well-being dispensed by the Muses to humans is of the same nature as that enjoyed by the gods, except that in the case of human beings its duration is intermittent and ephemeral. Similarly, the author of the *Nicomachean Ethics* writes: "The whole of the life of the gods is blessed, and that of man is so in so far as it contains some likeness to the divine activity" (10.8). Aristotle goes on to explain his thinking in *Metaphysics* 12.1072b: "Its [the prime mover's] life is like the best which we temporarily enjoy. It must

NOTES TO CHAPTER I

be in that state always (which for us is impossible), since its actuality is also pleasure." 17. Aristotle *Metaphysics* 1000a. Hesiod and the other mythologists "make the first principles Gods or generated from Gods, and say that whatever did not taste of the nectar and ambrosia became mortal. . . . For if it is for pleasure that the gods partake of them, the nectar and ambrosia are in no sense causes of their existence; but if it is to support life, how can the Gods who require nourishment be eternal?"

18. Hesiod *Theogony* 793–804: "Whoever of the deathless gods that hold the snowy peaks of Olympus pours a libation of her [the Styx's] water and is forsworn, lies breathless until a full year is completed, and never comes near to taste ambrosia and nectar but lies spiritless and voiceless on a strewn bed; and a heavy trance overshadows him. But when he has spent a long year in his sickness, another penance and an harder follows after the first. For nine years he is cut off from the eternal gods and never joins their councils or their feasts, nine full years."

19. Braudel, *La Dynamique du capitalisme* (quotes are from pp. 13, 14, and 13, respectively).

20. Roland Barthes, *Mythologies* [1957], trans. Annette Lavers (London, 1972).

21. Roland Barthes, *The Pleasure of the Text*, trans. by Richard Miller (New York, 1975), 53.

22. Ibid.

23. Braudel, *La Dynamique du capitalisme*, 13.

24. Michel de Certeau, *L'Invention du quotidien*, vol. 1: *Les Arts de faire* (Paris, 1980).

25. Paul Ricoeur, *Time and Narrative*, vol. 3, trans. Kathleen Blamey and David Pellaner (Chicago, 1988). "Everydayness is not confined to producing figures of fallenness; it functions as a reminder of the horizon . . . of the world, which the subjectivism of the philosophies of life– and also (we might add) the intimist tendency in Heidegger himself, seen in all his analyses centered around Being-towards-death–threatens to conceal from our sight" (295 n. 38).

26. *Iliad* 5.330–430.

27. Umberto Eco, *Apostille au nom de la rose* (Paris, 1988), 45–46. Salgarism, that is to say, writing like Salgari, the author of adventure stories for children, consists in making the most of a moment in the story, or a circumstance in the plot, in order to introduce a number of didactic comments: "Salgari's characters are in a forest, fleeing from enemies, when they trip over the root of a baobab tree, at which point the narrator suspends the action to give us a botany lesson on baobabs" (p. 46). The author of *The Name of the Rose* explains how he managed

to avoid such a procedure, which we, on the contrary, shall adopt, since it is well suited to the art of writing commentaries.

28. See Jean Pépin, *Idées grecques sur l'homme et sur Dieu* (Paris, 1971), 3.

Chapter 2

1. *Iliad* 8.143-44.

2. *Iliad* 8.201-11. One day Hera suggests to Poseidon that they should form a coalition of all the Olympians against Zeus, who has forbidden them to take part in the Trojan War. Zeus would thus be isolated and have to put up with Poseidon's resentment. Poseidon refuses, saying that Zeus is much too strong for them. *Iliad* 21.192 ff.: Zeus also shows that he is stronger than all the river-gods.

3. *Iliad* 20.367-68.   4. *Iliad* 17.446-47.

5. *Iliad* 24.525-26.   6. *Iliad* 1.588, 19.8.

7. *Iliad* 5.331-51.

8. This is a remarkable detail; it is not the consumption of meat that, in mortals, produces blood.

9. *Iliad* 5.339-42. On this point, see J. Jouanna and P. Demont, "Le Sens d'*ikhōr* chez Homère et Eschyle en relation avec les emplois du mot dans la collection hippocratique," *Revue des études anciennes* 83 (1981): 335-54; B. Zanini Quirini, "*Ichōr*, il sangue degli dei," *Orpheus* 4, vol. 2 (1983): 355-63; Nicole Loraux, "Le Corps vulnérable d'Arès," *Le Temps de la réflexion* 7 (1986): 335-54.

10. *Iliad* 6.211 and 19.105 (quotation; italics added).

11. *Iliad* 19.102.   12. *Iliad* 16.789-805.

13. *Iliad* 13.68-71.   14. *Iliad* 18.321, *Odyssey* 19.436.

15. *Iliad* 17.447.   16. *Iliad* 5.440-42.

17. *Iliad* 3.386-98.   18. *Iliad* 14.159-60.

19. *Iliad* 14.170-77.   20. *Odyssey* 6.220-24.

21. *Iliad* 1.314.   22. *Odyssey* 6.96, 220.

23. *Iliad* 14.178-86.   24. *Iliad* 14.187-88.

25. *Iliad* 14.214-17.

26. *Homeric Hymn to Aphrodite*, 55-56.

27. *Homeric Hymn to Aphrodite*, 91.

28. *Homeric Hymn to Aphrodite*, 85-91.

29. *Homeric Hymn to Aphrodite*, 90.

30. *Homeric Hymn to Aphrodite*, 34-39. On this text as a whole, see the excellent study by A. T. L. Bergren, "The Homeric Hymn to Aphrodite: Tradition and Rhetoric, Praise and Blame," *Metis* (1989).

31. A god's power sometimes rebounds against him- or herself, as has been noted in the case of Ares. This most violent of the Olympians

seems particularly exposed to the effects of war, to wounding, and even to the danger of death. See Loraux, "Le Corps vulnérable d'Arès."

32. *Iliad* 14.293-94.

33. *Iliad* 14.314-28. Sweet desire (*glukus himeros*) literally *holds* (*aireō*) Zeus, just as it *holds* (*aireō*) Anchises.

34. *Iliad* 3.441-46.

35. *Odyssey* 5.213.

36. *Odyssey* 5.215-20.

37. Here are some examples, chosen for their narrative importance. *Diaphragm* (*phrēn*): Hera asks Zeus to explain his plans to her: "I have not questioned you or inquired too closely in the past, but you are quite free to make whatever plans you wish. This time, though, I have a terrible fear in my mind [diaphragm] (*phrēn*) that you have been won over by silver-footed Thetis, the daughter of the old man of the sea" (*Iliad* 1.551-56).

Breast (*stēthos*): Poseidon asks Zeus for details of his plans and Zeus replies: "You have realized *the purpose in my mind* [breast] (*en stēthesi boulē*), Earthshaker, the reason why I called you together–I do care for them even as they die. But now I shall stay here, sitting in a fold of Olympos, where I can look on and delight my *heart* (*phrēn*). But the rest of you go down now to join the Trojans and the Achaians and give help to either side, as each of you is minded (*nous*) (*Iliad* 20.20-25, italics added).

Heart (*kēr*): Hera, crossed by Zeus, withdraws into silence, forcing her *heart* (*philon kēr*) (*Iliad* 1.569, italics added). Hermes describes Hector as a man dear to the *heart* (*kēr*) of the gods (*Iliad* 24.423, italics added).

38. Here is another collection of examples. *Mēnis* (rancor, or wrath, anger) is the very first word of the *Iliad*; it is as if the anger of Achilles coincided with the subject of the poem. But it is the anger, *mēnis*, of another, Apollo, the angry god (1.9) descending from Olympus, "angered at heart" (*chōomenos kēr*) (1.44), that determines the first event that is recounted: the rain of murderous arrows that ravages the Greek camp (1.75). Far from being a specific quality of particular Olympians, anger affects any god offended by being overlooked by human beings (5.178). *Menos*, fury, is the attribute of Ares (18.264). *Chōomenos*, angered, is what Zeus is when Hera fools him by delaying the birth of Heracles: "A sharp pain struck into Zeus's deep heart [diaphragm]. He immediately seized the goddess Ate in his *heart's fury* (*chōomenos phresi*), catching her by the shining hair on her head" (italics added). *Ochthein*, being angry, affects all the gods gathered in assembly (1.570).

39. *Iliad* 1.35. Irritation is a particular characteristic of sovereign

and paternal gods. This was to pose a daunting problem for the Christian theologians: How could God's anger be reconciled with his perfection? Lactantius did not hesitate to resume the attacks against the ideas of the Epicureans (a god must remain impassive) in order to justify the rages of the Father (*The Anger of God*).

40. Zeus's will governs the entire sequence of events that involve the gods and men. As for his intelligence (*nous*), see *Iliad* 20.25.

41. *Iliad* 7.25.   42. *Iliad* 8.6.

43. *Iliad* 20.32.   44. *Iliad* 2.3–5.

45. *Iliad* 2.814, 14.291, 20.74; *Odyssey* 10.305, 12.61.

46. *Homeric Hymn to Aphrodite* 113-16.

Chapter 3

1. *Odyssey* 6.42–46 (italics added).

2. *Iliad* 11.1-2.

3. *Iliad* 14.259.

4. *Iliad* 1.605-11.

5. An evening of feasting in Odysseus's palace, in Ithaca, ends with dancing and singing as the evening shadows lengthen. Then, "they each went home to sleep." The expression is identical to that used at *Iliad* 1.606, describing the gods going home to bed.

6. *Odyssey* 3.1-3.   7. *Iliad* 18.239-42.

8. *Iliad* 16.233 ff.   9. *Iliad* 19.98-100.

10. Penelope has rushed into the arms of Odysseus, whom she has at last recognized. "Rosy-fingered Dawn would have found them still weeping, had not Athene of the flashing eyes had other ideas. She held the night lingering at the western horizon and in the East at Ocean's Stream she kept golden-throned Dawn waiting and would not let her yoke the nimble steeds who bring us light" (*Odyssey* 23.241-45). Measurable time can be manipulated when, as here, it is a matter of a goddess's concern and of desire. Athena waits until the pair of lovers has enjoyed the delights of love, finished recounting their respective trials and tribulations, and had some sleep. Only then does she rouse Dawn and let her complete her daily journey (344-48).

11. *Iliad* 14.243-48.

12. *Iliad* 14.260-61.

13. Ovid *Metamorphoses* 13.581-82.

14. Ovid *Metamorphoses* 591-92. In the dramatic cosmology of the *Iliad*, Sun, plunging with his chariot into Ocean, attracts black Night. See Alain Ballabriga, *Le Soleil et le Tartare* (Paris, 1987).

15. Hesiod *Theogony* 123-24: "From Chaos came forth Erebus and black Night; but of Night were born Aether and Day, whom she con-

ceived and bare from union in love with Erebus." Day does not belong to the same lineage as the powers responsible for creating the duration of each day by moving as they do around the sky. Sun, Moon, and Dawn are all offspring of the marriage of Thaea and Hyperion. Dawn, when united with Astraeus, produced the Winds, the Stars, and the Morning Star (371-74). Day was thus one of the children of Night, along with everything which, for Hesiod, constituted the unhappy fate of the mortals. The idea that Day was engendered by Night, as the grandson of the original Chaos, is well in keeping with the gloomy image that Hesiod presents of daily time in his *Works and Days*.

16. Here are a few examples: "protect you from the day of slavery" (*Iliad* 6.463); "takes away the day of your freedom" (6.455). A warrior fights to "ward off the implacable day" (8.484). But "the fated day" comes anyway (*Odyssey* 10.175).

17. *Iliad* 8.71-72.

18. Dispelling all confusion between the functioning of the world and the daily life of the gods, Epicurus observes: "We are bound to believe that in the sky revolutions, solstices, eclipses, risings and settings, and the like, take place without the ministration or command, either now or in the future, of any being who at the same time enjoys perfect bliss along with immortality. *For troubles and anxieties and feelings of anger and partiality do not accord with bliss*, but always imply weakness and fear and dependence upon one's neighbors. Nor again, must we hold that things which are no more than globular masses of fire, being at the same time endowed with bliss, assume these motions at will" (Epicurus *Letter to Herodotus* 76, italics added). Happiness and physical or psychological movement are incompatible. Aristotle similarly declares: "God enjoys a single, simple pleasure perpetually. For there is not only an activity of motion, but also an activity of immobility, and *there is essentially a truer pleasure in rest than in motion*" (*Nicomachean Ethics* 7.14, italics added).

19. *Every day*: ēmata panta. Some texts, such as the one cited at the beginning of this chapter (*Odyssey* 6.42-46) suggest that the gods live plunged in constant bliss, as Pindar and Hesiod imagined them, before philosophy. The everydayness of the Olympians would thus consist solely of the experience of duration: homeostasis in the identical. However, a passage in the *Iliad* magnificently illustrates the impossible permanence, in the narrative, of that "always" saturated with happiness, showing that the expression "ēmata panta" is close to ēmati tōi, "on that day," and that the gods experience time as both continuous and discontinuous. When Hera wants to put Zeus to sleep, she promises Sleep that she will be grateful to him "always." But Sleep, distrustful of that

over-smooth "always," reminds the goddess of one particular date, "the day when" he was sorely punished for having put Zeus to sleep (14.235-276).

20. Ovid *Metamorphoses* 1.168-71.

21. The setting would certainly be sumptuous, but hardly more luxurious than the palace of a human being, for example, that of Menelaus in Sparta: "The lofty hall of illustrious Menelaus was lit by something of the sun's or the moon's splendor." The passing guests, Telemachus and Pisistratus, are dazzled by it. Telemachus whispers to his companion, "Look round this echoing hall, son of Nestor, friend of my heart. The whole place gleams with bronze and gold, amber and silver and ivory. . . . The court of Zeus on Olympos must be like this inside" (*Odyssey* 4.71-74). Menelaus, overhearing their conversation, replies that Zeus has no rivals on earth. But all the same, apart from the degree of splendor, the appearance of Olympus has to be inferred by analogy with that of the palaces of human beings.

22. For the gods described as *blessed*, see *Iliad* 1.339, 406, 599; 4.127; 5.340, 819; 6.141; 7.550; 14.72, 143; 15.38, 54; 24.23, 99, 377, 422. Frequently, the attribute appears as a noun: the *makares* are *the* blessed, *par excellence*.

23. *Odyssey* 6.46.   24. *Iliad* 4.28-29.
25. *Iliad* 4.56.   26. *Iliad* 18.372.
27. *Iliad* 24.525-26.   28. *Iliad* 18.53.
29. *Iliad* 24.104.   30. *Iliad* 18.7.
31. *Iliad* 21.123.

32. That, at least, is how Epicurus criticizes the traditional representation of the gods. See *Letter to Menoeceus* 123.

33. Pierre Vidal-Naquet, "The Time of the Gods and the Time of Men," in *The Black Hunter*, trans. Andrew Szegedy-Maszak (Baltimore, 1986) (quotation is on p. 41).

34. *Iliad* 1.208-9 (italics added).

35. Piero Pucci, *Odysseus Polytropos: Intertextual Readings in the "Odyssey" and the "Iliad"* (Ithaca, 1987).

36. *Iliad* 1.56.

37. *Iliad* 2.27.

38. *Iliad* 24.174.

39. That is the opinion, stated in all seriousness, of F. Codino, *Introduzione a Omero* (Turin, 1965), 168.

40. *Iliad* 5.899.

41. *Iliad* 5.885-86. On this point, see Nicole Loraux, "Le Corps vulnérable d'Arès," *Le Temps de la réflexion* 7 (1985): 335-54.

42. *Iliad* 5.857.   43. *Iliad* 5.860-61.

44. *Iliad* 5.872-74.
45. *Iliad* 5.885-87.
46. *Iliad* 5.382-400.
47. *Iliad* 8.140-41.
48. *Iliad* 21.379-80.
49. *Iliad* 21.462-67.
50. *Iliad* 5.31-34.
51. *Iliad* 5.856-57.

Chapter 4

1. Euripides *Helen* 1639-42.
2. *Iliad* 3.156-58.
3. *Iliad* 3.164-65.
4. As is explicitly declared by Plutarch (*On the Pythian Oracles* 22).
5. *Iliad* 1.54.
6. *Iliad* 1.55.
7. *Iliad* 1.93-129.
8. *Iliad* 1.182-84.
9. This account is also part of the antecedents to the Trojan War and does not appear in the *Iliad*.
10. *Odyssey* 12.348-51.
11. *Odyssey* 12.385-88.
12. *Odyssey* 21.257-68.
13. Euripides *Iphigenia in Aulis* 24-25.
14. Euripides *Iphigenia in Tauris* 17-24.
15. "The other gods had their sacrifices to feast on, and it was only to the daughter of great Zeus that he made no offering. Either he forgot or he ignored her—but it was a great blindness in his heart" (*Iliad* 9.530-50).
16. We will examine this story in more depth in Part II: The Gods at the Service of the City. On the lack of recognition to which Dionysus is frequently exposed, see Marcel Detienne, *Dionysos at Large*, trans. Arthur Goldhammer (Cambridge, Mass.: Harvard University Press, 1989).
17. *Homeric Hymn to Demeter*.
18. Ovid *Metamorphoses* 9.322.
19. Ovid *Metamorphoses* 6.5 ff.
20. *Iliad* 24.608-9.
21. *Iliad* 24.607.
22. *Odyssey* 11.576-81.
23. Pindar *Pythian Odes* 2.
24. *Odyssey* 11.582-92.
25. Pindar *Olympian Odes* 1.
26. *Odyssey* 11.593-600.

Chapter 5

1. Xenophon *Symposium*; Plato *Symposium*; Plutarch *Banquet of the Seven Sages* and *Table Talk*; Athenaeus *Deipnosophistai*.
2. *Iliad* 23.46.
3. *Iliad* 19.161-66.

4. On the eating patterns of Homeric mortals, see Athenaeus *Deipnosophistai* 1.19.

5. *Odyssey* 15.371-73.

7. *Iliad* 1.458-61.

9. *Iliad* 1.464-66.

11. *Iliad* 1.474.

6. *Iliad* 1.451-52.

8. *Iliad* 1.462.

10. *Iliad* 1.472-74.

12. The great sacrifices in the *Iliad* are addressed to one or several deities. See 1.450 (the great sacrifice to appease Apollo); 3.103-9 (lambs sacrificed for Earth, Sun, and Zeus before concluding a pact); 2.400-401 (before engaging in battle, the Greeks each sacrifice to a different god); 6.311 (the Trojan women promise Athena a heifer if she will break the spear of one of their enemies); 7.314-18 (Agamemnon sacrifices an ox to Zeus); 10.571 (a sacrifice is offered to Athena after two scouts make a dangerous expedition to the enemy camp). The very idea of sacrifice, considered from the point of view of the gods, corresponds to the satisfaction of a need. The rite is perfect when the god to whom it is addressed reckons that his altar lacks for nothing (24.66-70). At the same time, from the point of view of the sacrificers, the banquet associated with the offerings is perceived as an occasion when "no man's desire [heart] went without an equal share in the feast" (*Iliad* 1.468). The two words altar (*bōmos*) and heart (*thumos*) are interchangeable in that statement.

13. *Odyssey* 14.418-38. In this case, even grammatically, the receiver of the offering is the host, who is indicated in the dative.

14. Porphyry *Treatise on Abstinence*.

15. *Iliad* 19.264-65.

17. *Iliad* 7.465-75.

19. *Iliad* 2.400. See 3.270.

21. *Odyssey* 3.331-36.

23. *Odyssey* 3.430-36.

16. *Iliad* 24.621-28

18. Hesiod *Theogony* 535-41.

20. *Iliad* 6.311.

22. *Odyssey* 3.377-78.

24. *Commentary on the Iliad* 1.460.

25. Porphyry *Treatise on Abstinence* 2.7.3.

26. Porphyry *Treatise on Abstinence* 2.10.2.

27. Porphyry *Treatise on Abstinence* 2.42.3.

28. Origen *Contra Celsus* 8.60.6.

29. *Odyssey* 12.29.

30. *Iliad* 1.468.

31. *Iliad* 1.601-2.

32. *Homeric Hymn to Apollo* 1.120-34.

33. *Homeric Hymn to Hermes* 1.247-51.

34. *Homeric Hymn to Demeter* 1.233-39.

35. Pindar *Pythian Odes* 9.108-11.

36. *Iliad* 19.347-54.
37. *Iliad* 19.30-33.
38. *Iliad* 1.601.
39. *Homeric Hymn to Apollo* 10.
40. *Iliad* 15.84-88.
41. Plato *Republic* 2.363c-d.
42. See Giulia Sissa, *Le Corps virginal* (Paris, 1987).
43. Plato *Laws* 900b.
44. Aristotle *Metaphysics* 1074b.
45. Aristotle *Metaphysics* 1074b.
46. Aristotle *Nicomachean Ethics* 10.8.7.
47. Seneca *Letters to Lucilius* 53.11.
48. *Iliad* 1.575-79.
49. Hesiod *Works and Days* 109-19.
50. Plutarch *Table Talk* 9.14. The word "sympotic" refers to the symposium, the moment when the participants drink together.
51. *Palatine Anthology* 9.504.
52. *Homeric Hymn to Apollo* 186.
53. *Homeric Hymn to Hermes* 166.
54. Aristophanes *Birds* 186.
55. Aristophanes *Birds* 1515-24.
56. Aristophanes *Birds* 723-36.
57. Aristophanes *Birds* 752-53.
58. Lucian *Zeus the Tragedian* 13.
59. Lucian *Zeus the Tragedian* 22.
60. Lucian *Zeus the Tragedian* 21.
61. Lucian *The Double Indictment, or Trial by Jury* 1-3.

Chapter 6

1. *Iliad* 1.202-5.
2. *Iliad* 1.207-14.
3. *Iliad* 1.216-18.
4. *Iliad* 1.81-83.
5. *Iliad* 1.177.
6. *Iliad* 1.334-44.
7. *Iliad* 2.16.
8. *Iliad* 2.279.
9. *Iliad* 1.55 (italics added).
10. *Iliad* 8.335.
11. *Iliad* 10.482.
12. *Iliad* 11.544.
13. *Iliad* 13.43.
14. *Iliad* 13.72.
15. *Iliad* 14.135.
16. Cf. *Iliad* 1.206-14.
17. *Iliad* 2.375-78.
18. *Iliad* 3.65-66.
19. *Iliad* 9.377.
20. *Iliad* 9.254-58.
21. *Iliad* 9.341-43.
22. *Iliad* 1.357-62.
23. Plato *Republic* 3.
24. *Iliad* 19.90-131.
25. *Iliad* 1.386.
26. *Iliad* 1.387.

Chapter 7

1. *Iliad* 1.493-503.
2. *Iliad* 1.495.
3. *Iliad* 2.333-35.
4. *Iliad* 1.499; cf. 5.753-54.
5. *Iliad* 8.5-9.
6. *Iliad* 8.10-17.

7. *Iliad* 8.41-53.

9. *Iliad* 5.890-93.

11. *Iliad* 13.298-303.

13. *Iliad* 11.72-77.

8. *Iliad* 5.715-16.

10. *Iliad* 1.176-77.

12. *Iliad* 5.830-34, 5.455.

14. Zeus has promised the Greeks that they will avenge Menelaus by capturing Troy, but he loves the Trojans because their sacrifices are so generous.

15. *Iliad* 8.54.

17. *Iliad* 12.67-68.

19. *Iliad* 1.561.

21. *Iliad* 2.14-15.

23. *Iliad* 9.37-38.

16. *Iliad* 11.80.

18. *Iliad* 8.140-43.

20. *Iliad* 1.601-4.

22. *Iliad* 2.38.

24. *Iliad* 2.101-9.

25. Clement of Alexander *Protreptica* 2.37.1.

26. *Iliad* 2.110-18.

28. *Iliad* 12.164.

27. *Iliad* 9.17-25.

29. Plato *Republic* 2.21.

30. *Iliad* 2.110-14 (italics added).

31. *Iliad* 9.16-21.

33. *Iliad* 2.157-65.

35. *Iliad* 2.413-14.

37. *Iliad* 2.480-83.

39. *Iliad* 13.153-61.

41. *Iliad* 14.342-45.

43. Lucian *Zeus Rants* 24.

45. *Iliad* 4.60.

47. *Iliad* 18.364.

49. *Iliad* 24.65-70.

32. *Iliad* 2.155.

34. *Iliad* 15.60-71.

36. *Iliad* 2.478-79.

38. *Iliad* 15.41-44.

40. *Iliad* 15.53-54.

42. *Iliad* 15.93-103.

44. *Iliad* 15.185-93.

46. *Iliad* 8.358-60.

48. *Iliad* 24.56-61.

50. *Iliad* 15.204-17.

Chapter 8

The material in this chapter was first published in *L'Ecrit du temps*, 1988.

1. Cicero *On the Nature of the Gods* 1.7.

2. See the comparative study by R. Pettazzoni, *L'Essere supremo nelle religioni primitivi* (Turin, 1957).

3. Marcel Granet, *The Religion of the Chinese People*, trans. Maurice Freedman (Oxford, 1975), 122.

4. Ibid., 125 (italics added).

5. Ibid., 129.

6. K. Schipper, *Le Corps taoiste* (Paris, 1982), 19.

7. Lactantius *The Anger of God* 13, 20.

8. Psalms 96:4-5.

9. I have borrowed this word from Paul Ricoeur, *Time and Narrative*, vol. 3, trans. Kathleen Blamey and David Pellaner (Chicago, 1988).

10. Origen *Against Celsus* 6.50, 60, 61, 62.

11. Philo of Alexandria *Legum allegoriae* 1.2.

12. Plato *Timaeus* 37d-e.

13. This whole question is remarkably well presented and discussed by F. Boespflug, *Dieu dans l'art* (Paris, 1984).

14. F. A. Pouchet, *Hétérogénie ou traité de la génération spontanée* (Paris, 1859), 95.

15. Ibid., 99-101.

16. Ibid., 97.

17. Ibid., 97.

18. Cicero *On the Nature of the Gods* 1.2.

19. Cicero *On the Nature of the Gods* 1.16.

20. Cicero *On the Nature of the Gods* 1.17.

21. Cicero *On the Nature of the Gods* 1.19.

22. Cicero *On the Nature of the Gods* 1.9.

23. Cicero *On the Nature of the Gods* 1.20.

24. Cicero *On the Nature of the Gods* 1.40.

25. Cicero *On the Nature of the Gods* 1.19.

26. Cicero *On the Nature of the Gods* 1.9.

27. Epicurus *Vatican Sayings* 71.

28. Epicurus *Vatican Sayings* 33.

29. Epicurus *Vatican Sayings* 59.

30. Epicurus *Vatican Sayings* 68.

31. Epicurus *Vatican Sayings* 69.

32. Epicurus *Letter to Menecaeus* 135.

33. Theophrastus *Characters* 16 (the superstitious man). Plutarch *On Superstition*.

34. Cicero *On the Nature of the Gods* 1.20.

35. Psalms 139:16.

Chapter 9

1. Aelian *Varia Historia* 12.61. See the analysis by A. Jacquemin, "Boreas ho Thourios," *Bulletin de correspondance hellénique* 103 (1979): 189-93.

2. Aelian *Varia Historia* 12.61.

3. Herodotus 7.188-89.

4. Pausanias 8.26.1.

5. See Marcel Detienne, *Dionysos at Large*, trans. Arthur Goldhammer (Cambridge [Mass.], 1989), 33-41.

6. According to an inscription dating from the period of Augustus, which mentions "penteteric mysteries" founded by the city: R. Hodot,

"Décret de Kymé en l'honneur du prytane Kléanax," *J. Paul Getty Museum Journal* 10 (1982): 165-80.

7. [Theocritus] *Lēnai* (Bacchae) 76.5-6. In Erchia, a deme in Attica, Dionysus shared an altar with Semele, and the women would gather there to sacrifice to both of them on the same day. The references may be found in Detienne, *Dionysos at Large*, 71 n. 45.

8. [Apollodorus] *Library* 3.14.1.

9. *Iliad* 4.40-43, 51-55.   10. *Iliad* 15.187-93.

11. Hesiod *Theogony* 71-74.   12. Hesiod *Theogony* 390-96.

13. Hesiod *Theogony* 881-85.

14. See the essay on the division of the *timai* by J. Rudhart, "A propos de l'hymne homérique à Demeter," *Museum helveticum* 35 (1978): 1-17.

15. These traditions are studied in Marcel Detienne, "Les Danaïdes entre elles ou la violence fondatrice du mariage," in *L'Ecriture d'Orphée* (Paris, 1989).

16. See U. Kron, *Die Zehn attischen Phylenheroen: Geschichte, Mythos, Kult und Darstellungen* (Berlin, 1976), 84-103.

17. Clearchus of Soles frag. 73 Wehrli [= Athenaeus 13.555c]. Father *and* mother: Schol. Aristophanes *Ploutos* 773.

18. [Apollodorus] *Library* 3.14.1. On the olive tree, the ephebe, and the city, see Marcel Detienne, *L'Ecriture d'Orphée* (Paris, 1989), 71-85.

19. The version followed by Varro, cited by Augustine in *City of God* 18.9. Was this a matter of Poseidon's anger or was it the result of a deal made with Athena? On her love of the male, but without union in the institutional sense of marriage, see Aeschylus *Eumenides* 737-38.

20. We return to the subject of women and autochthony in Chapter 14, which gives a full account of the adventures of Erechtheus and those associated with him.

21. Pausanias 2.1.6.

22. Plutarch *Theseus* 6.1: the first fruits of the harvest were for him.

23. Pausanias 2.33.2 (Calauria-Delphi), 10.5.6 (Calauria-Delphi); Strabo 8.374 (Calauria-Delos).

24. *Iliad* 21.435-69.

25. Plato *Critias* 109b, 113b-c.

26. See J. Rudhart, "La ville dans la pensée religieuse hellénique," in *Du mythe, de la religion grecque et de la compréhension d'autrui* (Geneva, 1981), 92-101.

27. Apollo, the architect and founder of the walls of Troy and many other edifices.

28. Hesiod frag. 1.6-8 ed. Merckelbach and West.

29. *Odyssey* 8.559-63. See Marcel Detienne and Jean-Pierre Vernant, *Cunning Intelligence in Greek Culture and Society*, trans. Janet Lloyd (Hassocks [Sussex], 1978), 238-42.

30. *Odyssey* 6.10. See Claude Mossé, "Ithaque ou la naissance de la cité," in *Annali dell' Istituto universitario orientale. Archeologia e storia antica*, vol. 2 (Naples, 1980), 7-19.

31. See G. Vallet, "Bilan des recherches à Megara Hyblaea," *Annuario della scuola archeologica di Atene* 50 (1982): 174-81; Vallet, "Ville et cité: Réflexions sur les premières fondations grecques en Occident," in *L'Idée de la ville*, ed. F. Guéry (Paris, 1984), 56-64; and M. Gras, "Aspect de la recherche sur la colonisation grecque. A propos du Congrès d'Athènes: notes de lecture," *Revue belge de Philologie et d'Histoire* 64 (1986): 5-21.

32. An expression used by Timaeus of Tauromenium, but probably of earlier origin. See S. Mazzarino, *Il pensiero storico classico²*, vol. 1 (Bari, 1966), 235-37.

33. M. Caswitz, *Le vocabulaire de la colonisation en grec ancien* (Paris, 1985), 69-72, 103-7.

34. On the phenomenon of Pan-Hellenism (festivals, cults, the representation of the gods, systems of values), see, for a precise and general study, Gregory Nagy, "Hesiod," in *Ancient Writers*, ed. T. J. Luce (New York, 1982), 43-73.

35. *Titanomachie*, frag. 6 ed. Allen [= *Homeri Opera*, vol. 5 (Oxford), 111]. The text is studied by Nagy, "Hesiod," 61.

36. Well noted in particular by Walter Burkert, *Griechische Religion* (Stuttgart, 1977), 331-43 [= *Greek Religion, Archaic and Classical*, trans. John Raffan (Oxford, 1985)].

37. *Iliad* 2.400.

38. *Odyssey* 23.279-81: the oracle of Tiresias. Upon his return, Odysseus would have to leave again to journey to inland Greece, far from the sea, to sacrifice three victims (a bull, a ram, and a stud boar) to Poseidon, then return to Ithaca to make a sacrifice of sacred burnt offerings to *all* the gods. Eumaeus, an example of sacrificial piety in the midst of all the impious, greedy suitors, reminds Odysseus of two essential rules: not to *forget* the gods (*Odyssey* 14.421, italics added) and to address prayers to all of them (14.423).

39. *Iliad* 9.533-98.

40. *Iliad* 5.428-30.

41. Herodotus 2.4: the Egyptians were the first to use the real names of the Twelve Gods. They also invented altars, statues, and temples.

42. Herodotus 2.52-53.

43. Hyginus *Fable* 143, 274.8 ed. Rose.
44. Pausanias 1.26.5, 8.2.3. See Jean-Louis Durand, *Sacrifice et labour en Grèce ancienne* (Paris, 1986), 29.
45. *Iliad* 21.462–67.
46. Hesiod *Theogony* 796–97.
47. See previous discussion in Introduction.
48. See discussion in Chapter 13.

Chapter 10

1. The subject is studied in the excellent *L'Impensable polythéisme: Etudes d'historiographie religieuse*, ed. F. Schmidt (Paris, 1988). One detail is worth noting: Aeschylus predates Philo, who, for his part, speaks of *polytheia* and uses the adjective *polytheos*. The "multiplicity of gods" is a *Greek* category, at least as ancient as Aeschylus; it is therefore not affected by any "monotheist" pressure.
2. For a discussion of the dating, see A. F. Garvie, *Aeschylus Supplices: Play and Trilogy* (Cambridge, 1969), 1–28.
3. See Louis Robert, "Héraclite à son fourneau: Un mot d'Héraclite dans Aristote (*Parts of Animals*, 645a)," in *Annuaire de l'Ecole Pratique des Hautes Etudes, IVe section* (Paris, 1965–1966), 61–73.
4. R. Martin, *Recherches sur l'agora grecque* (Paris, 1951), 169–74; C. Picard, "Les 'agoras des dieux' en Grèce," *Annual of the British School at Athens* 46 (1951): 132–42.
5. Aeschylus *Suppliant Maidens* 189 (*pāgos . . . agōniōn theōn*), 208–21, 222 (*koinobōmian*).
6. Aeschylus *Suppliant Maidens* 465.
7. Aeschylus *Suppliant Maidens* 482 (*enchōrion*), 493 (*polissouchoi*).
8. Aeschylus *Suppliant Maidens* 424.
9. See Jean-Pierre Vernant, "Hestia-Hermes: The Religious Expression of Space and Movement in Ancient Greece," in *Myth and Thought among the Greeks* (London, 1983), 127–76.
10. Pausanias 7.22.4.
11. See, in general, the inquiry by E. Di Filippo Balestrazzi, "L'Agyieus e la città," in *Centro di ricerche e documentazione sull'antichità classica, Atti (1980–1981)* (Rome, 1984), 93–108.
12. The ritual of the *kolossoi* in Cyrene: J. Servais, "Les Suppliants dans la 'loi sacrée' de Cyrène," *Bulletin de Correspondance hellénique* (1960): 112–47. See Jean-Pierre Vernant, *Myth and Thought Among the Greeks* (London, 1983), 127–76.
13. Jack Bazin, "Retour aux choses-dieux," *Le Temps de la réfléxion* 7 (1986): 253–73; Marc Augé, *Le Dieu objet* (Paris, 1988); see also the

collective volume, *Objets du fétichisme, Nouvelle Revue de Psychanalyse* 2 (1970).

14. A. Zempléni, "Des êtres sacrificiels," in *Sous le masque de l'animal*, ed. M. Cartry (Paris, 1987), 267-317.

15. Emmanuel Laroche, "La Réforme religieuse du roi Tudhaliya IV et sa signification politique," in *Les syncrétismes dans les religions de l'Antiquité*, ed. F. Dunand and P. Levêque (Leiden, 1975), 87-95. In about 1250, the same king Tudhaliya IV had the pantheon sculpted in stone at Yazlikaya. In two natural chambers with vertical walls open to the sky, about fifty gods and goddesses in procession face one another. See Emmanuel Laroche, "Pierre inscrite: Yazilikaya, un sanctuaire rupestre hittite," in *Dictionnaire des Mythologies*, vol. 2, ed. Yves Bonnefoy (Paris, 1981), 265-66.

16. Tablet AO 5376 in the Louvre Museum, reproduced in the catalogue of the *Naissance de l'écriture* exhibition (Paris, 1982), 219.

17. Jean Bottéro, "Les Noms de Marduk, l'écriture et la 'logique' en Mésopotamie ancienne," in *Ancient Near Eastern Studies in Memory of J. J. Finkelstein, Connecticut Academy of Arts and Sciences* 19 (1977): 5-28.

18. "L'Oracle de Claros," in *La Civilisation grecque de l'Antiquité à nos jours*, vol. 1, ed. C. Delvoye and G. Roux (Brussels, 1966), 305-12.

19. Before a consultation, to purify oneself, one sacrificed to the god and also to "all those whose names were inscribed on the altar" (Pausanias 1.34.5).

20. See P. Roesch, "L'Amphiaraion d'Oropos," in *Temples et sanctuaires*, ed. G. Roux (Lyons, 1984), 173-84.

21. *Homeric Hymn to Hermes* 128.

22. See the excellent summary by E. Will, *Le Dôdékathéon: Texte (Exploration archéologique de Délos, fasc. 22)* (Paris, 1955), 178-84. See also Charlotte R. Long, *The Twelve Gods of Greece and Rome* (Leiden, 1987).

23. H. A. Thompson and R. E. Wycherley, "The Agora of Athens," in *The Athenian Agora* (Princeton, 1972), 14:129-36.

24. See Will, *La Dôdékathéon*, 178-79.

25. Pindar *Olympian Odes* 10.22-58 (25: *bōmōn hexarithmon ektissato*, and 49: *dōdeka*).

26. Pindar *Olympian Odes* 10.45.

27. Pindar *Olympian Odes* 51-55.

28. See Pausanias 6.22.9: the sanctuary of Artemis *Alpheiaia* in Elis.

29. Schol. Apollonius Rhodius *Argonautica* 2.533.

30. *Odyssey* 8.321-42.

31. *Homeric Hymn to Hermes.*

32. In Delphi and in Troy.

33. See O. Kern, *Die Inschriften von Magnesia am Meander* (Berlin, 1900), 98:41-44: portable statues and an altar on the *agora*. It is worth noting that the calendar of the people of Magnesia was consecrated to the Twelve Gods. See J. and L. Robert, *Bulletin épigraphique*, in *Revue des études grecques* 77 (1973).

34. Pausanias 1.40.3.

35. Pausanias 10.5.1-2.

36. Alcaeus, frag. 129 Lobel-Page [= *Poetarum Lesbiorum fragmenta*² (Oxford, 1963), 176-77]: "Common" sanctuary (*xunon*).

37. In Alcaeus, frag. 129.9, an "eater of raw flesh," at least. Son of Semele in frag. 346.3. But son of Thyōne in Sappho, frag. 17.10, all Lobel-Page. In Rhodes, Dionysus with the phallus of figwood is called *Thyōnidas*, "the son of Thyone."

38. See *Homeric Hymn to Dionysus* 1.1-2, 55-56.

39. Pausanias 2.19.6.

40. Harpocration, *s.v. Kolōnaitas:* Schol. Sophocles *Oedipus at Colonus*, 56. See Marie Delcourt, *Héphaistos ou la légende du magicien* (Paris, 1957), 192-93.

41. W. Volgraff, "Le décret d'Argos relatif à un pacte entre Cnossos et Tylissos," *Verhandeling der koninklijke Nederlandsche Akademie von Wetenschappen, Afd. Letterkunde, LI*, no. 2, Amsterdam, 1948, pp. 1-105.

42. Frag. 6.29-31.

43. Frag. 5.30-34.

44. F. Sokolowski, *Lois sacrées d'Asie Mineure*, no. 32 (Paris, 1955), 52-53.

45. See M. Detienne, "Apollon und Dionysos in der griechischen Religion," in *Die Restauration der Götter: Antike Religion und Neo-Paganismus*, ed. R. Faber and R. Schlesier (Königshasen, 1986), 124-32.

46. Heraios: F. Sokolowski, *Lois sacrées des cités grecques* (Paris, 1969), 1, A, 19-20. Damatrios in: *Inscriptions de Lindos* 183, ed. C. Blinkenberg. Sokolowski also mentions a Zeus Aphrodisios in Paros (IG, XII, 5, 220, 2).

47. L. Deubner, *Attische Feste*² (Berlin, 1956), 155-57.

48. Georges Daux, "La grande démarchie: Un nouveau calendrier sacrificiel d'Attique (Erchia), *Bulletin de Correspondance hellénique*, 1963: 606 (A 40-43) and 629 (commentary).

49. Pausanias 2.10.4-6.

50. The connection with the white poplar comes from Pausanias 2.10.6.

51. Pausanias 2.10.1. Phaistos introducing the "foreign" rite: Pausanias 2.6.6-7.

52. Pausanias 2.10.1.

53. Herodotus 2.44.

54. Jean Pouilloux, "L'Héraclès thasien," *Revue des études anciennes* (1974): 305-16. See the critical analyses of C. Bonnet, *Melaart: Cultes et mythes de l'Héraclès Tyrien en Méditerranée* (Louvain-Namur, 1988), 346-71, which prompts one to reconsider the double cult status of Heracles in Thasos.

Chapter 11

1. Three passages come to mind here: *Iliad* 1.423-25 and *Odyssey* 1.22-26 and 7.201-15. Their importance for defining the relations between the gods and men have been excellently analyzed by C. Kérény, *The Religion of the Greeks and Romans*, trans. C. Holme (London, 1962) [= *La Religion antique: Ses lignes fondamentales*, French trans. Y. Le Lay (Geneva, 1957)], pp. 128-59 (in particular, pp. 138-39). This is a text for which I should like to express my tardy admiration; likewise, Kérény's analyses of *theoria* (the role of "vision" in men's perception of the gods (pp. 98-117 in the French translation). It was initially the observations of Giulia Sissa that persuaded me to reconsider an all too familiar sacrificial model. See below, n. 42.

2. Hesiod, frag. 1.6-8 ed. Merkelbach and West. The only difference between them is that of their "vital force," the unequal *aiōn*. On the Ethiopians, see Alain Ballabriga, *Le Soleil et le Tartare: L'image mythique du monde en Grèce arachaïque* (Paris, 1986), 107-10; Jean-Pierre Vernant, *Manger au pays du soleil*, in Marcel Detienne et al., *La Cuisine du sacrifice en pays grec²* (Paris, 1983), 239-49.

3. Hesiod *Works and Days* 197-200.

4. Hesiod *Works and Days* 252-53.

5. See W. Fahr, *Theous nomizein: Zur Problem der Anfänge des Atheïsmus bei der Griecher (Spudasmata, vol. 26)* (New York, 1969). Two approaches to belief: in the form of "truths," a program of truth, P. Veyne, *Did the Greeks Believe in their Myths?*, trans. Paula Wissing *(Chicago, 1988)*; on the mode of "making believable" in general, Michel de Certeau, *L'Invention du quotidien:* vol. 1: *Les Arts de faire* (Paris, 1980), and the collective volume *Collection de l'Ecole française de Rome*, vol. 51: *Faire croire* (Rome, 1981). Worth reading for the quality of thought: F. Héran, "Le rite et la croyance," *Revue française de sociologie* 27 (1986): 231-63.

6. See C. Malamoud, "La Déesse Croyance," in *Michel de Certeau*, ed. Luce Giard (Paris, 1987), 225-36.

7. See J.-C. Schmitt, "Du bon usage du 'credo,'" in *Faire croire*, 337-61.

8. The disparity between Christianity and the gods of Greece has been passionately refuted by W. Otto in a whole series of books. As an introduction, see Marcel Detienne, "Au commencement était le corps des dieux," preface to *Les Dieux de la Grèce: La Figure du divin au miroir de l'esprit grec*, by Walter F. Otto (French translation) (Paris, 1981).

9. Jean Rudhart, *Notions fondamentales de la pensée religieuse et actes constitutifs du culte dans la Grèce classique* (Geneva, 1958), 141-42.

10. Hesiod *Theogony* 417: *kata nomon*.

11. Plato *Laws* 4.716d-717a.

12. *Sylloge*³, 286.1-5: decree of *isopolitia* between Olbia and Miletus (ca. 334 B.C.).

13. H. Engelmann and R. Merkelbach, *Die Inschiften von Erythrai und Klazomenaï* (Bonn, 1972), no. 2, B, 1, 16-17, but with the correction by Haussoulier and Wilhelm. Cf. the commentaries of B. Haussoulier, "Inscriptions de Chios et d'Erythrée," *Revue de philologie* 33 (1909): 11-12.

14. Hesiod *Works and Days* 127-39.

15. See Jean Rudhart, "Les Définitions du délit d'impiété d'après la législation attique," *Museum helveticum* 17 (1960): 87-105.

16. The verb "to be" is explained in Plato's *Apology* 261.3-4, and above all in the *Laws* 10. See the information collected by Fahr, *Theous nomizein*.

17. Sophocles *Oedipus the King* 661.

18. In general, see Detienne et al., *La cuisine du sacrifice en pays grec*², in particular 7-35.

19. Cf. Jean-Louis Durand, "Du rituel comme instrumental," in Detienne et al., *La cuisine du sacrifice en pays grec*², 178-79.

20. Herodotus 2.41.

21. On the sacrificial banquet in epic, see S. Said, "Les Crimes des prétendants, la maison d'Ulysse et les festins de l'*Odysée*," in *Etudes de littérature ancienne* (Paris, 1979), 9-49.

22. See the analyses of Jesper Svenbro, "A Megara Hyblaea: Le Corps géomètre," *Annales E.S.C.* (1982): 953-64 (in particular, p. 954), and Guy Berthiaume, *Les Rôles du Mageiros: Etude sur la boucherie, la cuisine et le sacrifice dans la Grèce ancienne* (Leiden, 1982), 50-51.

23. See Jean-Louis Durand, "Bêtes grecques: Propositions pour une topologie des corps à manger," in Detienne et al., *La cuisine du sacrifice en pays grec*², 151.

24. Plato *Phaedrus* 265e.

25. Berthiaume, *Les Rôles du Mageiros*.

26. See Louis Robert, *Le Sanctuaire de Sinuri près de Mylasa*, vol. 1 (Paris, 1945), 49-50.

27. See Plutarch *Moralia* 642e-f.

28. Schol. Pindar *Olympian Odes* 7.152b.

29. Claude Vial, *Délos indépendante (314-167 av. J.-C.): Etude d'une communauté civique et de ses institutions* (Athens, 1984), 18-20.

30. Ludwig Deubner, *Attische Feste*[2] (Berlin, 1956), 26.

31. Paul Roesch, *Etudes boétiennes* (Paris, 1982), 243-54.

32. See Louis Robert, "Un Décret d'Ilion et un papyrus concernant des cultes royaux," *Mélanges C. B. Welles*, 1966, pp. 184-186; J. and L. Robert, "Bulletin épigraphique," *Revue des études grecques* 405 (1977): 390.

33. See Stephen G. Miller, *The Prytaneion* (Berkeley, 1978). Delos file: Vial, *Délos indépendante*, 203-10.

34. Inscriptions published in 1953 by M. N. Kontoléon, with commentaries by J. and L. Robert, "Bulletin épigraphique," *REG* 181 (1955): 253.

35. Plutarch *Solon* 24.5.

36. Hermeias *in* Athenaeus 4.149d [= frag. 112 Tresp, *Die Fragmente der griechischen Kultschrifsteller*].

37. J. Bousquet, "Convention entre Myania et Hypnia," *Bulletin de correspondance hellénique* 89 (1965): 665-81.

38. Georges Daux, *Delphes au Ie et au IIe siècles* (Paris, 1936), 335-41.

39. See Jean-Pierre Vernant, "A la table des hommes: Mythe de fondation du sacrifice chez Hésiode," in Detienne et al., *La cuisine du sacrifice en pays grec*[2], 37-132 (in particular 43-44).

40. This data, briefly commented on here, led to C. Kérényi reaching a number of conclusions on sacrifice and the relations between men and the gods that I found unconvincing at the time of *La Cuisine du sacrifice*. I was wrong, and would like to express my admiration for his analyses: *The Religion of the Greeks and Romans*, trans. C. Holme (London, 1962), [= *La Religion antique: Ses lignes fondamentales*, French trans. Y. Le Lay (Geneva, 1957)], pp. 128-49 (in particular, pp. 137-40).

41. An excellent collection of data is provided by L. Weniger, "Theophanien: altgriechische Götteradvente," *Archiv für Religionswissenschaft* 22 (1923-1924): 18-22.

42. Callimachus *Hymn to Apollo* ed. F. Williams, 1-10 (italics added).

43. Plutarch *Greek Questions* 36.299a-b. See Marcel Detienne, *Dionysos at Large*, trans. Arthur Goldhammer (Cambridge [Mass.], 1989), 55-56.

44. Pausanias 6.26.1.

45. Plato *Laws* 2.653d. This text is the central focus of Pierre Boyancé's *Le Culte des Muses chez les philosophes grecs*[2] (Paris, 1972), 170-75. My translation of the passage from the *Laws* is based on his commentary as well as on L. Robin's version in the Pléiade edition of Plato. (Translator's Note: The English Loeb translation has been adapted here.)

46. Plutarch *Moralia* 1102a.

47. Plato *Laws* 4.716d-717a, 6.771d.

48. Plato *Symposium* 188c.

49. See Chapter 5 above and H. Jeanmaire, *Dionysos: Histoire du culte de Bacchus*[2] (Paris, 1970), 28-31.

50. Sophocles, frag. 548 Radt.

51. See D. Gill, "Trapezōmata: A Neglected Aspect of Greek Sacrifice," *Harvard Theological Review* 67 (1974): 117-37, and the mobile table of vases in J.-L. Durand, *Sacrifice et labour en Grèce ancienne* (Paris, 1986), 116-23.

52. See L. Bruit, "Sacrifices à Delphes: Sur deux figures d'Apollon," *Revue de l'histoire des religions* 201 (1984): 339-67 (in particular, pp. 362-67).

53. *Odyssey* 7.201-4.

54. The verb *antiaō*: "to answer a call, present oneself, confront, stand before, be there." It is a verb that, at the sacrifice to Poseidon, indicates the "presence" of Athena (*Odyssey* 3.435-36) and Apollo (*Iliad* 1.67).

55. For example, Apollo, seated, with his head turned toward the altar and sacrificers: bell-shaped, Attic red-figure krater, Agrigentum 4688 (reproduced in Durand, *Sacrifice et labour en Grèce ancienne*, 129, fig. 51); or Athena present at the sacrifice to her: Acropolis Museum, Athens, 581 (the document is analyzed by D. Willers, *Zu den Anfängen der archaïschen Plastik in Griechenland* [Berlin, 1975], plate 31).

56. On the manifestations of gods, deities visibly making their actions manifest during festivals, sacrifices, and banquets where the "table of the gods" is open to all: A. Laumonier, *Les Cultes indigènes de*

Carie (Paris, 1958), 272, 365. See P. Roussel, "Les Mystères de Pana-mara," *Bulletin de correspondance hellénique* 51 (1927): 123-37.

Chapter 12

1. B. D. Meritt, "Inscriptions of Colophon," *American Journal of Ar-chaeology* 56 (1935): 361-71; Louis Robert, *Opera minora* (1969), 2:158-59; R. Martin, *L'Urbanisme dans la Grèce antique*[2] (Paris, 1974), 55-56.

2. Pausanias 4.26.1-27, 8. See I. Malkin, *Religion and Colonization in Ancient Greece* (Leiden, 1987), 104-6.

3. The "despair" of the Messenians, Aristomenes' epic, and the anger of Artemis are analyzed in P. Ellinger, *La Légende nationale pho-cidienne: Artémis, les situations extrêmes, et les récits de guerre d'anéan-tissement*, in *BCH*, Supplement 25 (Athens-Paris, 1993).

4. Nevertheless, it appears that the Messenian cults were not aban-doned and continued until the fifth century, as Anthony Snodgrass notes (but without providing details) in "Les Origines du culte des héros dans la Grèce antique," in *La Mort, les morts dans les sociétés an-ciennes*, ed. Gherardo Gnoli and Jean-Pierre Vernant (Cambridge, 1982), 117.

5. See the essays by Snodgrass, "Les Origines du culte des héros dans la Grèce antique," 107-19; and "Etablir un lien avec un ancien habitant du territoire" (117).

6. Michel Casevitz, *Le Vocabulaire de la colonisation en grec ancien* (Paris, 1985), 195-208.

7. Pausanias 4.27.5: *boulēsetai . . . epichōrēsai.*

8. An alternative put forward by Plato *Laws* 5.738a.5-6.

9. As was easily done between Greeks or others with gods of the same rank.

10. *Erēmos*, deserted "infinitely long ago," as Plato's *Laws* puts it (4.704c.6-7), in connection with the founding of a city in a radical fash-ion, "like a colony." Historians and archaeologists are actively correct-ing this view of empty spaces. It was certainly an imaginary view, but it was that of the founders, the men who invented the city between the eighth and seventh centuries B.C. I am entirely in agreement with Ivad Malkin, "La Place des dieux dans la cité des hommes: Le Découpage des aires sacrées dans les colonies grecques," *Revue de l'histoire des reli-gions* (1987): 331-52.

11. The altar, *bōmos*, is said to be aromatic, *thuēeis.*

12. *Iliad* 4.48, 24.69.

13. An aromatic altar and *temenos: Iliad* 8.48, 23.148; *Odyssey* 8.363.

14. See David W. Rupp, "Reflections on the Development of the Altar in the Eighth Century B.C.," in *The Greek Renaissance of the Eighth Century B.C.*: Tradition and Innovation, ed. R. Hägg (Stockholm, 1983), 101-7.

15. The sense of *eudmētos*, from the verb *demein*. Alongside *teūchein*, the work of an architect and builder.

16. See *Iliad* 1.440, 448.

17. *Iliad* 1.47.

18. *Homeric Hymn to Apollo* 388-510.

19. Thucydides *History of the Peloponnesian War* 6.3.1. See Malkin, *Religion and Colonization in Ancient Greece*, 140.

20. Pindar *Olympian Odes* 7.20-95.

21. Callimachus *Hymn to Apollo* 55-64, with the detailed comments of Frederick Williams (*Callimachus, Hymn to Apollo* [Oxford, 1978]).

22. *Odyssey* 6.9-10.

23. The founder of the Cretan colony in the form of a philosophical city (in Plato *Laws* 5.738d) plans to distribute land beginning by giving "choice plots" (*exaireta temenē*) to the gods, daimons, and heroes.

24. *Homeric Hymn to Apollo* 298 (*naon naiein*).

25. See the analyses by Michel Casevitz, "Temples et sanctuaires: Ce qu'apprend l'étude lexicologique," in *Temples et sanctuaires*, ed. Georges Roux (Lyons, 1984), 81-95.

26. *Iliad* 8.48.

27. *Iliad* 23.147.

28. *Odyssey* 6.263-66 (a stone-built *agora* surrounding the sanctuary of Poseidon, the *Posideion*).

29. *Iliad* 6.88-93.

30. I am following the spirited analyses of C. Rolley, "Les grands sanctuaires panhelléniques," in *The Greek Renaissance of the Eighth Century B.C.*: Tradition and Innovation, ed. Robin Hägg (Stockholm, 1983), 109-14.

31. See Ibid., 113-14.

32. Louis Gernet, *Le Génie grec dans la religion* [1932] (Paris, 1970), 164-79.

33. Georges Roux, *L'Amphictionie, Delphes et le temple d'Apollon au IVe siècle* (Lyons-Paris, 1979), vii-ix, 1-19.

34. Strabo 9.419 and Hyperides *Speech on Delos*, in Athenaeus *Deipnosophistai* 10.424e (cited by Gernet, *Le Génie grec dans la religion*, 167).

35. The first use of the term *Panhellenes* is in Hesiod *Works and Days* 528. See Gregory Nagy, "Hesiod," in *Ancient Writers*, ed. T. J. Luce (New York, 1982), 44.

36. The *agōn* as analyzed by V. Ehrenberg, *Ost und West* (Prague, 1935), 63–96.

37. *Homeric Hymn to Apollo* 146–55 (according to the text, attested by Thucydides 3.104).

38. *Homeric Hymn to Apollo* 146–55.

39. Georges Roux has produced some of the best reflections on these problems: "Trésors, temples, *tholos*," in *Temples et sanctuaires*, ed. Georges Roux (Lyons, 1984), 153–71.

40. See Georges Roux, *Delphes, son oracle et ses dieux* (Paris, 1976), 19–51 (on the Delphic pantheon).

41. Roux, "Trésors, temples, *tholos*," 171.

42. These ideas have been analyzed in depth by Jean-Pierre Vernant, *Myth and Thought among the Greeks* (London, 1983), 305–21.

43. Ibid., 318.

44. Callimachus *Hymn to Artemis* 237–39.

45. See Jean Rudhart, "La Ville dans la pensée religieuse hellénique" [1979], in *Du Mythe, de la religion grecque et de la compréhension d'autrui* (Geneva, 1981), 92–101.

46. E. A. E. Reymond, *The Mythical Origin of the Egyptian Temple* (Manchester, 1969).

47. See *L'Espace du Temple*, vols. 1–2, ed. Jean-Claude Galey (Paris, 1985–1986) (in particular, Galey, Introduction, 1:9–22, and M.-L. Reiniche, "Le Temple dans la localité: Quatre exemples au Tamilnad," 1:75–119).

48. See Reiniche, "Le Temple dans la localité."

49. *Iliad* 18.370 (together with the remarks of M. Delcourt, *Hephaïstos ou la légende du magicien* [Paris, 1957], 62–63).

50. See Georges Dumézil, *Archaic Roman Religion*, vol. 2, trans. Philip Krapp (Chicago, 1970), 586–87; and H. Bardon, "La Naissance d'un temple," *Revue des études latines* 33 (1955): 166–82.

51. On the minimal presence of diviners in accounts of colonization: Malkin, *Religion and Colonization in Ancient Greece*, 92–113. I would go even further than Malkin and say that Delphi rendered diviners superfluous.

52. See Marcel Detienne, "L'Espace de la publicité: Ses opérateurs intellectuels dans la cité," in *Les Savoirs de l'écriture: En Grèce ancienne*, ed. Marcel Detienne (Lille, 1988), 41–44.

53. Forbidden to all "strangers": F. Sokolowski, *Lois sacrées des cités grecques* (Paris, 1969), no. 96 (the religious calendar of Mykonos in about 200 B.C.), 25–26. These were the only cults in the calendar that were forbidden.

54. Thucydides 4.98.2.

55. In Thebes, power was associated with a secret tomb, that of Dirke, and with nocturnal sacrifices made without a fire, during which the chief magistrate passed on to his successor the insignia of power, a spear and a seal (Plutarch *De genio Socratis* 5.578b). In Athens, there was a tomb of Oedipus at Colonus, on the frontier (see, e.g., the analyses of André-Jean Festugière, "Tragédies et tombes sacrées" [1973], in *Etudes d'histoire et de philologie* [Paris, 1975], 47–68, and P. Vidal-Naquet's investigation into institutions and space, "Oedipus Between Two Cities: An Essay on *Oedipus at Colonus*," in *Myth and Tragedy*, trans. Janet Lloyd [New York, 1988], 329–60). Furthermore, according to Euripides' *Erechtheus*, the daughters of Praxithea, the Autochthonous Athenian Woman, who were buried together in an inviolable place, would protect the Athenian territory against its enemies, on condition that no opponent of Athens came to sacrifice to them "secretly." To do so would bring victory to the sacrificer and disaster upon Athens.

56. Plutarch *Solon* 9.1.

57. Herodotus 5.82–88.

58. An ironical return to their local clay, their own earth, which represents one aspect of the self-sufficient city. On "ceramics," vases and pottery as an invention of Athens, celebrated by *Critias*, see François. Lissarrague, *Un Flot d'images: Une esthétique du banquet grec* (Paris, 1987), 134.

Chapter 13

1. The key Greek word is *metecheīn*, fully analyzed by Denis Roussel, *Tribu et cité* (Paris, 1976). For a differential comparison between citizenship in Greece and in Rome, see P. Gauthier, "La Citoyenneté en Grèce et à Rome," *Ktema* 6 (1981): 167–79 (in particular, 171, on "participation" in a Greek city).

2. Roussel, *Tribu et cité*, 139–56. The rules governing the Labydai phratry in Delphi are analyzed in remarkable detail by G. Rougemont, "Lois sacrées et règlements religieux," in *Corpus des inscriptions de Delphes*, vol. 1 (Paris, 1977), nos. 9 and 9a, pp. 26–88.

3. See the data on the reinterpretation of archaeological aspects of Athens collected by Charles W. Hedrick, Jr., "The Temple and Cult of Apollo Patroos in Athens," *American Journal of Archaeology* 92 (1988): 185–210.

4. There were no gods for individuals in Greece.

5. J. Labarbe, "L'Age correspondant au sacrifice du 'koureion' et les données historiques du sixième discours d'Isée," *Bulletin de l'Académie*

Royale de Belgique, Classe des Lettres et des Sciences morales et poli-tiques 5th ser., 39 (1953): 358-94.

6. See Pierre Vidal-Naquet, *The Black Hunter* (Baltimore, 1986), 109-13.

7. Their selection has yet to be studied in relation to the configuration of each of them; see the data in Roussel, *Tribu et cité*, 133-37.

8. See David Whitehead, *The Demos of Attica* (Princeton, 1986), and R. Parker, "Festivals of the Attic Demes," *Acta Universitatis Upsaliensis, Boreas* 15 (1987): 137-47.

9. See Georges Daux, "Le calendrier de Thorikos au musée J. Paul Getty," *L'Antiquité classique* (1983): 150-74. Provisional text: 1.5, 38, 44.

10. I am following the observations of Parker, "Festivals of the Attic Demes," 140-43.

11. Isaeus frag. 5 ed. P. Roussel.

12. *IG* 2².1172.

13. *IG* 2².1204.

14. See Marcel Detienne, "L'Espace de publicité: Ses opérateurs intellectuels dans la cité," in *Les Savoirs de l'ecriture: En Grèce ancienne*, ed. Marcel Detienne (Lille, 1988), 64-72.

15. Aristotle *The Constitution of the Athenians* 54.3.

16. Detienne, "L'Espace de publicité," 67-70.

17. Aristotle *Constitution of the Athenians* 57.1.

18. See Marcel Detienne, "Hestia misogyne: La Cité en son autonomie," in *L'Ecriture d'Orphée* (Paris, 1989).

19. *Syll*³ 526.29-31.

20. M. Guarducci, ed., *Inscriptiones creticae*, 3.4.7, pp. 87-88.

21. See O. Kern, ed., *The Decree of the Cnossosians for Two Magnesian Benefactors: Inschriften von Magnesia*, no. 67 [= *Syll*³ 721.32-33].

22. Examples suggested by J. and L. Robert, *Bulletin épigraphique, Revue des études grecques* 345 (1973): 129-30.

23. "Acharnes stele," reproduced in Chrysis Pélékidis, *Histoire de l'éphébie attique: Des origines à 31 avant Jésus-Christ* (Paris, 1962), 112-13.

24. Ibid.

25. See the observations of P. Gauthier, "Le Droit de la cité à Athènes," *Revue des études grecques* (1986): 128-31.

26. Residence was certainly not a qualification for citizenship: Gauthier, "Le Droit de la cité à Athènes," 129.

27. See David Whitehead, *The Ideology of the Athenian Metic* (Cambridge, 1977), 86-89.

28. See A. Wilhelm, "Bürgerrechtsverleihungen der Athenen," *Athenische Mitteilungen* 39 (1914): 257-95.

29. Thasos decree of the third century B.C.: *Choix d'inscriptions grecques*, ed. Jean Pouilloux (Paris, 1960), no. 33, I. 4, pp. 124-126.

30. Herodotus 9.33.

31. [Demosthenes] *Against Neaera* 104 (italics added).

32. *Delphinion*, n. 149, cited by J. and L. Robert, "Une inscription grecque de Téos en Ionie: L'Union de Téos et de Kybissos," *Journal des Savants* (1976): 153-235 (in particular, 230-31).

33. M. Mitsos, "Inscription de Stymphale," *Revue des études grecques* 59-60 (1946-1947): 150-74.

34. L. 29-30; commentary: 155.

35. Data on the collection of "sacred things": G. Busolt and H. Swoboda, *Grieschische Staatskunde*[2] (Munich, 1920), 1: 514-16.

36. Decree of Histaea in honor of the banker Athenodorus of Rhodes: *IG* 11.4.1055 (italics added), translated with a commentary in *Choix d'inscriptions grecques*, ed. Jean Pouilloux (Paris, 1960), no. 7, 1. 25-26, pp. 42-44.

37. See C. Vatin, "Damiurges et épidamiurges à Delphes," *Bulletin de correspondance hellénique* 85 (1961): 236-55, and also Georges Roux, *L'Amphictionie, Delphes et le temple d'Apollon au IVe siècle* (Lyons-Paris, 1979), 62-65.

38. Strabo 4.1.5.

39. See L. Robert, *Hellenica* 5 (Paris, 1956), 64-69. The Greek text can be found in F. Sokolowski, ed., *Lois sacrées d'Asie Mineure* (Paris, 1955), no. 73, 6-8. The same rule seems to have applied to archons in Athens: Pollux 8.85 (cited by Sokolowski, 172 n. 1).

40. See Marcel Detienne, *Dionysos Slain*, trans. Mireille Muellner and Leonard Muellner (Baltimore, 1979), 74-77.

41. Lysias *Speeches* 6. In an editor's note (pp. 89-93) to this volume, Louis Gernet gives reasons for doubting that such a "diatribe" came from the pen of Lysias. But that makes no difference in the present context.

42. Lysias *Speeches* 6.33.

43. Aeschines *Against Timarchus* 23 describes the ceremonial of the city when it deliberated "upon the most serious business"–in order of importance, "sacred things," heralds and ambassadors, and "civil things": *hiera*, external relations, and *hosia*. A similar pattern is described in Aristotle's *Constitution of the Athenians* 43.6.

44. W. Volgraff, *Le Décret d'Argos relatif à un pacte entre Knossos et Tylissos* (Amsterdam, 1948), in particular, p. 89.

45. See Nicole Loraux, "Solon et la voix de l'écrit," in *Les Savoirs de l'écriture: En Grèce ancienne*, ed. Marcel Detienne (Lille, 1988), 95-129.

46. S. Dow, "The Law Codes of Athens," *Proceedings of the Massachusetts Historical Society* 71 (1953-1959): 3-35.

47. Lysias *Against Nicomachus* 25.

48. K. Clinton, "The Nature of the Fifth-Century Revision of the Athenian Law Code," *Hesperia, supplement 19* (1982): 27-37.

49. See the testimony of Porphyry *De Abstinentia* 4.22, and Ron S. Stroud, "Drakon's Law on Homicide," *University of California Classical Studies*, vol. 3 (Berkeley, 1968), 65-83.

50. Plato *Laws* 818a.

51. Sokolowski, *Lois sacrées des cités grecques* (Paris, 1969), no. 3, pp. 5-8.

52. Ibid., no. 96, 3 (in particular: *epanorthōn*).

53. F. Sokolowski, *Lois sacrées des cités grecques. Supplément* (Paris, 1962), no. 18B, pp. 11-14.

54. Xenophon *Oeconomicus* 5.12.

55. R. Martin, *Recherches sur l'agora grecque* (Paris, 1951), 174-94.

56. See Jean-Pierre Vernant, *Myth and Thought Among the Greeks* (London, 1983), 334.

57. See Marcel Detienne, *L'Ecriture d'Orphée* (Paris, 1989), 85-98.

58. According to Theramenes, who, when his life was threatened by Critias, rushed to the altar of Hestia on the agora: Xenophon *Hellenica* 2.3.52.

59. This remark was made by L. Gernet in L. Gernet and A. Boulanger, *Le Génie grec dans la religion* (Paris, 1932), 171, an exceptional book, quite the best in this field, and one to which I constantly refer.

60. A "clear vision" in the Greek sense of *enarges*, as used by Epicurus (*Epicurea*, ed. H. Usener III, p. 123), who declares "the gods exist, our knowledge of them is a clear vision." See the remarks of Paul Veyne, "Sémiotique des dieux du paganisme," *Poétique* 54 (1983): 131-33.

Chapter 14

1. A question discussed by the guests assembled by Plutarch in his *Table Talk* 9.6.741a-b.

2. *Asphaleios, gaièochos, themeliouchos*: E. Wüst, ed., *Paulys Realencyclopädie der classischen Altertumswissenscgaft*, XX, 1 (1953), s.v. "Poseidon," ca. 493-504.

3. See Chapter 9 above.

4. Marcel Detienne, "Les Danaïdes entre elles: Une violence fondatrice de mariage," in *L'Ecriture d'Orphée* (Paris, 1989).

5. Alcaeus frag. 129 Lobel-Page. See W. Pötscher, *Hera: Ein Strukturanalyse im Vergleich mit Athena* (Darmstadt, 1987), 14-19.

6. Marcel Detienne, "Potagerie de femmes ou comment engendrer seule," in *L'Ecriture d'Orphée* (Paris, 1989).

7. Varro, in Augustine *City of God* 18.9.

8. Schol. Aristophanes *Plutus*, 773.

9. Aeschylus *Eumenides* 737-38.

10. Pausanias 5.3.2.

11. See Luc Brisson, *Le Mythe de Tirésias: Essai d'analyse structurale* (Leiden, 1976).

12. See Claire Nancy, "Euripide et le parti des femmes," *Quaderni Urbinati di cultura classica* 17 (1984): 111-36.

13. This is a question implicitly raised in Nicole Loraux's fine book, *The Children of Athena*, trans. Caroline Levine (Princeton, 1993). This is a brave book that stands its ground and stimulates frank discussion, such as I have myself enjoyed with the author. It discusses the meaning of the story of Praxithea, the relation between founding and autochthony, the question of whether there truly was "no authochthony for women," and the pertinence of another question concerning mythology, namely, "who profited" from such or such a story.

14. *The Flounder*, by Günter Grass, a great mythological book (trans. Ralph Manheim and published by Harmonsworth, Penguin, 1979).

15. See, for example, Vigdis Soleim, "A Greek Dream: To Render Women Superfluous," *Social Science Information* 25, no. 1 (1986): 67-82.

16. Loraux, *Children of Athena*, 8-11, 16-18.

17. Ibid., 135.

18. *Homeric Hymn to Apollo* 311 (quotation); 314-320.

19. Well worth reading: Nicole Loraux, *The Invention of Athens: The Funeral Oration in the Classical City* (Cambridge [Mass.], 1986).

20. See "Autochthony, an Athenian Topic," in Loraux, *Children of Athena*, 37-72.

21. *Iliad* 2.547-51: *tiktein . . . zeidōros*.

22. Again see Loraux, *Children of Athena*, and *Invention of Athens*.

23. As well as the works of Colin Austin, "De nouveaux fragments de 'l'Erechthée' d'Euripide," in *Recherches de Papyrologie* (Paris, 1967), 4: 11-67, with a splendid commentary; see also P. Carrara's excellent edition of this play, *Euripide, Eretteo* (Florence, 1977).

24. Frag. 18.90-91 ed. P. Carrara.

25. It was by no means forgotten and even fueled the rivalry between the priestesses of Athena and the priests of Poseidon-Erechtheus, all chosen from the same *genos*, the family of the Eteoboutadids, but from lineages which, apparently, never intermarried. See R. S. J. Garland, "Religion's Authority in Archaic and Classical Athens," *Annual of the British School at Athens* 79 (1984): 77-78. On the altar of forgetfulness, which Loraux singles out in the Erechtheion, and on the political discourse that provides an exegesis on it, see "L'Oubli dans la cité," *Le Temps de la réflexion* 1 (1980): 213-42.

26. According to Phanodemes, in *F. Gr. Hist.* 325 Fr. Jacoby: The First-born and Pandora *heautās sphagēnai*, with their throats slit.

27. Frag. 18.96-97 ed. P. Carrara.

28. In agreement with H. Van Looy, "L'Erechtée d'Euripide," *Mélanges Marie Delcourt* (Brussels, 1970), 121.

29. See B. G. Dietrich, *Death, Fate and Gods* (London, 1965), 102-4; Paul Roesch, *Etudes béotiennes* (Paris, 1982), 215-16.

30. Frag. 10.8 ed. P. Carrara.

31. Frag. 10.5-10 ed. P. Carrara: *ktizein*.

32. See J. Taillardat, *Les Images d'Aristophane* (Paris, 1965), 391-93.

33. Frag. 18.11-14.

34. *IG* I².24.

35. Lycurgus *Against Leocrates* 98.

36. Frag. 8.1-2 ed. P. Carrara, whose interpretation (62) is adopted here: force, *kratos*.

37. Frag. 10.38-39.

38. Frag. 10.34-35.

39. Frag. 10.15.

40. Frag. 10.38-39: *pro gaias*.

41. *Ion* 278: *pro gaias sphagia parthenous ktaneīn*.

42. And Athena, who speaks to Praxithea of "your husband, Erechtheus" (Frag. 18.16, 66, 90).

43. Frag. 10.43-45.

44. Frag. 10.50-51: *locheumata*.

45. Demarates in *F. Gr. Hist.* 42 Fr. 4 Jacoby.

46. Frag. 18.67-89.

47. This is not Pandora the dummy, Hesiod's artifact-woman. The names Pandora and Protogenia have come down to us through Phanodemes *F. Gr. Hist.* 325 Fr. 4 Jacoby), who took an expansive view and mentions a large family of six daughters.

48. As Aristides notes, ed. Dindorf, I, p. 191.

49. Frag. 10.32-35.

50. Frag. 18.73-74.

51. Frag. 18.75-82.

52. The Sorbonne papyrus is too dilapidated at 82.

53. Frag. 18.87.

54. Frag. 18.83-86. See the remarks on "sacrifices without wine": J. Bingen, "Euripide, Erechtée, 84," *Chronique d'Egypte* 43 (1968): 56-58.

55. Aeschylus *Eumenides* 107.

56. See Carrara, *Euripide, Eretteo*, 86.

57. Frag. 18.48 ed. P. Carrara.

58. Frag. 18.90-94 ed. P. Carrara.

59. Poseidon and Erechtheus were associated in an Athenian cult long before their "fusion" was noted (or invented?) by Euripides. The data and reconstructions are presented in M. Lacore, "Euripide et le culte de Poséidon-Erechthée," *Revue des études anciennes* (1983): 215-34.

60. On a victim taking the name of his murderer or a murderer taking the name of his victim (as does Apollo, who becomes Hyakinthos), see Lacore, "Euripide et le culte de Poséidon-Erechthée," 217 n. 4.

61. Rather than becoming an autochthonous god, as Lacore notes, ibid., 233.

62. Frag. 10.46-49.

63. Frag. 10.95 (*eksanorthōsa bathra*). A similar formula is used of a radical type of foundation, a formula beneath which, there too, another gradually becomes detectable when a god, clearly Apollo, "once again raises" (*anorthōn*) and "refounds" (*pālin katoikizei*) the city of the Magnesians, the city that Plato discusses in his last work, the *Laws* (11.919d). See Marcel Detienne, "Qu'est-ce qu'un site?" in *Tracés de fondation*, ed. Marcel Detienne (Paris-Louvain, 1989), 93: 1-6.

64. Contradicting the pessimistic conclusion that there is no feminine form of autochthony, and also qualifying the timid conclusions of those who underline the role played by women in the transmission of autochthony: "[the Athenian woman] transmits autochthony" (Brulé, *La Fille d'Athènes*, 395).

65. See the analyses by Brulé, *La Fille d'Athènes*; also, P. Brulé, "Arithmologie et polythéisme: En lisant L. Gerschel," in *Les grandes figures religieuses. Lire les Polythéismes* (Paris, 1986), 1: 35-47.

66. Brulé, *La Fille d'Athènes*, 29.

67. Chrysis Pélékidis, *Histoire de l'éphébie attique* (Paris, 1962), 111-13.

68. Philichorus, *F. Gr. Hist.* 328 Fr. 105 Jacoby.

69. See Brulé, *La Fille d'Athènes*, 31. This is a book of which I was wrongly somewhat dismissive in the 1989 French edition of the present work. Brulé's approach to his subject via Artemis and feminine initiatory procedures suggests that we should now explore other aspects, both of these stories and of the relations between Athena, Aglauros, and Artemis.

70. See F. Vian, *Les Origines de Thèbes: Cadmos et les Spartes* (Paris, 1963), 206-15.

71. Situated to the east of the Acropolis; see the topographical data in G. S. Dontas, "The True Aglaurion," *Hesperia* 52 (1983): 48-63.

72. The formula used by Philichorus (*F. Gr. Hist.* 328 Fr. 105 Jacoby). The *propylaia* of the *polis*, in the sense of the Acropolis surrounded by its walls, the city in its reduced, condensed, essential form.

73. Also according to Philichorus (*F. Gr. Hist.* 328 Fr. 105 Jacoby).

74. In passing, Brulé describes Aglauros as autochthonous, but does so without conviction (*La Fille d'Athènes*, 113). The notion of feminine Athenian autochthony would have oriented his inquiry quite differently.

75. See Brulé, *La Fille d'Athènes*, 32-33.

76. Inscription published in 1983: *Hesperia* 52, no. 1 (1983): 1-12. These are not the sacrifices made to the traditional gods by the ephebes upon "entering" their military service, in the Prytaneum (which is given a new address by Dontas in "The True Aglaurion," 60 n. 37: "20, Tripodon Street.") See Pélékidis, *Histoire de l'éphébie attique*, 217-18.

77. Agraulos, the wife of Ares: a tradition connected with the Areopagus, [Apollodorus] *Library* 3.14.2; Hellanicus, *F. Gr. Hist.* 329a Fr. Jacoby.

78. *Evagoras* 47. See Jean Pouilloux, "Syncrétisme religieux à Salamine de Chypre?" in *Les Syncrétismes dans les religions de l'Antiquité* (Leiden, 1975), 76-86.

79. Porphyry *De Abstinentia* 2.54.

80. In Rome, a javelin blow killed the "October horse" in the course of a festival of Mars (the Roman Ares) that was of a manifestly warrior nature. See Georges Dumézil, *Fêtes romaines d'été et d'automne* (Paris, 1975), 145-49; see also, for the pleasure of an exceptional analysis centered on the tail and the head, "Les Derniers soubresauts du cheval d'octobre" (pp. 181-219).

81. M. Guarducci, "Una nuova dea a Naxos in Sicilia e gli antichi legami fra la Naxos siceliota e l'omonima isola delle Cicladi," *Mélanges de l'Ecole française de Rome* 97, no. 7 (1985): 7-34.

82. The oath of the ephebes, dating from the fourth century B.C., is

engraved on a stele of Acharnes, a deme in Attica, and takes the form of a dedication by "the priest of Ares and Athena Areia."

83. Aristophanes *Women at the Thesmophoria* 533; Bioo of Proconnese, *F. Gr. Hist.* 3b Fr. 166 Jacoby.

84. Marcel Detienne, "Violentes 'eugénies': En pleines Thesmophories: des femmes couvertes de sang," in Marcel Detienne et al., *La Cuisine du sacrifice en pays grec*[2] (Paris, 1981), 183-214.

85. See Brulé, *La Fille d'Athènes*, 34-38.

86. Whereas it is Aglauros, the priestess of Athena, who invents the clothing (*kosmos*) of the gods (*Anecdota graeca* 1.276); it has been suggested that "laundering" came later, with the Plynteria, commemorating her death (Brulé, *La Fille d'Athènes*, 105-13).

87. Schol. Pindar *Pythian Odes* 4.106a, 2.112.17 ff., citing Mnaseas of Patara (*Fragmenta historicorum graecorum* 3.150 ed. Müller).

88. Text published in *Hesperia* 52, no. 1 (1983): 12-14, ed. Dontas.

89. See the texts analyzed by M. Detienne, *The Gardens of Adonis*, trans. Janet Lloyd (Princeton, 1994), 113.

90. See Pélékidis, *Histoire de l'éphébie attique*, 112-13.

91. Pausanias 1.8.4.

92. See Pélékidis, *Histoire de l'éphébie attique*, 211-56, who provides a detailed epigraphical analysis of the ephebes' participation in "the religious and agonistic life of the city."

93. *IG* 2[2].1039.5-6, 57; 2221.21 (Pélékidis, *Histoire de l'éphébie attique*, 256).

94. The timing is uncertain. No date for the swearing of the oath is known. Possibly it was in the month of Pyanepsion, when "the festival of the return" was held, as P. Vidal Naquet suggests in *The Black Hunter* (Baltimore, 1986), 116.

95. Aristotle *Constitution of the Athenians* 42.3.

96. Plutarch *Lycurgus* 26.1.

97. With his measure concerning the "agronomes," the guardians of the *agros*, the open territory, in the *Laws*, Plato elaborated a method marking out the space that would make it possible for the young men to get to know the whole country in thorough detail, in the course of two years.

98. See Pélékidis, *Histoire de l'éphébie attique*, 271.

99. See, in general, on this aspect of the ephebe as a secret prowler, a "black hunter," Vidal Naquet, *The Black Hunter*, 85-157; and the article entitled "The Black Hunter Revisited," *Proceedings of the Cambridge Philological Society*, no. 212 (1986): 126-44.

100. I am following Pélékidis, *Histoire de l'éphébie attique*, 211-56.

101. See G. Barbieri and J.-L. Durand, "Con il bue a spalla," *Bolletino d'Arte* 29 (1985): 1-16 (in particular, 9-14).

102. See Philo *Quod omnis probus liber sit* 140, and Ludwig Deubner's remarks in *Attische Feste*, 2nd ed. (Berlin, 1956), 214.

Chapter 15

1. See Chapter 9 above.

2. *The Derveni Papyrus*, ca. 17.8-10.

3. The *mixis* or Mixture, Aphrodite-Harmonia: both throughout the *Homeric Hymn* in her honor and in Empedocles' poem (see Jean Bollack, *Empédocle*, vol. 1: *Introduction à l'ancienne physique* [Paris, 1965].

4. Plutarch *Roman Questions* 264b and other elements in Marcel Detienne, s.v. "Mariage (Puissances du . . .)" in the *Dictionnaire des mythologies*, ed. Yves Bonnefoy II (Paris, 1981), 65-69. See the collection of data with a rich introduction in *L'Amore in Grecia*, ed. Claude Calame (Rome-Bari, 1983). In her *Dionysos* (Paris, 1985), Maria Daraki sets the Anthesteria at the center of an overall analysis that we need not pause to consider here, except to point out that the invasion "of unadulterated sexuality" into the ritual of the Anthesteria, criticized by Maria Daraki, appears nowhere (except perhaps in a misunderstanding over *summeixis* and on one small Lucanian vase on which the figures have been very much redrawn). The wild sex of Dionysus is nowhere to be found. Much else is also absent from this *Dionysus*.

5. For example, in Dumézil, *Archaic Roman Religion*, trans. Philip Krapp (Chicago, 1970), and his *Fêtes romaines d'été et d'automne* (Paris, 1975).

6. See Marcel Detienne and Jean-Pierre Vernant, *Cunning Intelligence in Greek Culture and Society*, trans. Janet Lloyd (Hassocks [Sussex], 1978), 187-214.

7. Hesiod *Theogony* 187-206. See J. Rudhart, *Le Rôle d'Erôs et d'Aphrodite dans les cosmogonies grecques* (Paris, 1986).

8. See M. Olender, "L'Enfant Priape et son phallus," in *Souffrance, plaisir et pensée*, ed. J. Caïn and A. de Mijolla (Paris, 1983), 141-64; M. Olender, "Priape le mal taillé," in *Le Temps de la réflexion* 7 (1986): 373-88.

9. Philipe Borgeaud, *The Cult of Pan in Ancient Greece*, trans. Kathleen Atlass and James Redfield (Chicago, 1988), 116, 132.

10. Henri Jeanmaire, *Dionysos: Histoire du culte de Bacchus*[2] (Paris, 1970), 42, in agreement with Ludwig Deubner. In his own way, Walter F. Otto (*Dionysos: Le Mythe et le culte*[2] [1948], French translation by P. Lévy [Paris, 1969], 181-89) noted the place of sexuality in Dionysism,

but did not really give the phallus its due. It is obscured by too many mothers, nurses, and "authentic femininity."

11. Ludwig Deubner, *Attische Feste* (Berlin, 1956), 138–42.

12. On the civic ceremonies and their meaning, see Simon Goldhill, "Anthropologie, idéologie et les Grandes Dionysies," in *Anthropologie et théâtre antique*, ed. Paulette Ghiron-Bistagne (Montpellier, 1987), 55–74; "Great Dionysia and civic ideology," *Journal of Hellenic Studies* (1987): 58–76.

13. Deubner, *Attische Feste*, 141, and Russell Meiggs and David Lewis, *A Selection of Greek Historical Inscriptions* (Oxford, 1988), no. 49, 1, pp. 11–13.

14. Philippe Bruneau, *Recherches sur les cultes de Délos* (Paris, 1970), 312–19.

15. Schol. Aristophanes *Acharnians* 242. See the (female) *phallophoros*, following the three *liknophoroi*–who carry the sacred winnowing basket–in the inscription on the *thiasos* of Torre Nova in the Metropolitan Museum in New York.

16. Herodotus 2.48.

17. See Marcel Detienne, *Dionysos at Large*, trans. Arthur Goldhammer (Cambridge [Mass.], 1989), 3–12, 30–32.

18. Schol. Aristophanes *Acharnians* 243.

19. Detienne, *Dionysos at Large*, 31.

20. Pausanias 10.19.3.

21. Bruneau, *Recherches sur les cultes de Délos*, 312–14.

22. Martin P. Nilsson, *Griechische Feste* (1906), 280–82.

23. Schol. Lucian *Dialogue of the gods 1–5* pp. 211, 14–212, 8.

24. Priapism: Galen 7.728, 10.967-68, 13.318, and Satyriasis: 19.426. Attention is drawn to these texts in M. Olender's analyses of Priapus, in *Souffrance, plaisir et pensée*, ed. J. Caïn and A. de Mijolla (Paris, 1983), 148.

25. François Lissarrague, "De la sexualité des Satyres," *Métis* 2, no. 1 (1987): 63–90.

26. See Olender, "L'Enfant Priape et son phallus," and "Priape le mal taillé."

27. See the data and interpretations of Olender, ibid., until such time as his forthcoming synthesis appears.

28. Aristophanes *Acharnians* 259-60; also Plutarch *On the Love of Riches* 8.527d.

29. F. Vian, "Mélampous et les Proitides," *Revue des études anciennes* (1965): 25–30.

30. See, in particular, the analyses by F. Frontisi-Ducroux, "Images

du ménadism féminin: Les Vases des 'Lénéennes,'" in *L'Association dionysiaque dans les sociétés anciennes*, ed. O. de Cazenove (Rome-Paris, 1986), 165-76.

31. François Frontisi-Ducroux, "Les limites de l'anthropomorphisme: Hermès et Dionysos," *Le Temps de la réflexion* 7 (1986): 193-211.

32. Munich 8934: M. Robertson, "A Muffled Dancer and Others," *Mélanges A. D. Trendall*, Sydney, 1979, pp. 129-134 (pl. 34, 3-4).

33. Athens 9690: Hélène Metzger, *Recherches sur l'imagerie athénienne* (Paris, 1965), 50-51.

34. See Detienne, *Dionysos at Large*, 50-64.

35. Ibid., 57-61.

36. Aristotle *Movement of Animals* 703b.3-26.

37. Aristotle *Parts of Animals* 4.11.689a.20-31.

38. Iamblichus *On the Mysteries* 1.11, together with the remarks of Pierre Boyancé, "Dionysiaca," *Revue des études anciennes* (1966): 43-44.

39. For example, by writing a treatise on postures, a favorite topic in pornography for the men and women of ancient Greece, such as that by Philaenis, a talented woman on whom we now possess some information, thanks to D. W. J. Vessey, "Philaenis," *Revue belge de Philologie et d'Histoire* 54 (1976): 78-83.

Translator's Note

The following English translations of Greek and Latin texts have been used:

**Loeb Classical Library,
London and Cambridge (Mass.)**

Apollodorus, trans. Sir James George Frazer, 1967.

Aristophanes, *Birds*, trans. Benjamin Bicklay Rogers, 1968.

Aristotle, *The Constitution of the Athenians*, trans. H. Rackham, 1962.

Aristotle, *Metaphysics*, trans. Hugh Tredinnick, 1961.

Aristotle, *Nichomachean Ethics*, trans. H. Rackam, 1962.

Callimachus, *Hymns and Epigrams*, trans. A. W. Mair, 1969.

Cicero, trans. H. Rackham, 1967.

Demosthenes, trans. A. T. Murray, 1964.

Diogenes Laertius, *Lives of Eminent Philosophers* (for Epicurus, *Letter to Herodotus*), trans. R. D. Hicks, 1979.

Hesiod, *Theogony* and *Works and Days* (also including *The Homeric Hymns*), trans. Hugh G. Evelyn White, 1960.

Lucian, trans. A. M. Harmon, 1968.

Lysias, trans. W. R. M. Lamb, 1967.

Ovid, *Metamorphoses*, trans. Frank Justus Miller, 1970.

Pausanias, *Description of Greece*, trans. W. H. S. Jones, 1966.

Pindar, *Odes*, 2 vols. (vol. 1: *Olympian* and *Pythian*; vol. 2: *Nemean* and *Isthmian*), trans. Sir John Sandys, 1966.
Plato, *Laws*, trans. R. G. Bury, 1926.
Plato, *Phaedrus*, trans. Harold North Fowler, 1966.
Plato, *Timaeus*, trans. R. G. Bury, 1929.
Seneca, trans. Richard M. Gummere, 1967.

Penguin Classics, Harmondsworth

Herodotus, trans. A de Sélincourt, 1954.
Homer, *The Iliad*, trans. Martin Hammond, 1987.
Homer, *The Odyssey*, trans. E. V. Rieu, rev. P. C. H. Rieu and Peter Jones, 1991.

The Complete Greek Tragedies,
The University of Chicago Press

Euripides, *Iphigenia in Aulis*, trans. Charles R. Walker, 1958.

Cambridge University Press

Epicurus, *Vatican Sayings*, trans. A. A. Long and D. N. Sedley (in *The Hellenistic Philosophers*, vol. 1, 1987).

Index

Also published by Stanford University Press:

Daily Life in China on the Eve of the Mongol Invasion, 1250–1276, by Jacques Gernet
Daily Life in Rembrandt's Holland, by Paul Zumthor
Daily Life in Russia under the Last Tsar, by Henri Troyat
Daily Life in Spain in the Golden Age, by Marcelin Defourneaux
Daily Life of the Aztecs on the Eve of the Spanish Conquest, by Jacques Soustelle

Library of Congress Cataloging-in-Publication Data

Sissa, Giulia, 1954–
   [Vie quotidienne des dieux grecs. English]
   The daily life of the Greek gods / Guilia Sissa and Marcel Detienne ; translated by Janet Lloyd.
     p.   cm.
   Includes bibliographical references and index.
   ISBN 0-8047-3613-8 (cloth)–ISBN 0-8047-3614-6 (pbk. : alk. paper)
    1. Gods, Greek. 2. Homer. Iliad. 3. Mythology, Greek. 4. Greece–Social life and customs. I. Detienne, Marcel. II. Title.

BL782.S5713 2000
292.2´11–dc21   99-087856

Typeset at Stanford University Press in 10/12.5 Bodoni